The United States vs. Russia, 2009-2019:
The Last Ten Years of an Old Geopolitical Game

Nicholas Dima

The United States vs. Russia, 2009-2019:
The Last Ten Years
of an Old Geopolitical Game

Nicholas Dima

St. James's Studies in World Affairs

Academica Press
Washington - London

Library of Congress Registration Information

Name: Dima, Nicholas.,
Title: The United States vs. Russia, 2009-2019: The Last Ten Years of an Old Geopolitical Game
Description: Washington, DC : Academica Press, 2020. | Identifiers: LCCN: 2019954539 | ISBN 9781680532241 (hardcover : alk. paper) | ISBN 9781680531244 (paperback : alk. paper)
LC record available at https://lccn.loc.gov/ 2019952687

Contents

Chapter 1
Russia's Near Abroad and US's Interests 1
The Russian-Georgian Conflict; U.S.-Georgia Relations; The Russian Invasion of Georgia: One Year Later; EU Report about the War; Russia and Ukraine; *Red Famine: Stalin's War on Ukraine* (Book Review); Azerbaijan and U.S. Policy; Turmoil in the Republic of Moldova; Belarus: Still an Outpost of Tyranny.

Chapter 2
Moscow's Challenges and Washington's Answers 57
Obama's "Mission Impossible" to Moscow; Secretary Clinton's Mission to Eastern Europe and the Caucasus; Biden's Moldova Visit; Russia's Geopolitical Challenge to NATO; German Chancellor Visits Moldova.

Chapter 3
Post-Soviet Russian Federation 85
Twenty Years since the Fall of the Berlin Wall; Moscow's Victory Day Military Parade; The Dismemberment of the Soviet Union.

Chapter 4
Poland-A Special Case 115
Intermarium: The Land between the Black and Baltic Sea (Book Review); Lech Walesa-Vaclav Havel: New Russian Revisionism; Katyn Tragedy Redux; The Lie of Katyn.

Chapter 5
Ukraine, New Challenges 133
Putin Asserts Russia's Regional Power; The EU's Vilnius Summit; *World Order* (Book Review); Ukraine: A New Battleground; American Illusions and Russian Delusions.

Chapter 6
The United States, Romania and Russia 153
In Europe's Shadow (Book Review); U.S. and Romania: Security and Mutual Interests; Russia's Opposition to U.S. Missile Defense in

Romania; Moldova: Between Russia and the West; Fixing a U.S. Diplomatic Gaffe; EU Enlargement, Russia and U.S. Policy.

Chapter 7
New Russian Maneuvers and Policies... 175
Putin's Ukraine Policy is Dividing Europe; The Black Sea: New Battleground between Russia and NATO; Russia, NATO and the New Ukrainian Defense Policy; Putin Meddling in Eastern Europe and the Middle East; The Kurds and the Question of 'Kurdistan;' Is Turkey Changing Sides? Waiting for Russia's Next Move; New Russian Maneuvers.

Chapter 8
Europe's Never Ending Struggle 201
Heart of Europe: A History of the Holy Roman Empire (Book Review); Europe's New Challenge: Wake Up or Break Apart! Ethnic Fragmentation: The Case of Catalonia; Squeezing the Buffer Zone between NATO and Russia; Eastern Europe: An Area Divided; A Little Publicized Meeting; Is Romania Approaching a Second Revolution?

Chapter 9
Recent American Policy and Attitudes.. 223
Obama's Multicultural America and the Transformation of a Nation; Facing a Crucial Election Year: Will Traditional Values Survive?; President Trump's Foreign Policy: The Case of Eastern Europe; Trump Hosts Romania's President; Thoughts at the End of an Important Year; America's Policy in Eastern Europe: U.S. Romanian Common Interests.

Chapter 10
America and the Process of Globalization 239
About Globalization; Globalization and the American Patriots; Globalization: The Process; The Current Refugee Crisis in Europe; America and Brexit; U.S. and the World.

Chapter 11
Global Problems in a New Global World.. 259
A World in Disarray: American Foreign Policy and the Crisis of the Old Order; *Winning the Third World:* Sino-American Rivalry During the Cold War; *A.I. Super Power:* China, Silicon Valley, and the New World Order (Critical Book Reviews).

Closing Thought 273

Preface

Nicholas Dima started writing for the Selous Foundation in 1989, beginning with the publication of his memoir *Journey to Freedom*, "an autobiographical description of the effects of communist dictatorship on a nation, a family, and an individual." His is the story of physical and spiritual escape. While the author's journey was fraught, his native Romania suffered more than four decades of Soviet occupation from 1947, when the "People's Republic" was declared in the aftermath of World War II, through Christmas December 25, 1989, marking the demise of Romanian dictator Nicolae Ceaușescu.

Enduring four years imprisonment in some of the most notoriously harsh prison and labor camps in the Socialist Republic of Romania following a failed escape attempt with youthful companions, Nicholas Dima navigated a Soviet-style educational system, eventually graduating with an advanced degree from Bucharest University. By 1968 he had successfully escaped to the West immigrating to the United States, where he received a Ph.D. from Columbia University before going on to become a prolific writer, journalist at Voice of America, and professor at the John F. Kennedy Special Warfare Center and School of the U.S. Army at Fort Bragg.

In his capacity as professor, writer, and reporter, Dr. Dima met some of the most prominent leaders of America and Eastern Europe, as well as many scholars and public opinion leaders. He published several books and numerous articles, while offering countless lectures. He voiced his views on American Radio and TV in addition to East European Radio and TV stations, universities and public institutions.

Upon his retirement, Dr. Dima was among the first free-lance writers for the Selous Foundation's emerging online publication *SFPPR News & Analysis* at the onset of the Russian invasion of Georgia in

August-September 2008. Carrying on to 2018, his work now makes this book possible.

**Ralph J. Galliano, Director at the
Selous Foundation for Public Policy Research, Washington DC.
October 29, 2019.**

Chapter 1
Russia's Near Abroad and US's Interests

East Europe continues to remain a region of confrontation between the security interests of the United States and the geopolitical ambitions of Russia. In addition, this confrontation reaches into the Middle East, and in view of the convergence of interests between Moscow and Beijing, it acquires global dimensions.

This collection of articles, published previously mostly by the Selous Foundation for Public Policy Research, offers the views of the author about some of the chief events that occurred in the region involving the United States, Russia, and the European Union. The articles are presented mainly chronologically and by countries or geographic areas. Whereas individual articles were written separately and years apart, the reader will find occasionally some repetitions and some different styles, but that does not affect the substance of the articles. The collection should be of interest to specialists of the area and also to political analysts who want to know the recent past. Political decision makers may also review the past events to opt for better future decisions.

Geographically, East Europe is the area located between Germany and Russia to the north stretching from the Baltic Sea to the Black Sea. After the dismemberment of the USSR, we also refer to the former European Soviet republics, now independent, as part of East Europe. They are the three Baltic Republics, Estonia, Latvia and Lithuania, currently members of EU and NATO, as well as Belarus, Ukraine, Moldova and the three Caucasian republics. While relinquishing direct control over the Baltic Republics, Moscow continues to cling stubbornly to Ukraine, Belarus, Moldova and the Caucasian region. Moscow calls it "The Near Aboard." This is the battleground now between Russia, NATO, and the United States. After the dissolution of the USSR Moscow showed its determination to hold on to this area first in Moldova shortly after it became independent and then in Georgia and Ukraine. We start with Moscow's interventions in these two countries and with America's political and diplomatic responses.

The Russian-Georgian Conflict. September 2, 2008.

The former Soviet Union was set up allegedly as a union of sovereign republics and the republics were based on the main ethnic groups living in old Russia. However, the vast expanse of land occupied by tsarist Russia was inhabited by hundreds of large nationalities or small ethnic groups. There was no way to grant union-level republics to all of them. In addition, many regions were ethnically very much mixed. And more importantly, the goal of the new Soviet leadership was to control the country, not to grant independence to its ethnic components. To give a modicum of satisfaction to the smaller ethnic groups, Moscow granted them various degrees of cultural and administrative autonomy within the larger union republics where they resided. In this regards certain criteria were set up, but they were rather arbitrary and chiefly reflected Moscow's interests. For Stalin, who was the first commissar for nationality problems and later the ruthless leader of the USSR, everything had to suit his personal hold on power. Coming from Georgia and the ethnically very mixed Caucasus, Stalin was indeed a master of divide and rule. For example, in theory the Soviet constitution allowed for the secession of the union republics. Based upon this illusory provision, Stalin who hated the Tatars, argued that the Tatars should not be granted a union republic because being surrounded by Russian territory ostensibly they could not secede.

Initially, the entire Caucasus region was incorporated into the USSR as a single republic. Later, the communist leaders who came from this region convinced Moscow to split it into three union-level republics, namely Georgia, Armenia and Azerbaijan. The northern reaches of the Caucasus, inhabited by a host of smaller ethnic groups, were incorporated into Russia as autonomous republics, and Russia itself was organized as a federation. According to the Soviet laws, the union-level republics had considerably more prerogatives, at least on paper, than the autonomous republics. And there were further territorial divisions in the USSR, such as ethnic Oblasts (regions) and Okrugs (rural areas), which were provided with very limited rights.

Abkhazia and South Ossetia were organized as autonomous republics within Georgia, but as long as Georgia itself was under Moscow their autonomy was rather meaningless. The situation changed radically when Georgia declared its independence. To further complicate the regional geopolitical landscape, there is also a North Ossetia autonomous republic just north of South Ossetia, but within the Russian Federation. The Ossetians would like to unite the two areas into a single country, but for the time being they prefer to remain with Russia. In 1991, in order to bring Georgia back into the Russian fold, Moscow helped Abkhazia and South Ossetia fight a war to establish their independence from Tbilisi.

Georgia is a rather small country having an area of 69,700 sq. km. or 27,000 sq. mi. In 2006 it had a population of 4.7 million which makes it more or less comparable to South Carolina. But Georgia's geopolitical location is very important to Russia. It occupies a mountainous area south of the main Caucasian range and it has a rather large frontage for its size at the Black Sea. Georgia also borders Russia to the north, Turkey to the south and Armenia and Azerbaijan to the southeast making it a key country in the Caucasus. From a strictly geographic point of view, Georgia can be considered part of Asia, but from a cultural point of view Georgia and Armenia, both of them old Christian nations, consider themselves part of Europe.

From a geopolitical point of view Georgia is important to Russia in two ways. An independent Georgia would block Russia's direct access to Armenia, its remaining ally in the Caucasus, which would reduce considerably Moscow's influence in this part of the world. The entire region is close to the sensitive and oil-rich Middle East and the now dangerous south Asia. And if Georgia were to join NATO, as it strongly expressed its intention to do so, this would further reduce Russia's sphere of influence. In addition, the conflict also has an important economic dimension. Russia is currently the chief supplier of oil and gas to Western Europe and as such it controls nearly all of the oil and gas pipelines to Europe. The recently built oil and gas pipelines from Baku in Azerbaijan to Ceyhan in Turkey cross Georgian territory, however. If Russia loses control over Georgia, it will also start to lose energy control and political leverage over Western Europe. At the same time, the American oil companies that already have big vested interests in the Caspian Sea basin risk losing their positions. All these factors were behind the recent war in Georgia.

Moscow's struggle to maintain control over the Caucasus began immediately after the dissolution of the USSR in December 1991.Officially, Moscow developed a new strategic concept known as the "far abroad" and the "near abroad." Consequently, Russia relinquished control over East Europe and the three Baltic states which were considered part of its far abroad area. Yet, this area which is now integrated in the North Atlantic Alliance led by the United States was to be watched carefully by Moscow. Indeed, the recent decision by NATO to deploy advanced weapons in Poland and the Czech Republic was met with a strong Russian reaction.

The concept of near abroad, encompassing the remaining former Soviet republics, has been played down in recent years, but it is obvious that Moscow considers this area as within its sphere of influence. The area stretches over Ukraine, Belarus and Moldova in Europe, former Soviet Central Asia, and the Caucasus region. In theory the new independent states that replaced the former Soviet republics are free to choose their way of development. In practice, they have been treated as vassal states. And this is a vast grey area surrounding the new Russian Federation. Most of their inhabitants, save a large proportion of ethnic Russians who moved there during the Russian dominated Soviet regimes, would prefer full independence, but Moscow found ways to block their aspirations. An important tactic was to incite various minorities to revolt against the new independent governments. Once they revolted, Russia intervened to allegedly reestablish peace in the area or to defend the Russian minorities, which in practice meant a new Russian occupation. In the Georgian case, Moscow worked through its Abkhazian and Ossetian proxies.

The conflict in Abkhazia began to brew immediately after Georgia declared its independence and from the beginning the Abkhazians had the full military and economic support of Russia. Then, the war against the government in Tbilisi escalated causing thousands of victims and huge numbers of refugees. Eventually, most ethnic Georgians were expelled and by 1993 the rebel Abkhazians with full Russian support were controlling the territory. A cease-fire, providing for Russian "peacekeeping" troops was signed in Moscow in 1994. Then Russia helped the secessionist region organize its own military forces and even a Black Sea navy stronger than Georgia's navy. The same ploy was used in South Ossetia. The result is that Georgia was practically broken, but the proud Georgians would not renounce their aspiration for freedom and territorial integrity. To this effect, in January 2004 they elected Mikhail Saakashvilli, a pro-Western and independent-minded young president determined to reintegrate the country and to join the European family of nations. It is not clear why the new government decided to enter South Ossetia on August 7, 2008 to retake it from the secessionists, but this event triggered a direct response from the Russian troops. It appears that it was a trap set up by Moscow to provide an excuse for its own military intervention. The Russians responded with traditional brutality against Georgia as a country, while their Ossetian proxies resorted to criminal acts against the Georgians as individuals. America and the West did not provide the support that Tbilisi needed and expected. The rest is recent history, but it could also be just the beginning of a new era.

Will Russia Succeed in Ousting Georgian President Saakashvili? December 7, 2008

There are indications that Moscow is taking steps to remove the president of Georgia with the consent of the West. On November 28, the Russian press agency ITAR-TASS (formerly the official Soviet news agency TASS) announced that friends of Georgia in NATO are very much discouraged about the prospects for President Mikhail Saakashvili, who could be deposed. Russia's permanent representative to NATO, Dmitry Rogozin, declared in a televised interview that Saakashvili himself realizes that Washington has taken the decision to have him replaced by another leader. The same source claims that the new president will most likely be the Speaker of the Parliament Nino Burdzhanadze, who allegedly has been approved by Washington. "I think, for the West, it will be a better alternative than mister Saakashvili," Rogozin concluded.

It should be emphasized at the outset that Russia is a master chess player and that the former KGB, presently FSB, is still hard at work. It is difficult to compete with Moscow in the area of disinformation. The Russian announcement may be just a ploy, but it could also reflect a confidential consensus with the United States, in view of the incoming Obama administration. Either way, the announcement represents at least a precondition set by Moscow to renormalize its relations with the West. And it is possible that the State Department conceded at Moscow's insistence to have Saakashvili removed from office.

Mikhail Saakashvili was elected president in January 2004 on a platform that emphasized total independence, recovery of the two breakaway Georgian provinces of Abkhazia and South Ossetia, a firm pro-Western and pro-American stand, and most importantly, a strong determination to join the North Atlantic Alliance. In reality, Moscow could not allow Georgia in the Caucasus area and Ukraine in Eastern Europe to join NATO. This is the reason Moscow became insistent. As it is known, with Russia's help, Abkhazia and South Ossetia declared independence from Georgia and over the last several years the two have continued to provoke the Georgian authorities. To make good on his campaign promises, on August 7, 2008, Saakashvili ordered his troops to enter secessionist South Ossetia. It is not clear why Saakashvili's government made this decision and chose this particular timing, but the Russian response was quick and devastating for Georgia. Looking back, it appears that it was a trap set up by Moscow to provide an excuse for its own military action. The brutal Russian intervention was denounced by the United States and Western Europe, following which the French President Nicolas Sarkozy was appointed by the EU to negotiate a cease fire. Initially, the West was very vehement against Russia and promised considerable financial assistance to Georgia. Saakashvili wanted more than promises, but the response of the United States and Western Europe stopped short of what he expected.

The official position of the United States was stated clearly by Secretary of State Condoleezza Rice on September 18 at the Washington meeting of the Marshall Fund: *"All sides made mistakes and miscalculations. But several key facts are clear... On August 7, following repeated violations of the ceasefire in South Ossetia, including the shelling of Georgian villages, the Georgian government launched a major military operation into areas of the separatist region... But the situation deteriorated further when Russia's leaders violated Georgia's sovereignty and territorial integrity and launched a full scale invasion across an internationally-recognized border... Russia's leaders established a military occupation that stretched deep into Georgian territory..."*

The official Russian reaction to Secretary Rice came without delay the very next day, when its Ministry of Foreign Affairs declared: *"It is not the first time that events provoked by Georgia's aggression against South Ossetia are crudely distorted in a speech by a member of the American leadership. Not particularly surprising, given Washington's predisposition to support the bankrupt regime in Tbilisi. There is no need to rebut yet again the false interpretation of what happened...The Georgian army and special forces killed hundreds upon hundreds of civilians in South Ossetia, most of whom were Russian citizens. It was an attack on Russia, and we had no choice but to use our self-defense right in full compliance with Article 51 of the UN Charter..."*

The truth of the matter is that ever since the collapse of the Soviet Union in December 1991 the new Russian Federation has made desperate efforts to regain its power status and to impose itself upon the "new world order." Following the surprise resignation of Boris Yeltsin, the ascent to supreme power in Moscow by a former KGB colonel, Vladimir Putin in January 1999, marked the beginning of the new Russian geo-politics. Having served two elective four-year terms as President of the Russian Federation, Putin is now prime minister, following the election of his hand-picked successor, Dmitry Medvedev, a lawyer by profession. Yet, Putin remains the power behind the throne and he has already prepared the terrain for a future presidential comeback. In the meantime, the Russian authorities have re-imposed quasi-totalitarian order at home and have muted the independent press and the political opposition. Internationally, with new financial resources resulting from the sale of high-priced oil and gas, Moscow launched a new policy.

In brief, Moscow wants its exclusive sphere of influence and international recognition. However, Russia does not want a confrontation with the West nor a new Cold War, which it may lose again. This is why Moscow has played its hand in a cool and calculated manner. It negotiated, it offered some small compromises and it proposed new energy deals to Western Europe, especially with Germany. At the same time, Moscow insisted categorically that its official recognition of independent Abkhazia and South Ossetia was final and non-negotiable. Slowly, the United States and the bigger Western European countries softened their stand and began to warm up to Moscow. The result is that President Saakashvili lost his attempt to reunify his country and at the same time his domestic backing diminished considerably. Apparently, Saakashvili had aggravated Georgia's situation without any guarantees of real international support, while his political adversaries, and most surely the Russian agents inside Georgia, organized public rallies and demanded that he step down. Putin, the architect of the new Russian geopolitics, could not be any happier. He actually declared that he wanted to catch Saakashvili and hang him.

In this regard, Putin had a discussion with French President Sarkozy when the two met in the *Kremlin on August 12*. *"I am going to hang Saakashvili by his balls,"* Putin crudely stated. *"Hang him?"* Sarkozy exclaimed in surprise, *"Yes, why not? Did not the United States hang Hussein?"* retorted Putin. *"But you do not want to become like President Bush,"* Sarkozy continues. *"Here you have a point,"* Putin replied. This "undiplomatic" dialog was reported by *The Times* of London and by the Russian daily, *Pravda*.

It is obvious that Moscow has marked solidly its sphere of influence and does not want to make any other concessions. If NATO wants Georgia and Georgia wants to be integrated into NATO, then it has to do it with its territory mutilated. For the time being, Russia is playing a strong hand while the U.S. position seems to be weak. The Russian message is clear. You send your military ships to Georgia, we send ours to Venezuela. You play hard ball with us in our neighborhood in the Caucasus area and we do the same in Latin America. Quid pro quo!

As the U.S. press has already reported, in November Russian President Dmitry Medvedev visited several Latin American countries and among them were Venezuela and Cuba. In Havana he met Fidel and Raul Castro and renewed Moscow's old ties with this still Communist country only 90 miles from the Florida Keys. In Venezuela, he signed several accords of cooperation with Hugo Chavez. And, in a show of power and posturing, the Venezuelan state-run news agency announced a

Russian-Venezuelan joint naval exercise. The just ended military exercise involved a Russian naval squadron led by the nuclear-powered cruiser *Peter the Great* and eleven Venezuelan ships. The American response was cautious.

America is presently at a turning point between two presidential administrations, while the world is changing rapidly. Western Europe needs Russia and Russia needs Europe. The United States also needs Europe, but it is caught between new players with new agendas and it has little room to maneuver. At the last NATO Summit in Brussels, held at the very beginning of December 2008, Condoleezza Rice conceded that Georgia and Ukraine were not ready for now to join the Alliance. Strangely, however, the chief American diplomat also warned the European countries not to enter any military activities with Russia, as if some odd links would be established, thereby bypassing the United States. Although, Secretary Rice added that Russia was invited to continue its cooperation with NATO.

In the chess game of global geopolitics, it appears that Moscow is winning the last move. If Russia insists that Saakashvili should be removed from office, it is possible that it already has received an approving nod from the West. However, his removal would be just a symbolic Russian victory because Ms. Burdzhanadze is also pro-West and pro-American.

U.S.- Georgia Relations: Regaining Territorial Integrity. February 2, 2009

On September 3, 2008, President George W. Bush stated that the United States applauded the actions taken by the European Union to help rebuild the independent and sovereign nation of Georgia, adding, "*I am announcing one billion in additional economic assistance to meet Georgia's humanitarian needs and to support its economic recovery.*" The White House also commended the European Union's commitment to deploy an independent OSCE mission to monitor developments in Georgia. At the same time, the president stressed that the international monitors "*must have access to the entire region of conflict, including South Ossetia and Abkhazia, in accordance with the cease-fire agreement.*" The same statement stressed that the U.S. expects Russia's

"full compliance in redeploying forces to their pre-August 7 positions…"
This expectation, however, is unrealistic.

The Republican position was commendable. Georgia badly needs financial assistance and moral support from the West, but what it needs the most is help to regain its territorial integrity. From this point of view the Western pledges do not meet Tbilisi's expectations. Furthermore, the new Democrat administration may park this issue on a back burner. What can the United States do in the Caucasus without risking an international conflict that could escalate?

The United States and Russia are now situated where the Western allies and the former Soviet Union were at the end of World War II. With the nod of the West, Moscow then annexed almost whatever territory it wanted. And in spite of its promises, Moscow transformed the occupied countries into ruthless totalitarian states and pawns in its geopolitical game. As Europe was split in 1945, so is the Caucasian region today. The United States may have the upper hand in Georgia and Azerbaijan, but Russia controls Armenia and vital parts of both Azerbaijan and Georgia. In the immediate post-war years of the last century, the United States saved Western Europe through the implementation of the Marshall plan, but for almost 50 years it did not do anything to help Eastern Europe. Will history repeat itself now in the Caucasus?

In May 2005, America and its allies marked the 60th anniversary of the end of the Second World War and for the first time ever condemned publicly the Ribbentrop-Molotov Pact of 1939 that led to the war. In addition, President George W. Bush denounced the Yalta Agreement of 1945 and the Soviet occupation of Eastern Europe. As reported by the Washington Post on May 8, 2005, Mr. Bush stated: *"The agreement at Yalta followed in the unjust tradition of Munich and the Molotov-Ribbentrop Pact. The captivity of millions in Central and Eastern Europe will be remembered as one of the greatest wrongs of history."* Will rebuilding the remaining territory of Georgia, following the Russian invasion of August 7, 2008, suffice? Will the Georgian citizens of Abkhazia and South Ossetia share the fate of Eastern Europe, which was abandoned behind the Iron Curtain for fifty years?

On January 9, 2009, U.S. Secretary of State Condoleezza Rice and her Georgian counterpart signed the United States-Georgia Charter on Strategic Partnership. The accord outlines cooperation in defense, trade, energy security and stresses that *"the United States supports Georgia's sovereignty and territorial integrity, as well as its aspirations for integration into the institutions of the Euro-Atlantic."* How will the U.S. help Georgia regain its lost territories when Russia's President Dimitry Medvedev declared unequivocally that *"Moscow's recognition of the independence of Abkhazia and South Ossetia is final and irrevocable?"* This rigid Russian stand threatens the position of Georgia as an independent and sovereign nation, as well as that of its president. On January 26, Mikhail Saakashvili stated that he will not step down as Moscow and some Georgian politicians insist. Yet, his tenure is very weak. And if he is replaced, the next president will have to be less pro-American. This is the price the West will pay for accommodating the new Russia. In a way, it is a repeat of 1945 East Europe.

In the current economic and financial situation in which the world finds itself, neither Russia nor the U. S. wants a new Cold War. However, the game between the two is intricate and dangerous, requiring a high degree of diplomatic experience on the part of the new Obama administration. Washington may want to chip away at Russia's sphere of interests, but Russia is an experienced chess player. Moscow fears encirclement and is determined to do everything to counteract it. For example, it is now playing America's European allies like a fiddle, enjoying already a measure of success. Russia is also extending its international reach into Syria, Yemen, Libya and Venezuela. And in late January, Moscow announced that it will open a naval base in Abkhazia, the very Georgian province that it helped to secede from Georgia. To regain credibility and loyalty, America will have to address the aspirations of the Georgian people, not only play on their fears and desperation. Most importantly, Washington will have to find a way to help Georgia regain control of its territory.

The Russian Invasion of Georgia: One Year Later.
August 24, 2009

Protesters demonstrating against the Russian occupation of South Ossetia last year compared the Russian invasion of Georgia to the Soviet invasions of Hungary in 1956 and Czechoslovakia in 1968, a time during the Cold War when Soviet tanks crushed freedom movements behind the Iron Curtain in Eastern Europe.

Georgian President Mikhail Saakashvili credits former President George W. Bush and his Secretary of State, Condoleezza Rice, with preventing the "annihilation" of the independent, democratic state of Georgia and the seizure of east-west oil and gas pipelines from the Caspian region. A major energy transit point located on the Black Sea, the former Georgian Soviet Socialist Republic has become the political target for former Russian president, Vladimir Putin, now prime minister, whom Saakashvili claims is intent on killing him and regaining Soviet empire in a geopolitical challenge to the West. For the former KGB colonel, the collapse of the Soviet Union was "the greatest geopolitical catastrophe" of the 20th Century.

Tragically, the short-lived Russo-Georgian war in August of 2008 left at least 390 Georgians dead and more than 30,000 homeless refugees. Provocations on August 7, 2008 by separatists caused Georgian forces to mount an assault on Tskhinvali, the capital of the Georgian province of South Ossetia, prompting a surprisingly swift Russian response. The war lasted five days with the Russian advance deep into Georgian territory stopping just short of Tbilisi. While President Dmitry Medvedev approved a French-led ceasefire on August 12th, Russian troops remain in South Ossetia in violation of the agreement. On August 26th, Medvedev announced the recognition of South Ossetia and Abkhazia as independent states. Today, only Nicaragua's Daniel Ortega has extended recognition.

Moscow's military action *"violated the core principles of the Helsinki Final Act, the charter of Paris, and the territorial integrity of a country that was a member of NATO's Partnership for Peace and the Euroatlantic Partnership Council – all in the name of defending a sphere of influence on its borders,"* wrote the leaders of Central and Eastern

Europe in a recently issued Open Letter. All the while, the Atlantic alliance stood by as thousands of Russian troops and tanks violated Georgian sovereignty and independence.

In an interview with Philip Pank of the Times of London reported on June 25, 2009, Saakashvili revealed that in his conversation at the time, President Bush told him, *"We will not allow them to enter Tbilisi."* According to the report, half-an-hour after that statement, the Russians backed down. The Russian military continues to occupy the two breakaway provinces of South Ossetia and Abkhazia, with some 10,000 troops stationed there, including tanks and heavy weapons. Daily provocations occur as Russian border guards and South Ossetian paramilitaries fire across the checkpoints. Less than one hour's striking distance from Tbilisi, Russia remains a threat. It's like living in Washington, DC with Russian troops occupying Annapolis, Maryland and preparing to invade our capital at any moment.

Today, Abkhazia is totally dependent on Moscow, while both breakaway provinces have for all intents and purposes been ethnically cleansed of their Georgian population. On the eve of the first anniversary of the ceasefire, Putin paid an unexpected visit to Abkhazia pledging $500 million in aid to pro-Kremlin supporters. "The situation has changed radically and there will be no return to the past," Putin declared. "Abkhazia does not need to be recognized by anyone but Russia." The leader of Russian occupied Abkhazia, Sergei Bagapsh, stated on Russian radio Ekho Moskvy on July 16th that it could become part of Russia by popular referendum. Further, he revealed that an important Iranian delegation had visited from July 11-14. The Romanian daily Ziua reported the Iranians also visited Abkhazia's Soviet-built nuclear facilities. This included the Vekua Institute of Physics and Technology located in the capital of Sukhumi.

A 34 year old Georgian blogger, highly critical of the Russian government, named Georgy, claims that on August 8, 2009 hackers launched a massive cyber attack to silence him. IT experts believe the attacks originated in Abkhazia. Reportedly, both sides used cyber attacks during the five day war.

Russia finds it offensive that Georgian troops continue to receive NATO training from U.S. Marines for deployment to Iraq and Afghanistan. In fact, Moscow suspended military cooperation with NATO following the invasion of Georgia. One year later, the Kremlin is still unable to come to terms with the independence of its former republics. Recent NATO exercises involving 1,000 soldiers representing 18 countries were carried out under severe protest from the Kremlin. President Medvedev described them as *"an overt provocation."*

In comparison, Moscow's war games were staged in and around Georgian territory from Monday, June 28th through Monday, July 6th, a day that coincided with President Obama's visit to Moscow, with 8,500 Russian troops, 200 tanks, 450 armored vehicles and 250 artillery pieces reportedly participating in their full field military exercises. The Caucasus 2009 war games also involved parts of the Russian air force including airborne troops and elements of the Black Sea Fleet stationed in Crimea. In the meantime just across the border in Georgia, 200 EU monitors guard against the threat of a Russian invasion, while Moscow continues to block observers in Abkhazia and South Ossetia.

William H. Courtney, U.S. diplomat and former ambassador to Georgia (1995-97), in praise of a new book on the subject entitled The Guns of August 2008: Russia's War in Georgia, states, *"In July 2008, Russia's military conducted a full field exercise of an invasion and then launched the real thing."* The Russian and Eastern European expert ends by saying, *"It leads to the disturbing conclusions that Russia may go beyond Georgia to subdue other neighbors, and that it may again use force against Georgia."*

The Columbia Law School graduate, Saakashvili, was largely responsible for the ouster of President Eduard Shevardnadze in what became known as the 2003 Rose Revolution. Shevardnadze, a former Soviet foreign minister, had been backed by the United States. Now 41 and president of small democratic country on the southern border of Russia, Mikhail Saakashvili remains defiant over the loss of Georgian territory to the Russians, yet, confident it will be recovered and that eventually Georgia will become a full fledged member of NATO and the European Union. Both moves are strongly opposed by the Kremlin.

EU Report Concludes Georgia Triggered War.
October 17, 2009

In December 2008 the Council of the European Union set up a special fact-finding mission to examine the causes of the August Russian-Georgian War. It was the first time that the EU had stepped in directly and actively to investigate an armed conflict. The mission was independent and international and at the end of its mandate its findings were presented in a detailed report by Ambassador Heidi Tagliavini, a Swiss diplomat and former head of the United Nations Observer Mission in Georgia.

In welcoming the presentation of the report, the EU Council noted in a press release that *"a peaceful and lasting solution to the conflicts in Georgia must be based on full respect for the principles of independence, sovereignty and territorial integrity as recognized by international law, including the Helsinki Final Act of the Conference on Security and Cooperation in Europe, and the United Nations Security Council Resolutions."*

Background

Chronologically, the August war lasted only five days. A cease-fire was reached under the EU's initiative chaired by French President Nicolas Sarkozy. The conflict left hundreds of people dead, displaced over 30,000 Georgians, and brought the U.S. and Russia into a brief Cold War-style confrontation. The conflict exposed Western Europe's and America's weakness, while strengthening Moscow's position in the Caucasian region. Despite wide-spread international opprobrium, Moscow recognized officially the independence of South Ossetia, which had caused this brief war, as well as of Abkhazia, the other Georgian break-away province.

The EU's official inquiry, known as the Independent International Fact-Finding Mission on the Conflict in Georgia, was conducted during a period of debate in Western Europe over how to back Georgia in its conflict with Russia. The results of the inquiry were published on September 30, 2009 in a document of almost one thousand pages, which can be found at *http://www.ceiig.ch/ Report.html*. Its findings were awaited with interest by many circles and especially by Russia and Georgia, which blamed each other for triggering the war. The main conclusions of the report were somehow anticipated. Yet, the way the findings were phrased made some analysts conclude that they were stretched to avoid challenging the Kremlin. The mainstream media in the East as well as in the West dedicated substantial commentaries to the report.

Report Findings

One of the main conclusions of the investigation was that "*the armed conflict was triggered by Georgia.*" However, the report stressed that "*Russia prepared the ground for war to break out and broke international law by invading Georgia as a whole.*" On September 30, BBC radio reported the same findings, but used different wording. It said that "*the onus of having actually triggered the war lies with the Georgian side, but the Russian side, too, carries the blame for a substantial number of violations of international law.*" Another BBC broadcast of the same period also claimed that the war was started by a Georgian attack that was not justified, but it added that the attack "*followed months of provocations, in which both sides violated international law.*"

It seems that from the outset the European investigators sympathized with Georgia, but they did not want to upset Russia with their findings. Other than that, the report found plenty of blame to go around, but in the end it left it up to the reader to decide which side was to be blamed. Maybe Tbilisi triggered the war, but it was Moscow that cornered Georgia and gave it no alternative but to defend its integrity.

In reality, if Georgia fired the first shot, it was Russia that created and exploited the conditions that led to war. For several years prior to the conflict, Russia encouraged separatist movements in Abkhazia and South Ossetia, trained their military forces, and hired mercenaries to challenge the Georgian authorities. At the same time, Moscow granted Russian citizenship and distributed Russian passports in massive numbers to Georgian citizens who sided with the Kremlin. Dutifully, the report mentions these acts. Later, Moscow claimed that it intervened in the conflict to defend those citizens it had hastily created. In fact, Moscow said that it invaded Georgia "*to protect Russian citizens"* and allegedly *"to stop a Georgian genocide."* The reality was quite different and the EU report acknowledges it in many ways.

The report found, for example, that Russia backed the Ossetian militias who committed atrocities and ethnic cleansing of Georgian villages. Actually, it found that "ethnic cleansing was practiced against ethnic Georgians in South Ossetia both during the war and after the conflict." Specifically, the report found that Russian military forces either "would not or could not control the South Ossetian militias." At the same time, the report found no evidence to back Russia's claims that it was Georgia that committed acts of genocide.

The report also faults the international community for failing to intervene with effective diplomacy when it was clear that the conflict was imminent. Yet, the report notes that the United States, Ukraine and Israel supplied economic and military aid to Georgia which allowed Tbilisi to consolidate its military forces. By implication, one may conclude that by helping Georgia militarily, those countries emboldened and encouraged the Tbilisi government. Inarguably, it was Georgia's right as an independent country and as a member of the United Nations, albeit not a member of the EU, to take whatever measures necessary to defend its sovereign territory.

The question is why only America, Ukraine and Israel helped Georgia? The answer is geopolitical. The U.S. is interested in the stability and integrity of the oil-rich Caucasian-Caspian Sea area. The Ukrainian government at the time was trying to do everything to weaken Russia's grip on its neighbors and implicitly on itself. As for Israel, the answer is more complex. One of the proposed reasons is the proximity of Georgia to Iran and Israel's intentions to neutralize Iran's nuclear ambitions by using Georgia as a way station. Yet, the report stops short of mentioning either the real causes of the war, or the grave consequences of a larger Caucasian conflict.

According to the Wall Street Journal of October 1, 2009, Russia and Georgia received the report with interest and both claimed vindication. Moscow claimed the report *"found that Tbilisi triggered the conflict."* But Tbilisi was quick to point out that according to the same findings *"Moscow acted illegally in the extent of its invasion"* and in addition *"its troops allowed ethnic cleansing on Georgian territory."* Actually, Georgia's president, Mikheil Saakashvili, stated that he had no choice but to order the shelling of South Ossetia's capital *"to stop imminent attacks on Georgian villages, to bring the region under Tbilisi's control, and to deter a Russian invasion already in progress."* From this point of view, certain Western analysts concluded that if sovereignty means anything, it means that leaders of a state have the right to take proper actions within their borders as they see fit to defend their countries. Within these confines, Georgia acted legitimately, the Wall Street Journal concluded. Indeed, why blame a small country defending itself against a colossus since according to the report *"the EU and the US consider that Abkhazia and South Ossetia have no right to secede from Georgia."*

The Georgian government also claimed that the European investigators ignored evidence that Russian soldiers were already in South Ossetia on August 7, 2008, when the war started. Accordingly, Georgia said it had acted in self-defense. Tbilisi's envoy to the European Union also stated that the inquiry had confirmed *"almost all the facts which Georgia had been alleging, but it erred by determining that Russia's military actions did not qualify as an invasion."* The report emphasized indeed the *"years of provocations, mutual accusations, military and political threats, and acts of violence"* that led to the war and urged readers to look beyond the issue of "who shot first." As for Russia, Moscow interpreted the findings differently. *"For the first time, the report directly names the causes of the conflict,"* said Konstantin Kosachev, chairman of the Committee on Foreign Affairs of the Russian Parliament. And as reported on October 1, by the Wall Street Journal, he stressed the fact that the report pointed to Georgia as a trigger of the war vindicated Russia's position in the eyes of the world.

However, Jorg Himmelreich, a German analyst with the German Marshall Fund, wrote in his article "Missing From the Georgia Report" published on October 3, 2009, that interpreting the five-day war was more complicated. In his opinion, the report has a major flaw: *"It fails to thoroughly analyze the decisive role that the United States played before, during and after the conflict."* Only a detailed assessment of President

George W. Bush's policy and its failures, he wrote, can fully explain the outbreak of the war. He continued: *"Once the war broke out President Bush decided against any U.S. military action, and instead encouraged President Sarkozy of France to seek a cease-fire."* He claims that this was a mistake because only the United States had the political clout and power *"to negotiate and enforce a serious peace agreement with Russia."* Himmelreich further added that *"Mr. Sarkozy deserves credit for stopping the war, but he had to accept onerous Russian conditions."* Thus, in his opinion, President Bush's failure was one of *"not doing rather than wrongdoing; not stopping Mr. Saakashvili and not taking the lead in the peace settlement."*

Washington's Position

One may say that the position of the previous U.S. administration was clear, but not firm enough. On September 18, 2008, during the ceasefire, the former Secretary of State Condoleezza Rice was the keynote speaker at the Marshall Fund meeting in Washington, DC. Her comprehensive speech addressed the state of American-Russian relations in light of the just ended Russian-Georgian War. Interestingly, she foresaw many of the ideas and a good part of the spirit of the EU report, revealing how difficult it is to solve anything in the so-called Russian "Near Abroad." The very next day the Russian Ministry of Foreign Affairs refuted Ms. Rice's statement, point by point. The two pronouncements were posted on the respective web sites of the State Department and of the Russian Embassy in Washington. The official positions of the two governments could not have been further apart. Yet, both countries were careful, were coldly polite, and avoided aggravating the situation and ending up in a renewed Cold War.

An independent analyst should emphasize that in cross-cultural relations each side mirrors its values, expectations, beliefs, as well as its past experience. In cross-political settings each side reflects and defends its "interests." In the Caucasus region, the United States is promoting Western interests in a more open and less aggressive way which mirrors America's experience. Russia is doing the same thing, but according to its own historical experience which is one of brutal force and aggression. In the case of Georgia, the main difference is that Russia was promoting its interests close to home while America was thousands of miles away. And Moscow continues to treat the Caucasian region as part of the Russian geopolitical sphere of influence. To counteract this, the United States must show clarity of purpose, strength and determination. Angry pronouncements or acts of accommodation would not do it. The result is that the Caucasian conflict continues to be today where it was before the publication of the EU report and where it was at the time of Ms. Rice's speech in Washington. Actually, Moscow is in a stronger position now than two or three years ago and the world community cannot do much about it. In a way, the international comments of the findings of the report have arrived at the same conclusions.

Conclusion

A Russian official, for example, said that he did not expect the conclusions of the EU report to have any major impacts on Western policy toward Russia or to change the status quo in the area of conflict. And he noted that the topic of Georgia came up only briefly during the recent meetings of the United Nations. This statement was quoted by Ellen Barry from Moscow in an article published by the Wall Street Journal on September 29, 2009. At the same time, Alexandr Gabuyev, a Russian journalist with the *Kommersant*, wrote that neither Moscow nor Tbilisi have managed to prove that their military actions in August 2008 were justified. According to him, however, the report indicates clearly that the EU will never support Russia's actions in the Caucasus and will never come to terms with the recognition of Abkhazia and South Ossetia. His remarks were aired by BBC News on October 1, 2009. As for Georgia, although she feels exonerated, according to the same broadcast, her chances of regaining control of the two breakaway regions are dim and the hopes of joining the EU and NATO are very slim.

Generally speaking, the EU findings are neither fully conclusive nor broad enough to settle the many unsolved problems regarding this war and the lingering bitter relations between Russia and Georgia. In fact, by blaming both countries, the report seems unlikely to resolve the debate over which bears more overall responsibility and how to settle the ongoing dispute. Yet, it should be noted that the Eastern European countries have insisted that Russia's policies in Georgia epitomized

Moscow's new and dangerous expansionist tendencies. And Himmelreich, the German analyst of the Marshall Fund, stressed that the Russian-Georgian war of August 2008 did not end the political conflict, adding that the conflict has all the potential to explode into a new armed confrontation any day.

The truth is that Russia is not giving up its geopolitical claims to the "Near Abroad" and is working tirelessly to regain its previous sphere of influence. The 2008 Caucasian war was chiefly a conflict for the control of a larger area with huge oil and gas resources stretching from the Black Sea to Central Asia. Russia is determined to regain control over a big buffer zone bordering NATO and the EU. Will the next battle between Russia and the West be over the former Soviet Central Asia? And will Moscow win again? In this regard, the new American administration will have to clarify its position and to take a firm stand if it wants to contain an expansionist Russia.

Russia and Ukraine: Part 1, November 17, 2008

The Russian-Georgian war of August 2008 opened the possibility of a new direction in Moscow's geopolitical attitude toward the former Soviet space and especially toward Ukraine. Following the collapse of the USSR, the Russians could not swallow their wounded pride and could not forget their former empire. For years after the 1991 dismemberment of the Soviet Union, Moscow continued to view the newly independent republics as its exclusive sphere of influence and called it the "Near Abroad." Moscow adopted similar, yet differentiated, policies in the large area that surrounds the new Russian Federation. With regard to the newly independent republics that now separate Russia from Europe, Moscow grudgingly allowed the three Baltic republics to gain their independence. At the same time, Moscow managed to secure the allegiance of Belarus and to transform Moldova into a puppet state. Ukraine, however, Russia's true link and bridge to Europe, remained a big question mark.

Had Russia given up its territorial ambitions, it would have relinquished any old claims and would have established friendly relations with all the newly independent countries that replaced the Soviet Union. But it is obvious that Russia did not renounce its imperial goals. For example, in the new Eastern European geopolitical configuration, Moscow sees Moldova as a stepping stone toward the Balkans, and more importantly, as a safe outpost behind Ukraine. For Russia, Ukraine is the real Gordian knot. In fact, it is hardly possible for Russia to see itself as a superpower, or even as a regional power, without Ukraine. Will Moscow forgo in the foreseeable future its claim over this important European country?

Ukraine is the Cornerstone of Eastern Europe. As one of the largest and most important countries of Europe, Ukraine has the misfortune to exist in the shadow of a colossal bear that in the past had embraced to death all its neighbors. The two east Slavic nations, Russia and Ukraine, are related from an ethnic and linguistic point of view and for centuries have evolved in close association. These facts make a complete separation very difficult. With the passage of time, numerous Russians have settled in Ukraine, while countless Ukrainians settled in Russia, the two peoples becoming virtually indistinguishable from each other. There are also millions of mixed marriages and numerous Ukrainians have adopted Russian as their native language. For its part, Moscow tried hard to minimize any differences between Russians, Byelorussians and Ukrainians. In the past, Moscow used to refer to the Byelorussians by their proper name, "White Russians," but it referred to the Ukrainians as the "Small Russians." The reality is that throughout most of their history, the Russians looked down on the Ukrainians, mistreated them and grossly neglected their aspirations. Consequently, when the Soviet Union broke apart in December 1991, most Ukrainians rejected any new close association with Moscow. However, Ukraine is politically unstable, its population is very much ethnically mixed, and its territory was artificially assembled by Moscow.

Historically, much of today's Ukraine descends from the "Kievan Rus," a city-state that flourished one thousand years ago. In time, the state fell to internal conflicts and was successively subdued by the Islamic Tatars, by Russians and by Poles. As a result of those foreign invasions, to this day modern Ukraine reveals various influences. The Tatars, who settled chiefly in southern Ukraine and particularly in the Crimean peninsula where many of them still live, are of Asian origin and belong to the Muslim religion. The Tatars were later strengthened by the Ottoman Turks, also Muslims, who dominated for centuries the Black Sea and the southern area of Ukraine. Eastern Ukraine, located near Russia, became highly russified, a process facilitated by the Christian Orthodox religion shared by most Russians and Ukrainians. Western Ukraine, formerly under the Poles and part of it lately under the Austrians, became Catholic and highly westernized. Of all the foreign occupiers, the Tatars and the Turks were indirectly the most consequential for the present state. Trying to defend themselves against the Turks, in 1654 the Ukrainians appealed to Moscow for help and united their land with Russia. In practical terms, that led to the annexation of their country by Moscow.

The Twentieth Century was very turbulent for the Ukrainians. As junior partners to Russia, the only Ukrainians who could prosper under the tsars were those who served Moscow's interests and assimilated with the Russians. Small wonder, after the Bolshevik revolution Ukraine seized the opportunity and in 1918 proclaimed its short-lived independence. Four years later it was occupied again by the Red Army and was transformed into a Soviet Republic. The Sovietization was followed by seventy years of incredible suffering. Most Ukrainians, who were generally peasants, opposed the Soviet regime and particularly the collectivization of their land. As a consequence, the Soviet Union under Stalin engineered a murderous famine that claimed the lives of millions. That horror was so vivid among the Ukrainians that when Germany invaded the Soviet Union during the Second World War many of them sided with their new occupiers. This event led to a new Soviet revenge in the late 1940's when more millions were starved. After Stalin's death the situation returned to a modicum of normalcy, but any manifestations of Ukrainian patriotism were harshly suppressed. When finally the USSR imploded, Ukraine was among the first to proclaim its independence. Ever since, Ukraine's relations with Moscow have been difficult, revealing a deep mutual distrust. Nevertheless, Russia under Boris Yeltsin recognized Ukraine and Europe greeted the newly independent country.

Since its independence in August of 1991, Ukraine is one of the most populous and most endowed European countries. By size alone, 233,000 square miles, Ukraine is actually the largest country in Europe, but it is still dwarfed by the enormous size of neighboring Russia. Yet, Ukraine is a large, rich and important country in its own right.

Largest European countries

Country	Sq. Miles	Pop. Millions	Arable Land	Per capita GDP
Ukraine	233,000	46,9	58 %	$ 6,300
France	212,209	60,6	33 %	$ 28,700
Germany	137,847	82,4	33 %	$ 28,700
U. K.	94,526	60,4	26 %	$ 29,600

Source: The World Almanac and book of Facts 2006. New York, 2007

Ukraine used to be called the bread basket of Europe and under the Soviet years it did feed a large part of the population of the USSR. Although some of its soil fertility has been depleted by years of Soviet abuse, with 58 percent of its land as arable, Ukraine remains one of Europe's richest agricultural countries. Ukraine is also endowed with other important natural resources such as coal, iron ore and other metals, salt, sulfur, as well as oil and natural gas. Based on these resources and on its proximity to Russia, the former Soviet regime built a rather strong industry in Ukraine that included metallurgy, heavy industry, machine building, military equipment, aircraft industry, chemicals and others. However, a good part of these big industrial complexes were built in the east, where the ethnic Russians are predominant. Also on the negative side, the forced industrialization of Ukraine led to grave cases of air and water pollution, to several mine disasters and to the well-publicized Chernobyl nuclear accident. This unique accident caused by faulty Soviet designs and inadequate maintenance led to great loss of human lives and its effects were felt from Finland to Romania.

Despite its natural resources, Ukraine's economy is not considered developed by Western standards. Its GDP, for example, was only 300 billion dollars in 2004. By comparison, the GDP of Germany was $2.4 trillion, $1.8 trillion in the United Kingdom and $1.7 trillion in

France. That translates into a per capita GDP of more than four times bigger in Western Europe than in the Ukraine. Even in Russia the per capita GDP was considerably higher than in Ukraine, but that did not make the Ukrainians want to join Russia. On the contrary, after its newly acquired independence Kiev wanted to distance itself as much as possible from its former master and expressed its strong desire to join Europe and NATO.

Russia and Ukraine: Part II

Ukraine's attitude was decisive in sealing the destiny of the Soviet Union. In his book, Yeltsin: A Revolutionary Life, Leon Aron devoted several pages to how hard Boris Yeltsin had to negotiate a new relationship between Moscow and Kiev, with the Ukrainian leaders. Neither Mikhail Gorbachev nor Boris Yeltsin wanted or expected the dissolution of the Soviet Union and the dismemberment came as a shock to both the leadership and average Russians. To avoid a total disintegration, Gorbachev and Yeltsin proposed to replace the USSR with a Union of Sovereign States. Ukraine, however, rejected any further submission to Moscow and insisted on a simple "community of equal and independent republics," whose primary objective was to be economic. Even the road toward such a limited community was very bumpy. President Yeltsin declared that he could not conceive a new union without Ukraine, but on December 1, 1991, Kiev organized a referendum in which 80 percent of its people favored independence. Once again, Ukraine chose to go its own way, but contentious problems arose from the start. Among the problems that required further negotiations were the questions of: the Russian minority living in Ukraine; the sovereignty of Crimea; the nuclear arsenal left behind in the Ukraine; and, the ownership of the former Soviet Black Sea Fleet.

From a political point of view, during the first years after the Soviet collapse, Ukraine was led by former Communist Party bosses, including Leonid Kravchuck and Leonid Kuchma, who in many ways acted in concert with their former colleagues in Moscow. In December 2004, however, a younger, Western-leaning, non-Communist leader, Viktor Yushchenko, was elected president. Suddenly Ukraine appeared to be on its way to real independence and the new president acted immediately to prove it. As reported by Stratfor.com on August 13, 2008, the new leader "issued an edict mandating that all Russian naval and air forces traversing Ukrainian territory and in particular the Russian Black Sea Fleet give their Ukrainian counterparts a 72-hour notice on movement, destination, cargo and munitions details." The Russian Foreign Ministry immediately called the decision a serious anti-Russian move. Moscow would not easily relinquish its control over Ukraine and to this end it was determined to exploit all the weaknesses of its former vassal.

Ethnic, Cultural and Other Related Problems

The most difficult obstacle for the Russians to accept Ukraine's total separation and independence is probably historical and psychological. Aron argues that Ukraine occupies "a unique place in Russia's historic memory and national consciousness." The current generation of Russians cannot reconcile themselves with the loss of their former empire and Ukraine is the key to their European holdings. Hypothetically, it appears that Moscow might even be willing to sign some union accord with the European Union and possibly join NATO if Russia could hold on to its former domains and would be treated as an equal partner. But to let Ukraine join NATO and the EU is unconceivable for Moscow.

From an ethnic standpoint, almost one third of Ukraine's population is non-Ukrainian. Of its 49 million inhabitants about 20 percent are Russian and at least another 10 percent speak Russian as their mother tongue. Other important minorities are Tatars, Romanians, Poles, etc., who also prefer Russian as a means of cross-national communication. Linguistically, the Ukrainian language is now official and mandatory, but Russian remains widespread. In addition, many Russians and Russian speakers are concentrated in eastern Ukraine and in Crimea, where they outnumber the Ukrainians.

From a religious point of view, most Ukrainians are Eastern Orthodox Christians, but the Orthodox Church is almost equally split between those who belong to the Russian Patriarchate of Moscow and those who belong to the national Ukrainian Patriarchate, which is not even recognized by Moscow. The relationship between these two churches is uneasy to say the least.

Economically, eastern Ukraine was mostly developed during the Soviet years and Moscow is unwilling to relinquish its rights over this area. As a matter of fact, recently when Ukraine wanted to sell modern Soviet-era tanks manufactured in this region to a third country, Moscow claimed that it could not do so without its consent. From certain points of view, Russia's military hardware depends on this Ukrainian region, which begs the question of, 'what happens if this region threatens to fall into NATO's hands?'

Geopolitical Problems

The status of Crimea is another bitter bone of contention between Russia and Ukraine. During the early Middle Ages, Crimea was inhabited by Slavic people in the north and by Greeks and Italians living in city-states by the Black Sea in the south. Then, during the 13th and 14th centuries the peninsula was conquered by the invading Tatars who later allied themselves with the Turks. The Turks kept Crimea from 1478 until 1774, when it was occupied by Russia. Consequently, from 1774 until 1954 Crimea was part of tsarist and later Soviet Russia. During those centuries the proportion of Tatar inhabitants slowly diminished, while the number of Russians and Ukrainians increased. In 1954, on the anniversary of 300 years of Russian-Ukrainian "union," former premier Nikita Khrushchev gave Crimea to Ukraine probably as a gesture of good will. At the time, an independent Ukraine was beyond imagination.

Crimea is now an autonomous republic of Ukraine with its own constitution and parliament. The Peninsula has an area of 10,100 square miles and a population of about two million. Of these inhabitants 58 percent are ethnic Russians, 24 percent are Ukrainians and 12 percent are Tatars. The main port of Crimea is Sevastopol, where the remaining part of the former Soviet Black Sea Navy is based. For years following the Soviet collapse, this Navy became a contentious issue between Ukraine and Russia, but after difficult negotiations the two sides signed an agreement granting Russia most of the Navy and allowing it temporary lease of the harbor. However, the agreement is due to expire in 2017 and Kiev is not inclined to extend it, which means additional problems. The recent dispute over the Kerch Strait illustrates once again the precarious state of Russian-Ukrainian relations.

The Crimean Peninsula is separated from Russia to the east by the Kerch Strait which also closes the small Azov Sea. During the Soviet years, the Strait was controlled by Moscow and it made little difference who had nominal title to it. After the fall of the Soviet Union, Russia became very concerned, especially since Moscow and Kiev did not draw the maritime boundary through this Strait. According to Stratfor.com of November 10th article, Ukraine, Russia: The Importance of the Kerch Strait, Russia currently controls half of the Strait and rents the other half from Ukraine, in order to freely transport its goods into the Sea of Azov. Russia has also made several offers to rebuild the transport systems across the Strait, but Ukraine refused. Very recently, to prove that the land belongs to Ukraine, President Yushchenko ordered more troops into Crimea and additional patrol boats to watch the port of Sevastopol. The Ukrainian authorities declared, however, that they did not intend to wage war against Russia, but neither would they allow a replay of the South Ossetian scenario to take place in the Crimea.

International military specialists claim that in case of a conflict over the Kerch Strait Ukraine cannot possibly challenge Russia successfully. They also underline that during such a conflict most of the local Crimean population would side with Russia, which could lead to a civil war. The Kerch incident was rather small, but a small dispute like that could trigger a much larger one, given the strategic importance of this area to the Kremlin. Russia's fear is that an independent-minded Ukraine would allow NATO forces access to the Sea of Azov and thus encroach even further upon Russia's interests. In preparation for such an eventuality, Moscow is issuing Russian passports to many inhabitants of Crimea and this trend has accelerated after the recent Georgian war. If eastern Ukraine is highly influenced by Russia and would side with Moscow in a possible conflict, western Ukraine is a different story.

By historical standards, Western Ukraine is a relatively recent addition to the country with lands annexed, some of them very recently, from Poland, Slovakia and Romania. In the past, many inhabitants here belonged to Poland or Austria and some of them became Catholics and acquired a Western education. To this day, these people feel like they belong to Europe rather than to Russia. In fact, such people helped the modern Ukrainian renaissance and after the fall of the USSR have insisted on strong links to Western Europe. It was also in this part of Ukraine that presidential candidate and former Prime Minister Viktor Yushchenko found his largest mass of supporters. However, the difference between east and west Ukraine made the noted American scholar and Harvard professor, Samuel P. Huntington, write in his book, The Clash of Civilizations, that "Ukraine is a cleft country with two distinct cultures." Indeed, Ukraine is roughly split along the Dnepr River with the eastern part of the country being very much pro-Russian and the western part being pro-European. Accordingly, it is said that in case of a conflict, Ukraine could split along cultural and linguistic lines. And Moscow is all too willing to provoke such a split. In fact, it appears that Moscow is already preparing for such a scenario, as revealed in the Carpathian area of Ukraine.

In the westernmost corner of Ukraine one finds the Carpathian Oblast, a scenic mountainous area, which was acquired by the former Soviet Union mostly from Slovakia after the Second World War. The area is strategically located in the heart of Central Europe near Slovakia, Hungary, Romania and Poland. Economically, Ukraine promotes the Carpathians as a popular tourist and resort area. Politically, the Carpathians are an entirely different matter. This area is inhabited chiefly by Ruthenians, a population linguistically related to both Russians and Ukrainians, but still distinct of the two. Recently, the Rutherian leaders organized themselves into a regional council and after a meeting held in October of 2008 issued an unexpected statement. They stressed their decision to pursue their own independence following the Kosovo model. The leader of the council, Dimitri Sidor, is an Orthodox priest subordinated not to Kiev but directly to Moscow. According to the Ukrainian TV Channel 5, the Ruthenians insisted that if Kiev would not grant them autonomy by December 1, 2008, they would seek a separate independent state under the name of Carpathian Russia. In the meantime many Ruthenians began to ask Moscow to grant them Russian passports and citizenship and Russia was eager to oblige. A similar ploy was used in the two breakaway provinces of Georgia, before Moscow sent in the troops to allegedly defend the local Russian citizens.

To the west as well, Ukraine also has territorial disputes with Romania. In 1940, prior to the beginning of World War II, the USSR invaded the Romanian provinces of Bessarabia and Bukovina and annexed part of them to Ukraine. The leaders in Kiev are aware of this thorny issue and claim that Romania is presently Ukraine's worst enemy. Having obtained foreign lands that never before belonged to Ukraine, Kiev is now worried that in the new world order it might lose some of them. Indeed, a Russian-Ukrainian conflict will undoubtedly involve Moldova, where Russia maintains troops and military equipment on Ukraine's southwest flank. This will attract Romania, and would further complicate the Eastern European scene. With all these ethnic and territorial implications, Ukraine is caught in a real dilemma. Should it continue to pursue a pro-Western policy, Russia may simply decide to dismember it.

What Should the West Expect?

For the time being, the best Ukrainian policy to keep the country together is to preserve the status quo and to continue to act as a bridge between Russia and Europe. But as Huntington noted, a bridge is not a strong and desirable position and it can eventually break. That reality makes the Ukrainians want to anchor themselves to a strong shore, but they face a difficult dilemma; should it be with Russia or the West?

For now, Kiev and Moscow are mostly posturing and are rather careful not to cross the line. President Yushchenko may really want to join the EU and NATO, but the Ukrainian leadership is split on these issues and he does not have much support, even in Kiev. His chief ally, Prime Minister Yulia Tymoshenko, is also a Ukrainian patriot, but she seems to be an ambitious woman, who wants to become president herself. This is weakening the present political alliance. The former prime minister and contender to the presidency, Viktor Yanukovych, is avowedly pro-Russian having received strong support from Moscow, particularly from then-President and current Prime Minister Vladimir Putin, as evidenced by the 2004 election results from eastern Ukraine.

Parliamentary and presidential elections will be held in 2009, but it is unlikely that they will resolve the real Ukrainian dilemma.

At the recent EU-Russia meeting held in Nice, Russia's President Dimitri Medvedev appeared determined to keep Ukraine close to Moscow. As reported by Agence France Press (AFP), Medvedev declared that Moscow firmly opposed Ukraine inclusion in NATO. As also reported by AFP, Russia's ambassador to Brussels warned strongly against granting Ukraine and Georgia Membership Action Plans (MAP) to start negotiations for integration into NATO. Actually, during the 2008 NATO Summit held in Bucharest, the main European countries opposed the integration of Ukraine and Georgia in the Alliance. Strangely, the United States insisted on granting membership to the two countries, and U.S. Defense Secretary Robert Gates declared that negotiations could start even without going through the preparation stages. Should the U.S. insist on including Georgia and Ukraine in NATO, such an insistence may cause a split in the organization, which is what Moscow wants in the first place.

During the Bucharest Summit, Ukraine's ambassador to Romania declared that his country was very determined to join NATO. As reported by the Romanian Press Agency, Ukraine's ambassador underlined that to this end Ukraine was prepared to fight "till the last bullet." All these facts and statements made Moscow draw the line and put its foot down. From a Russian point of view, Ukraine will have to stay as it is or risk the consequences. Should Ukraine cross the line, the world should expect the unexpected. In all likelihood, Russia would invade the Ukrainian territory east of the Dnepr River, ostensibly to defend the Russian minority there and then it may accept to negotiate a settlement. Europe and the United States may not accept a replay of Georgia, but it is doubtful that NATO will intervene militarily, although Secretary of State Condoleezza Rice and Ukrainian Minister of Foreign Affairs Volodymyr Ohryzko signed the U.S.-Ukraine Charter on Strategic Partnership and Security in Washington on December 19, 2008. In the event of such a scenario, the United States and the North Atlantic Alliance will have to take a clear-cut position in order to save Western and especially American credibility.

Red Famine: Stalin's War on Ukraine. Anne Applebaum, Doubleday, NY, 2017, November 28, 2017

This book review is added to better understand the complex and painful relation between Russia and Ukraine. History is very much alive in East Europe! *Red Famine* is a much needed book at a time when Moscow is threatening again Eastern Europe. The book is mostly about the great famine of the 1930's, but it covers the history of Ukraine from 1917 to the recent Russian annexation of Crimea. Most of the facts are known, but placed within the political context of the time, and with full documentation, they make for a better understanding of Ukraine.

The Russo-Ukrainian conflict is old, complex, and not over yet. The famine triggered the most brutal clash between Moscow and Ukraine, but it was not the only one. Famines have been common throughout history. It happened in China under Mao, but it was the result of misguided policies. The 1930s famine was initially caused by Moscow's requisition of grains to feed the cities and to pay for industrialization. As early as 1920 Lenin had *'explicitly called for the requisition of all grain at any price'* (p. 59). In Ukraine, however, starving people into submission was a political weapon. The result was catastrophic. Over 6 million people died in the 1930s throughout the USSR, but four million died in Ukraine alone. In Kazakhstan also over a million people died. Most of them perished because they were forced to relinquish their nomadic ways, and in the process they lost their livestock and died. The Ukrainian disaster was purposefully caused by Stalin to destroy Ukrainian identity and nationalism; *'it was a case of genocide…'* (p. xxvii).

Practically, the famine started with the 1929 Soviet decision to collectivize agriculture.

To implement collectivism, Moscow sent 25,000 activists to the countryside to convince the peasants to join the kolkhoz. Most peasants opposed the process and were punished. Party activists would search for every kernel of grain hidden by the peasants. They poked the ground in search of caches of grain and confiscated livestock, and even pots and pans used for cooking. The results were gruesome. Class struggle was continuously emphasized and neighbor was instigated against neighbor. As for the idea of *social class*, Ilya Ehrenburg, a well-known Marxist journalist at the time, wrote about the victims... *'Not one of them was guilty of anything; but they belonged to a class that was guilty of everything.'* (p. 241). Such attitudes would justify mass arrests, deportations, executions, starvations, and finally, cannibalism...

Here are some testimonies: In a village visited by a Western agronomist in 1933 *'about half of the villagers were already dead. (p. 287)...'Dead villagers lay in the roads, along the road and paths. There were more bodies than people to move them.'* (p. 243)...*'Moribund people were thrown in common pits because... they would die anyway.'* (p.255)... *'By the late spring and summer cannibalism was wide-spread.'* (p. 256). In documented cases, parents killed and ate their children. *'Children were being hunted down as food.'* (pp. 257-259). *'It was one of the greatest man-made horrors in a century...'* (p. 337)

Few people dared speak against the official policy. Party leaders that questioned the orders coming from above were purged and even executed. The renowned Soviet novelist Mikhail Sholokhov wrote personally to Stalin and Stalin's answer was scary: *'You see only one side of the matter... Those who were starving were not victims... they were responsible for their terrible fate. They had caused the famine, and therefore they deserved to die.'* (pp. 294-295).

From an official Soviet point of view, the famine did not exist. It was never mentioned in the media and statistics about it were cooked. Foreign journalists were strictly controlled. Those who would mention the famine were denied visas. Those who wrote favorably about the Soviet Union were rewarded. For example, Walter Duranty, a *New York Times* correspondent in Moscow who was granted the privilege to interview Stalin, published an article titled mildly: *Russians Hungry, but not Starving.* (31 March 1933). It was part of a series about the *'successes of the collectivization and the first Soviet Five-Year Plan.'* In today's jargon, it would be described as truly "Fake News." Yet, for his articles Duranty received the Pulitzer Prize for journalism. Future President F.D. Roosevelt even praised Duranty's stories..! (p. 311).

Historically, Ukraine was the bread basket for Russia, but it was equally important geopolitically. In this regard, the Communists continued the old tsarist policies. Stalin himself denounced Ukrainian nationalism and was determined to annihilate it… '*In 1919 a peasant revolt in Ukraine had brought the White Army within a few days' march of Moscow; in 1920 chaos in Ukraine had brought the Polish army deep into Soviet territory… The USSR could not afford to lose Ukraine.*' (p. 185). Nationalism was the biggest enemy of the USSR. Intriguingly, these days, nationalism is a big enemy of globalization. Is this a coincidence?

As a native Romanian, I now understand better some events that I witnessed as a child or I read about. The land collectivization that occurred in Romania in the 1950s was modeled after the Soviet collectivization, albeit a less ruthless one. And, the famine in Soviet Moldova (former Romanian Bessarabia) and the mass deportations to Siberia in the 1940s were repeats of what happened in Ukraine. As for Ukraine, ever since the Middle Ages Russia has been and continues to be obsessed with controlling it. And, Moscow remains obsessed with maintaining control even now in the post-Soviet era. Regarding the former Soviet Union, President Reagan was right: The USSR was an evil empire. And, yet, some Western leftists still fantasize about Soviet Communism. And Ukraine continues to blame Russia for many of her ills, including the great famine of the 1930's. Reconciliation between the two countries is a tall order.

Azerbaijan and U.S. Policy. July 17, 2013

The new periphery of Russia in Europe consists of the Baltic republics (Estonia, Latvia and Lithuania), Moldova, and the South Caucasus republics of Azerbaijan, Georgia and Armenia. Ever since the collapse of the Soviet Union this area has constituted a bone of contention between Russia and the West. Although the Baltic republics have achieved worldwide recognition and Moscow has grudgingly renounced them, Moldova continues to exist in a state of limbo, while the South Caucasian republics remain a bitterly disputed area. As for Belarus and Ukraine, for the time being they remain under Russian control.

The immediate contending powers in the Caucasus are Russia, Turkey and Iran, but on a global level the real struggle for dominance is between Moscow and Washington. For now, Armenia has chosen to remain in Russia's sphere of influence, but based on its Diaspora, it has also cultivated good relations with America and Western Europe. Georgia, with its important geostrategic location on the Black Sea, has been victimized the most during the post-Soviet years. Of the three Caucasian countries, Azerbaijan, located in the South Caucasus, is the most important to America and the West because of its strategic location between Europe and Asia and, moreover because of its energy resources. Arguable, Georgia maintains its strategic importance as an energy export route, critical to keeping Russian ambitions in check. However, America's policy toward Azerbaijan, as well as toward most of the post Soviet newly independent republics, especially under the Obama administration, is perceived as confusing and incoherent. Thus, from the outset, one is confronted with some rather philosophical questions. Do superpowers have any moral obligations toward small countries? Should the United States, for example, pursue only its interests; or, should it also pursue overall humanitarian goals? In this regard, the U.S. and Azerbaijan offer a good case study.

In his article of June 11, 2013, "Geopolitical Journey: Azerbaijan and America," George Friedman of *stratfor* focuses on the importance of Azerbaijan from a geopolitical and energy perspective, while emphasizing the difference of perception between Washington and Baku and the resulting confusion. In Azerbaijan, writes the author, you *"listen to their desire to be friends with the United States and bewilderment at American indifference...Everyone is unhappy with the United States either for doing something or not doing something. In either case, they feel let down by the United States."* This is certainly a commentary on President Obama's foreign policy contradicting established relations with Azerbaijan, as presented by the State Department. And, Azerbaijan is not the only post-Soviet republic that feels let down by Washington. Consequently, America is losing friends and supporters.

The reality is that the stakes are very high in Azerbaijan. Russia is working hard to extend its grasp over the country. If Moscow could control the flow of Azeri gas and oil towards Europe, it would acquire a higher degree of influence over the old continent to the detriment of the United States. Turkey, an increasingly stronger regional power which depends on Azeri oil, would like to recreate Azerbaijan in its secular image and tie it to the West. At the same time, Iran with its very sizable Azeri minority, is set on turning Azerbaijan into an Islamic republic in its own image, meaning another anti-American outpost. And this is not unlikely, given that 96 percent of the Azeri population is Islamic, of which 85 percent is Shi'a, the primary faith of Iran.

And then what will America do? Washington is caught in a geopolitical game with Moscow, in a play of interests with American private corporations, and in a web of complicated moral/humanitarian issues. As a result, America's policy is perceived as weak and indecisive, with Moscow gaining the advantage.

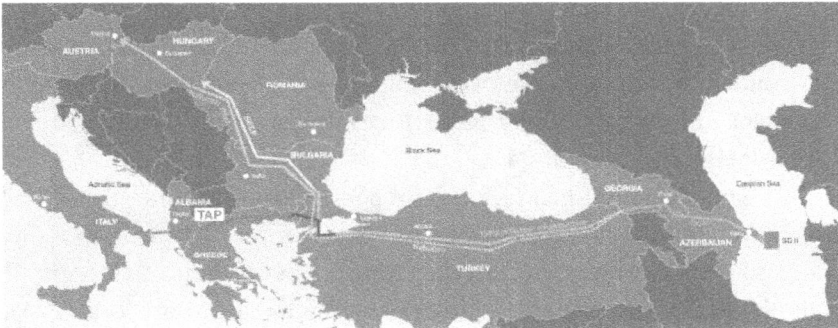

Source: Liquida.It.

The Nabucco project, for example, a pipeline designed to bring energy to Central and Western Europe thus reducing Russia's influence over the continent, is being abandoned in favor of a smaller Trans-Adriatic Pipeline (TAP) much less threatening to Moscow's dominant energy interests. At the same time, after implementing the so-called "reset" of U.S.-Russia relations, the 2008 Russian aggression against Georgia and the occupation of Nagorno-Karabakh of Azerbaijan by Armenia, with Russian help, have already been forgotten. In this uneasy situation, Azerbaijan is begging for American friendship and understanding. Baku needs moral and political support and wishes to buy American arms to strengthen its position. Yet, the United States remains uncommitted. In his article, Friedman admits that nations have no friends and *"the United States must pursue its interests."* But, can Washington pursue its interests, in this case, without hurting the Azeri people and, in the end, without hurting its own interests? Where does this leave the United States?

According to Friedman, in the future, the European Union will become weaker and Russia will get stronger and will try to regain its previous control over Eastern Europe. Nevertheless, he adds, America's foreign policy remains cautious, uncertain, and without foresight. It is indeed a skill and an art to combine objective national interests with subjective friendships with smaller countries that need America's help. But a friend in need is a friend indeed, and this is the core of the matter. Last year I was interviewed by a Romanian TV station and the interviewer, a known pro-Western journalist, presented me with the sad reality of today's Romanian economy and asked me whether it would not have been better for the country to remain with Russia. My answer was short and to the point. "Knowing the Russian-Romanian relationship, ever since the two countries made their first contact, would you trust Russia?" His answer, sadly, was no!

The change of heart of several persons may not alter the attitude of a nation, but the change of heart of many people, may lead to radical changes. The strongly pro-American former government of Georgia, for example, has been replaced by a new one inclined toward Russia. And this trend may be repeated in other countries at the Russian periphery, as well, if America continues to ignore the pleas for friendship and assistance of these countries. It is important to pursue national interests, but is also important to cultivate and maintain friendships. U.S. policy makers are divided between realists and idealists, with the former pursuing national interests and the latter emphasizing friendship and humanitarian aims, but the two approaches are not mutually exclusive. Can it be done in this instance?

Mr. Friedman argues that *"sometimes the United States does inexplicable things. Sometimes it fails to do necessary things. When the United States makes a mistake it is mostly other countries that suffer or are placed at risk."* Azerbaijan is a case in point, but it is hardly the only one. Georgia and Moldova are in a similar situation. Their people expect American support, but except for friendly declarations the awaited support does not really come. George Friedman claims *"the United States can afford to support only countries that take primary responsibility for their national security on themselves."* Yet, how can small countries like Georgia, Azerbaijan or even Moldova help themselves against the Russian giant? They do need a friend like America, but for the most part they see Washington as only pursuing American interests. And, Mr. Friedman's conclusion is worth stressing. *"The United States must adopt a strategy of early and low-risk support for strategic partners rather than sudden, spasmodic military responses to unanticipated crises."* The implied advice for Washington, as well as my own opinion as an American of Romanian origin, is to "follow your interests, but do not overlook the extended hand of friendship of those who need you. Otherwise, one day the mighty America may face the world virtually alone."

Turmoil in the Republic of Moldova. May 4, 2009

Europeans have very long memories and understanding current conflicts often requires incursions into their history and culture. The socio-political conflict that occurred recently in the Republic of Moldova is one of them. The post-Soviet republic is just the truncated eastern part of the old Romanian Principality of Moldova, a part that was better known as Bessarabia. An American scholar wrote in 1944 that Bessarabia was "the most critical territorial problem bequeathed to the present generation as a direct legacy of the old-age Eastern Question." The territory was a problem then, is still a complicated one today 65 years later, and will remain a problem for as long as the world ignores its real significance.

Background

The province, located between the Prut and Dnestr Rivers, was occupied for the first time by tsarist Russia in 1812. At the time, its population was overwhelmingly Romanian although they called themselves Moldovans (Moldoveni in Romanian). The modern name of Romania was adopted following the union of Moldova and Vallachia in

1859. Part of the province was reintegrated with Romania after the Crimean War ended in 1856, but it was annexed again by Russia in 1877. Following the Bolshevik Revolution of 1917, the province voted to reunite "once and for all" with Romania, but the new Soviet authorities did not recognize the union.

In 1940, after the Ribbentrop-Molotov Pact of 1939, the Red Army invaded Romania and annexed this province once again. The annexation was followed by mass arrests, deportations, summary executions and other unspeakable atrocities. It has been estimated that about one million people, mostly ethnic Romanians, suffered at the hands of the Soviet regime. To further weaken the Romanian character, the annexed province was dismembered and its northern and southern areas became part of Ukraine. At the same time, and to complicate the issue, a slice of land located on the left bank of Dnestr River was given to a newly formed Soviet republic. Ever since, this trans-Dnestr piece of land, has remained a hub of Communist activities led by its Russian minority.

Throughout the entire Soviet period Moscow tried to relocate many local Romanians, chiefly to Kazakhstan, and to bring in ethnic Russians. Despite this Soviet relocation policy, when the USSR began to implode in 1989, about 65 percent of the population of the republic remained ethnic Romanian. During the Soviet years, however, the local people were forced to call themselves Moldovans and to use the Cyrillic alphabet instead of Latin in their writing. This was the only cultural difference between them and Romania.

When I visited there as a Voice of America (VOA) reporter in 1989, the local scene was explosive. Huge masses of people were demonstrating with Romanian flags, asking openly for a change of language and alphabet and indirectly for reunification with Romania. At the time, Romania was still under the Communist regime of Ceausescu, who was afraid of losing his own power. Shortly thereafter, Communism was overthrown in Romania and Ceausescu was executed. He was replaced with Ion Iliescu, a disgruntled Communist who had studied in Moscow where he had been a colleague of Mikhail Gorbachev. To win the presidency of Romania, Iliescu agreed to leave Moldova in the Russian sphere.

Ever since its post-Soviet independence, Moldova has been a Russian puppet state. However, because Moscow did not trust the Romanian majority of the republic, it encouraged its trans-Dnestr region to proclaim separate independence. And to consolidate its position in 1992 the self-proclaimed Dnestr Moldavian Republic went to war with Moldova. During a short war its local forces were helped by the Russian 14th Army located in Tiraspol, used tanks and armored cars, and also occupied the town of Tighina (Benderi in Russian) on the right bank of the Dnestr. The war caused about one thousand victims and according to Helsinki Watch dislodged over 100,000 people.

Since the beginning, Moscow assisted and controlled this region, which remained nominally Communist and a hub for underground arms trafficking and illicit activities. Even as late as April 17, 2009, Russia's foreign minister declared that Moscow would continue to assist this breakaway region. As for Moldova, a Russian journalist wrote that Moscow was spending more money there than on any other former Soviet republic to keep it within its sphere. The stakes are geopolitical.

Russian Geopolitics

Since the dismemberment of the Soviet Union, Moscow's geopolitical game has changed tactically, but strategically it has remained very much the same. Initially, Russia still wanted to play a strong hand in the Balkans, but the breakup of Yugoslavia and the reorientation of Bulgaria toward the West, blocked Moscow. The Kremlin also alluded that it might agree to let Romania regain Moldova provided Romania would not join NATO. Then, when Romania joined NATO, Moscow tried to oppose the installation of American military forces on its territory. Losing its grasp on the Balkan Peninsula, Moscow concentrated on its regional position. What became clear then was that in no way would Russia allow Ukraine to join NATO. From this point of view, Moldova and its trans-Dnestr region acquired a renewed importance as pawns on the Western flank of Ukraine. And since Moldova itself is not safe, Moscow is backing the Dnestr republic.

EUROPE'S PRO-RUSSIAN ENCLAVES

Recent Events

Over the past 20 years, the majority of the people of the Republic of Moldova have rediscovered their Romanian roots. However, Moldova fell into economic decay, corruption and extreme poverty. By any measurement, Moldova is the poorest European state and its people are desperate. A large number of them have left for the West, and a multitude applied for Romanian citizenship. Under such dire conditions and with strong backing from Moscow, in 2001 the local Communists regained power. They were and still are led by Vladimir Voronin, a former KGB general and an unreformed Communist. Since his rise to power, the socio-economic situation of Moldova has deteriorated even further. Despite being president, Voronin's position is not strong politically. As pro-Russian, he had hoped to receive Moscow's support to regain control of the trans-Dnestr region. Moscow, however, needs this region for its own geopolitical designs. Russia maintains the remnants of the former 14th Soviet Army with some 3,000 troops and huge quantities of munitions in this self-proclaimed republic. For the time being, Voronin is still useful to Moscow, but he is also expendable.

In recent years, the population of Moldova became increasingly stressed and dissatisfied, and the younger generation is more and more vocally pro-Romanian, pro-democracy, and pro-European. The last hope of the population was the election of April 5th for which several opposition parties were prepared to challenge the Communists. As for Voronin and his party, throughout their years in power, their biggest fear was Romania. They continuously denounced, accused, and attacked Romania as having designs on Moldova. Indeed, Romania has been offering scholarships to young Moldovans and has granted Romanian citizenship to some applicants. Nevertheless, as a member of NATO and the European Union, Romania has been very careful with its former province. Nonetheless, the Moldovan Communists kept accusing Bucharest of interference. In a way, the Communists are right! The biggest "interference" is that the majority of the people of both countries are Romanian and that cannot be hidden anymore. At the surface, what triggered the April protests and the clashes with the police were the cries of the population that the Communists have again rigged the election. But this is only the proverbial tip of the iceberg. It was only the latest cries of the population who were fed up with living under the Communists, away from Romania, and under Moscow.

The election was held on Sunday April 5th and the next day the Communists announced that they had obtained over 50 percent of the votes. The truth is that the Communists have the upper hand because most of the young people have gone to work abroad and they do not vote. At the same time, the retirees and those who still work at home, are under the thumbs of the former Communist bosses who control the economy. No one, however, believed that the vote count was honest.

This was the straw that broke the camel's back. Monday after the election crowds of young people began to gather in downtown Chisinau for peaceful protests. The next days, there were over 20,000 demonstrators. The Communist regime answered with brutality. The demonstrators became more unruly too, and the two sides began to collide. The demonstrators carried a sea of Romanian flags and chanted:

"We are Romanians; we want to be with Romania." Voronin and his Communists were enraged. Security police began to club the students and to arrest them. Many journalists, especially from Romania, were expelled from the scene and all Moldovan students studying in Romania and wanting to return to Chisinau were stopped at the border. Yet, the clash with the police escalated. The demonstrators singled out the parliament and the government's building as symbols of Communism and stormed them. They occupied the tall building of the parliament and raised the Romanian flag. Later, with police brutality escalating, the students set the building afire and at least two floors were trashed before the blaze was extinguished. Twenty years ago, Moscow helped overthrow Ceausescu. Some observers see the same scenario now in Chisinau. If so, what is Russia's goal?

Since the 20th of April, it has been reported that some 200 students have been arrested and at least three of them were tortured to death in police custody. Their names and pictures were published in the press. At the same time, several young female students were badly beaten, sexually abused, and raped by the police. During the student revolt, Romania was rather quiet except for the people who organized peaceful demonstrations of support. Chisinau, nevertheless, expelled the Romanian ambassador, Filip Teodorescu, making him a scapegoat. In response, the president of Romania, Traian Basescu, summoned the Parliament, denounced the Communist government of Moldova, and asked the legislature to immediately pass a new law that grants Romanian passports to many Moldovans.

The Western European media covered the conflict to a limited degree only. But it did mention that Moldova was a non-state, implying that the very need for its existence is questionable. Officially, the European Union and the United States appealed for calm, for negotiations, and for a peaceful resolution. The European Parliament also decided to fully investigate the turmoil. Unwisely, however, the U.S. and the EU refuse to acknowledge the real problem. The problem is that Moldovans are Romanians and they want to rejoin their true country. On the other hand, Russia, which is aware of the reality, is practical.

Moscow suggested that it would allow the return of Moldova to Romania if Bucharest would recognize the independence of the Dnestr Republic.

The leadership of the European Union is not unified on this issue and is unwilling to accept the reality. For its part, Washington has an ambiguous attitude which in the end could turn against America's security interests. Washington wants military bases in Romania and Romanian soldiers in Afghanistan, but it ignores the feelings and aspirations of the Romanian nation. As for now, the age-old Eastern European question of Bessarabia is still an open wound. One day, though, Russia itself could decide to return the province to Romania, and America will be left on the sidelines. Only then will Washington understand that its top advisors have not acted with America's best interests in mind.

A Small Country in Limbo. November 15, 2009

Following the rigged April 7 elections and the bloody street protests that followed, Moldova organized new general elections held on July 29. The communists still obtained the largest number of votes, but no longer the majority they claimed after the April elections. As a matter of fact, the April elections were denounced as rigged by most international observers, by many Western countries, and by the European Union. The only country that defended them was Russia, but even some Russian journalists criticized them. The reality is that Moldova has become a bone of contention between Russian and Western interests. The new July 29 election results have not solved or clarified much. Yet, they brought to power a pro-Western coalition that wants to join the European Union.

According to Western observers, the July elections were generally fair, but not necessarily democratic. The Moldovan Communist Party, which controls much of the economy, the police and military forces, as well as a large part of the media, remained influential. While the United States, the European Union, and Romania supported the democratic opposition, Moscow backed the communists. Yet, Moscow was also prepared for an alternative. As a result, the Communists obtained 44.7 percent of the votes along with 48 parliamentary seats. Together the opposition obtained about 52 percent of the votes and 53 parliamentary seats. However, the opposition represents a fractured bloc of parties. The largest is the Liberal-Democrat Party, which obtained 16.4 percent of the votes. The next are the Liberal Party, with 14.4 percent, the Democrat Party, with 12.6 percent, and "Our Moldova" alliance, which received 7.4 percent. Consequently, no one party alone could form the new government or elect the new president. It is worth mentioning that Moldova has a uni-cameral legislative with 101 seats and a candidate needs an absolute majority of 61 votes to be elected president.

After the July election, the local and the international press pointed out that the opposition parties must join forces to be able to form a coalition and to govern this small and very poor former Soviet republic. Indeed, the opposition parties could form the new government if they join forces, but they still need the support of some communist legislators to elect the president. And regardless of any cooperation between the democratic bloc and the communists, some analysts claim that the new government could only move Moldova from a pro-Russian course undertaken under the communists to a neutral one. In fact, as reported by the paper *Ziua* of 4 August, the Muscovite publication *Kommersant* wrote that the elections showed there are in fact two opposing Moldova; one pro-Western and pro-Romanian, and another one pro-Russian. The journal stressed, however, that the pro-Russian faction of Moldova is losing ground.

The *Financial Times* of London, the *Kommersant*, and other publications, have already reported that the new Moldovan government appears to be in the hands of Marian Lupu, the new president of the Democrat Party. Marian Lupu, a 43 young man ethnic Romanian, is a former member of the Communist Party and the ex-speaker of the Moldovan Parliament under the previous communist government. He became politically active following the collapse of the Soviet Union and grew up as a realistic and pragmatic man. Initially, he opposed joining NATO, stressed neutrality for Moldova, and favored better relations with both Romania and Russia. The *Financial Times* also mentioned that Lupu is an able and charismatic leader who managed to attract a large number of Romanian speaking voters as well as many Russian-speaking citizens. Lupu became the key politician in the post-election period making himself indispensable to the opposition. And although he recently ruled out any cooperation with the communists, it will be very difficult to avoid them.

Moldova attracted international attention immediately after the July elections. As reported by Moldova.Org (USA) on August 6 the U.S. Helsinki Commission organized a session of hearings called "Moldova's Recent Elections: Prospects for Change in Europe's Poorest Country." The topic of discussion was Moldova's future. The same day Moscow reduced by almost 50 percent the price of gas deliveries to Moldova. The European Union announced that it would restart the negotiations on a new cooperation accord. However, the EU asked Chisinau to reestablish its relations with Romania and to abolish the visa requirements for the Romanian citizens. Then, unexpectedly, China announced it was ready to loan Moldova one billion dollars to finance all of its economic projects. The loan conditions were extremely favorable at three percent interest over a period of 15 years, with a grace period of five years. Why this sudden Chinese interest in Eastern Europe? According to *Ziua* of 17 August, an Indian economist stated that apparently China is getting ready to replace Russia in the post Soviet space.

In the meantime, the new Moldavian authorities celebrated the anniversary of its Declaration of Independence and the adoption of Romanian as the official language of the republic. The linguistic movement known as *"Limba noastra cea Romana"* or "Our Romanian Language" was extremely important in the reawakening of the local national spirit in the late 1980's. In a desperate move to counter the new pro-Romanian and pro-Western trend, the chief of the Communist Party, Vladimir Voronin, flew to Soci on the Black Sea to meet Russia's President Dmitry Medvedev. According to *Ziua*, the meeting took place on August 22. However, the Kremlin leader did not encourage Voronin and said that Moscow was ready to work with the new coalition in Chisinau. In an unexpected change of attitude, Medvedev even stressed that Russia wanted to work with Moldova within the limits of the established international diplomatic norms. Then, as reported by Moldova.org and *Ziua*, the new Parliament of Moldova met in its first session on August 28. The communist legislators boycotted the session, called Lupu a traitor and refused to lend him any support. Nevertheless, the parliament went ahead with its agenda and unanimously elected Mihai Ghimpu as the new speaker of the legislative body.

At 58, Ghimpu is the chairman of the Liberal Party, and was among the signatories of Moldova's Declaration of Independence. His late brother, Gheorghe Ghimpu, spent five years in the Siberian Gulag for having claimed that the so-called Moldavian language was just Romanian. On September 11 former communist president Voronin resigned and Mihai Ghimpu was elected interim president of the republic. The communists again denounced the new government and some local Russians even warned that a civil war may be in the making if the new authorities move the republic toward Romania, EU and NATO. Analysts in Moscow stressed, however, that neither of these perspectives is an imminent possibility. They even claimed that the European Union does not want new and poor members like Moldova. Yet, the Russian Duma warned that if Moldova moves toward union with Romania, Moscow would officially recognize the independence of the breakaway Dnestr Republic.

As temporary president, Ghimpu, another ethnic Romanian, was cautious in approaching Romania without upsetting Moscow too much. He declared, however, that Moldovans are simply Romanians, but the Romanians live now in two different states. In an interview published by *Timpul* (The Times) of Chisinau on 21 September he said: *"We know very well what happened in 1940 when the Soviet Union occupied this territory. The Soviets could not say that they freed the Romanians form under the Romanians, so they invented the Moldavian nationality…"*

In the same interview Ghimpu asked Moscow to withdraw its troops from Moldova. It is worth remembering that Russia maintains military units and very large quantities of equipment in the Transdnester region of Moldova on the left bank of the Dnestr. Ghimpu also addressed the accusation that he is a "unionist," meaning union with Romania, and therefore against Russia. He answered by stating, *"If I plead for truth and justice, for my true identity, does that not mean I am against someone else…?"* I am not against the Russian Federation or against the Russian *language,* he continued, *and for me the word "union" has positive connotations. "I am for the truth and I want to tell people the truth,"* Mr. Ghimpu said in closing his interview.

In the meantime, and as reported by *Ziua* of 23 September, the newly appointed prime minister, Vlad Filat, declared for the German radio Deutche Welle that the former communist president Vladimir Voronin is a criminal and that he and his thugs should be sued and imprisoned. But the communist leader did not easily accept his party's loss of power. He went to Moscow for new consultations and suggested that new elections be held. However, Moscow's attitude was luke-warm. Russia can indeed manipulate Moldova, but it is also aware of its pro-Western trend and it fears that any new elections could further weaken the positions of its Moldovan allies.

Since the defeat of the communists, Moldova implemented a policy of rapprochement towards Romania and the West. Thus, Chisinau followed the EU request and again allowed the Romanian citizens to visit Moldova without prior visas. At the same time, it reversed a previous decision and announced that the citizens of Moldova, including officials, are allowed to hold double citizenship. Previously, one of the biggest fears of the communists was that if Moldovans were allowed double citizenship most of them would become Romanian citizens. According to Romanian laws, the people living in the lands annexed by the Soviet Union in 1940 are entitled to citizenship, if their parents or grandparents were Romanian citizens before the annexation. Meanwhile, the parliament tried twice to elect a permanent new president and each time the communists boycotted the session and the attempts failed. Yet, fearing that in a new election they may lose their seats, a number of communist legislators indicated that they may vote for a president designated by the democratic opposition. Such a move would further split the communist party.

As for the future, Moldova will probably continue to remain in a limbo until a strongly pro-Romanian generation comes of age, or until another international agreement decides its fate. On the other hand, given Moldova's geopolitical importance for Russia, Moscow will most likely bitterly oppose its integration into NATO, as it has for any and all of its former Soviet republics. With regard to reunification with Romania, there is no doubt that this remains the ideal of most Moldovan Romanians. And given Romania's membership in the European Union, many non-Romanian ethnics may also prefer this option. Overwhelmingly, Romanians from both Romania proper and Moldova believe in reunification.

Belarus: Still an Outpost of Tyranny. May 10, 2011

Former Secretary of State Condoleezza Rice during her January 2005 Senate confirmation hearing labeled Belarus as one of several remaining "outposts of tyranny" saying that America stood with the oppressed people on every continent. Speaking in Lithuania the following April, Rice thought it a good idea for ex-Soviet Republics to "throw off the yoke of tyranny.

This was no less evident on the evening of December 20, 2010, the day after polling results gave Alexander Lukashenka nearly 80 percent of the vote among nine presidential candidates, when tens of thousands amassed to demonstrate their opposition in Minsk's Independence Square. But they were met with brute force and violence by Belarusian riot police. Demonstrators gathered to denounce the elections with shouts of "Freedom! "Down with Lukashenka!" and "Down with Gulag!" a reference to the Soviet-era labor camps.

Often referred to as the "Last Dictator of Europe," Belarusian President Alexander Lukashenka, at 59, poses as a populist leader, considers himself the father of the nation, enjoys songs about himself, and has no intention of quitting. While suppressing any dissent at home, he toys with ideas of approaching the West and occasionally irritates Russia with his attitude and statements. (In a way, it is what Ceausescu of Romania did for many years before alienating himself completely from the people followed by a show trial and execution). Some journalists compare Lukashenka's leadership style to both Stalin and Hitler. According to *Newsin* and as reported by *Romania Libera* of April 14, last year even Moscow criticized him. In a series of TV broadcasts, Moscow described Lukashenka as "psychologically unstable and as a man at the limits of his rationality who cannot stand to be contradicted in any form."

During his 16 years as president, Lukashenka has maintained himself in power with the help of the security apparatus, which in Belarus is still called KGB, as during the old Soviet era. His regime has rigged elections, suppressed the media, expelled several foreign ambassadors and caused the disappearance of opposition leaders. Many people are convinced that those opposition leaders were victims of secret death squads.

Domestic and foreign analysts point out that Alexander Lukashenka was little known before the collapse of the Soviet Union, but he manipulated the new system cleverly to attain power. For example, after being elected president, a constitutional amendment was passed that lifted the two-term limit placed on the presidency outmaneuvering the opposition at every subsequent election, when in December 2010 he was reelected to a 4th term. The 2010 election was described by Fred Weir of the Christian Science Monitor as violent and fraudulent. He reported that immediately after the election the state-dominated media declared Lukashenka the winner with an unprecedented 79.7 percent of the votes. The newspaper added that in spite of a strong opposition and mass democracy demonstrations, allegedly none of his opponents won more than 3 percent of the votes.

Believed to be connected to the December 2010 disputed presidential election results that rocked Minsk with mass demonstrations, the April 11, 2011 explosion that shook Minsk's *Oktyabrskaya* subway station reportedly killed 13 people and wounded more than 200. The explosion attracted worldwide attention to this small post-Soviet republic which had declared its independence in August 1991, after the disintegration of the former Soviet Union.

Belarus is a rather small country surrounded by Russia, Ukraine, Poland, Lithuania and Latvia. It has almost 10 million inhabitants and a surface area of about 80,000 square miles or roughly the size of the state of Kansas. Historically, the country was dominated by its neighbors, and in more recent times it was annexed by Russia and then by the USSR. The Belorussian people are of Slavic origin and are closely related ethnically, culturally and linguistically to the Russians.

Post-Soviet Belarus is confronted with a number of severe problems

First and foremost, geopolitically, Moscow cannot accept a fully independent Belarus, or for that matter even a fully independent Ukraine, as recent events have proven. In one way or another, Moscow considers and treats the two East Slavic countries as extensions of Russia. As a result, any attempt by Belarus to act contrary to Russian interests, such as joining NATO or the EU, would be blocked by Moscow.

Second, Belarus does not have a tradition of sovereignty or political democracy, and its geographic location adjacent to Russia and far from Western Europe makes it even more difficult to act independently or to develop a democratic political system.

Third, the Belorussian economy was developed mostly under the Soviet regime and is highly integrated with the Russian economy. Among others, Belarus depends on Russia for energy and raw materials, as well as a market for its goods. Despite objections from Western governments, Belarus has largely continued its Soviet-era policies, such as state ownership of the economy. Furthermore, in 2000, Minsk and Moscow signed a treaty for greater economic and political cooperation calling for a monetary union, single citizenship and a common foreign and defense policy. However, the implementation of the treaty was marred by various disputes. Yet, by comparison to Russia, Belarus is a poor country. Its per capita GDP, for example, is about half of Russia's. Consequently, while politically many Belorussians would like to adopt Western values and principles, the aforementioned factors continue to link the country to Moscow. In addition, the post-Soviet regime, which has been led for over 16 years by Alexander Lukashenka, has contributed a great deal to keeping the country in limbo. Lukashenka has kept Belarus in an uneasy state between a past that cannot be easily escaped and a future that so far has remained beyond reach.

While Belarus ostensibly provides Russia with a protective buffer from the West, deep within its borders lies the notorious site of the Katyn Forest where, in 1940, the Soviet KGB under Stalin's direct orders massacred Poland's elite officer corps. More recently, the 2010 flight commemorating the 70th anniversary of Katyn that was destined for

Minsk crashed in Smolensk, just across the Russian border, carrying Poland's political establishment headed by President Lech Kaczynski. The Polish delegation consisting of 94 high-ranking civilian and military officials, including a dozen members of parliament, the president of the national bank, all the heads of Poland's armed services and the head of the national security bureau, all of whom were to meet with Russian Prime Minister Vladimir Putin for a special memorial ceremony. The entire Polish delegation perished in the accident.

Before the Minsk subway station explosion on March 29, Amnesty International demanded the release of a Belarusian student who had just been sentenced after his 2010 arrest. It was the third such conviction in a week. *"It's chillingly clear that the three activists have been sentenced on the basis of trumped up charges just because they dared to criticize elections that were plagued by irregularities,"* wrote Nicola Duckworth. He added, "These men are prisoners of conscience jailed for the peaceful expression of their views and they must be immediately and unconditionally released."

Some of those arrested were still detained in April 2011 and many local and international organizations demanded that they be freed. It was in this tense atmosphere that the April bomb explosion occurred.

Apparently, the European Union and NATO are open to further eastern expansion if the countries under consideration qualify for membership. Nevertheless, due to its undemocratic behavior, in 1997 the Council of Europe barred Belarus from membership. Any negotiations about joining the EU or NATO are currently out of the question; of course, Lukashenka serves Moscow's purposes.

Vice President Biden described the situation saying: *"The people of Belarus have demanded and they deserve basic rights. We have condemned the government of Belarus for the repression of its own citizens. We've joined the European Union in imposing sanctions against that government, and we call for the immediate release of all political prisoners."*

The current American stand is also well reflected in the most recent Human Rights Report released by the State Department in April 2011. The report indicts both the country's leadership as well as Belarus' form of government: *"Since his election as president in 1994 Lukashenka has consolidated his power over all institutions and undermined the rule of law through authoritarian means, including manipulated elections and arbitrary decrees. Subsequent presidential elections were neither free nor fair, and fell well short of meeting international standards.... During the year authorities continued to commit frequent, serious abuses in a system bereft of checks and balances, and dominated by the president... The government failed to account for past politically motivated disappearances. Security forces beat detainees and protesters, used excessive force to disperse peaceful demonstrators, and reportedly used torture during investigations... Authorities arbitrarily arrested, detained, and imprisoned citizens for criticizing officials, participating in demonstrations, and other political reasons..."* And the report continues on a similar note.

Despite intense foreign and domestic criticism, Alexander Lukashenka and his regime are digging in and continue to maintain total control of the country. At the same time, they accuse the West and the local opposition of trying to sabotage Belarus. Various articles posted by Google in April this year show that the Organization for Security and Cooperation in Europe (OSCE) made a request to send a special international mission to Belarus to investigate the violations of human rights. Minsk rejected such a mission, accusing the West of double standards, and resorted to even more repression.

Immediately after the tragic incident of April 11, Lukashenka ordered an investigation of the opposition leaders whom he labeled "enemy of the people" and who in his words represent a "fifth column" of foreign interests. Also, according to recent BBC News broadcasts, Lukashenka congratulated the police on their "brilliant" operations and called for a thorough "cleansing" of the Belorussian society. As recently as April 15 *Agence France Press* (AFP) announced that the authorities had just reprimanded two leading Minsk newspapers for their coverage of the subway bombing. A few days later, on April 21, the same agency reported that President Lukashenka stated the deadly Minsk attack was caused by the *"disgraceful and excessive democratic measures installed by Belarus after the last presidential elections in order to please the West."*

The Jamestown Foundation's, Eurasia Daily Monitor (April 19, 2011—Volume 8, Issue 76) stressed, *"On virtually every opposition website reporting on the tragedy, the comments section is replete with suggestions that Lukashenka himself was responsible for the attack, seeking a diversion from his current economic problems."*

The reality is that after 20 years of political repression, mismanagement and state control of the economy, Belarus is in dire straits. *Stratfor Global Intelligence* of April 4, for example, wrote: *"Moody's financial ratings agency downgraded several Belarusian banks and downgraded the local currency deposit ratings of three state-owned Belarusian banks."* It was the latest in a series of financial and economic setbacks for Belarus. As a result, people rushed to the banks to exchange their rubles and began to form again long lines in front of food stores as during the old Soviet years. Moreover, STRATFOR underlined that the current situation could give Russia a new opportunity to strengthen its control over Belarus.

What can be expected in this situation? Politically, Belarus may embrace a certain degree of democracy at some future date, but economically it will remain tethered to Russia for a long time to come and likely remain in Moscow's sphere of influence. Geopolitically, it is hardly imaginable that Moscow would relinquish its control over Minsk.

Chapter 2
Moscow's Challenges
and Washington's Answers

Since the end of the Cold War relations between Washington and Moscow have fluctuated from open and amicable to cool and suspicious. Presently, they seem to be contradictory and difficult to grasp, though, one thing is sure: Russia is doing everything to keep the "Near Abroad" under its control while harassing American interests globally wherever it can.

Obama's "Mission Impossible" to Moscow. July 21, 2009

As a presidential candidate, Senator Barack Obama envisioned a new foreign policy of dialogue with the leaders of countries with which Washington had adversarial relations. As president, however, he committed America not only to a policy of "engagement," but also to one of "accommodation" with the hostile governments of Cuba, Venezuela and Iran, along with a "restart" of U.S.-Russian relations, to paraphrase Secretary of State Hillary Clinton.

President Obama's mission to Moscow likely hoped to achieve a rapprochement following last year's cooling off period with the U.S. and the EU, caused primarily by Russia's military aggression against the Republic of Georgia. From Moscow's point of view, the situation was more complex. Sensing the probable NATO expansion into its Soviet-era sphere of influence or its "near abroad," Moscow was determined to regain hegemony over its former republics. Thus, it strengthened its position in the Caucasus and it stiffened its attitude toward Ukraine, Georgia and Moldova. Furthermore, Moscow made it clear that it strongly opposed the American plan of placing a missile defense system in Poland and the Czech Republic. And to make sure that its new geopolitical policy would succeed, Moscow also strengthened its control of oil and gas supplies to Western Europe. By the time President Obama arrived in Moscow, Russia's leadership knew very well what it wanted and what it could compromise.

At the outset it can be said that President Obama's goals were set too high, while Moscow's were more down to earth. According to the interview given to the Russian newspaper *Novaya Gazeta* on July 6th, Mr. Obama stated: *"My government is completing a comprehensive review of all of our missile defense programs, including those in Europe. Given the threats around the world, especially those growing from North Korea and Iran, our goal is to enhance missile defense for the United States and our allies in Europe and elsewhere...When discussing our plans for Europe, we first and foremost are seeking to build a missile defense system that protects the United States and Europe from an Iranian ballistic missile armed with a nuclear warhead. We are not building and will not build a system that is aimed to respond to an attack from Russia. Such thinking is simply a legacy of the Cold War. We have not yet decided how we will configure missile defense in Europe. But my sincere hope is that Russia will be a partner in that project."*

Russia, however, does not see eye to eye with Washington. From Moscow's point of view, a new missile defense system placed in Eastern Europe represents a threat to Russia's interests. Actually, as reported by Agence France Presse (AFP) and published by Ziua on July 10th, at the recent G8 summit, President Medvedev declared without equivocation that if the U.S. installs the missile shield in Poland and the Czech Republic, Moscow will install the mobile Iskander-M ballistic missile system in the Kaliningrad enclave, now a Russian oblast and a geographic quirk from the World War II-era Potsdam Conference. Situated on the Baltic Sea, Kaliningrad lacks a connecting land route to Russia but offers Moscow a warm water port and a strategic location in North-Eastern Europe sandwiched between Lithuania and Poland. As opposed to Washington, Moscow does not perceive the nuclear programs of Iran and North Korea as priorities or imminent threats to its interests.

With few exceptions, from the beginning, Washington's and Moscow's positions were impossible to reconcile. As a matter of fact, the Russian press and the well-known political analysts in Moscow close to the Kremlin did not express any enthusiasm toward President Obama's visit or his goals.

According to the news agency Ria Novosti, the Russian political analysts were more skeptical than their American counterparts that Russian-U.S. ties could be "reset" or restarted during President Obama's visit. Sergei Karaganov, chairman of the Council for Russia's Foreign and Defense Policy, and a reputed analyst, said "the underlying nature of the concept of a 'reset' was extremely fragile. Russia does not see real changes in U.S. policies and believes they are more of a cosmetic nature." More specifically, he stressed that the Americans were "unwilling to make substantial changes in their policies, including over NATO expansion and the signing of a Russian proposed pan-European security treaty."

Viewed as substantial summit achievements by the White House, Obama and Medvedev signed a Joint Understanding on the mutual reduction of their nuclear arsenals. The agreement specifies: *"each Party will reduce and limit its strategic offensive arms so that seven years after entry into force of the treaty and thereafter, the limits will be in the range of 500-1100 for strategic delivery vehicles, and in the range of 1500-1675 for their associated warheads."* This compares to 1600 strategic launch vehicles and 2200 warheads under the expiring START and Moscow treaties.

Moscow also agreed to allow the U.S. to supply its troops in Afghanistan by crossing Russian air space. But this agreement permits the Kremlin a modicum of control over the American supply route and indirectly it confirms Russia's domination over the former Soviet Central Asia. The United States and NATO can continue to use the U.S.-built air base at Manas, in the former Soviet Republic of Kyrgyzstan, but only with an increase in rent from $17 million to $60 million a year. But to please Moscow, as reported by Ziua on July 8th, Kirghizstan's President Kurmanbek Bakiyev also agreed to grant Russia a new military base at Osh in the southern part of the country.

Although the Obama White House insists there is no linkage between this arms reduction of strategic offensive weapons and the development of a strategic defensive weapons system in Poland and the Czech Republic, President Medvedev sees it differently. In fact, the Joint Understanding specifies in point-5: "A provision on the interrelationship of strategic offensive and strategic defensive arms." Both Barack Obama and Dimitry Medvedev signed the new arms treaty.

As for the delicate questions of expanding NATO into Georgia and Ukraine, Moscow gave the president a clear "Nyet." And for cooperation against North Korea and Iran's nuclear ambitions, Moscow's answer was vague, which in reality is also a diplomatic NO. Furthermore, Medvedev has already spoken out against expanding sanctions against Iran, describing them as "counterproductive." Moscow has its own agenda. According to Newsweek of July 20, the Russians have completed the Iranian Bushehr nuclear reactor and are now about ready to supply Iran with "a state of the art missile defense system." The system costs $700 billion and "would make a U.S. or Israeli air strike … considerably more difficult."

During his meetings with President Dmitry Medvedev and Prime Minister Vladimir Putin, the power behind the throne, Mr. Obama discussed a series of delicate European and international issues. According to Ziua of July 8th, during the Obama-Putin meeting the Russian Prime Minister underlined that Ukraine and Georgia "are very important to Russia." This prompted Mr. Obama to promise that he will "keep this in mind." Pravda on July 8, reported that President Obama had concluded the two-day summit with conciliatory words for Moscow's leaders. He praised Russia's contribution to culture and art and only mildly challenged the Kremlin to change its behavior.

Indeed, during his remarks at the graduation ceremonies for the New Economic School in Moscow, President Obama said: "*State sovereignty must be a cornerstone of international order. Just as all states should have the right to choose their leaders, states must have the right to borders that are secure and to their own foreign policies... That's why we must apply this principle to all nations — and that includes nations like Georgia and Ukraine. America will never impose a security arrangement on another country... And let me be clear: NATO should be seeking collaboration with Russia, not confrontation."*

The conclusion is also clear; for now, the two above mentioned countries – Georgia and Ukraine – are being drawn inexorably into Russia's sphere of influence.

The signal sent by Washington to the world after the recent Moscow summit is not one of strength. Only months ago Russia invaded Georgia, threatened Ukraine, interfered in Moldova's elections, tightened its control over oil and gas supplies to Europe and flexed its muscles internationally. The United States and the European Union reacted with verbal indignation, but not much else. In the meantime, Russia continued to pursue, unabated, its new geopolitical course. President Obama's mission to Moscow legitimized Russia's gains, while the Kremlin gave up nothing of substance.

In addition, Obama's visit to Moscow appeared to neglect the interests of some of America's staunchest allies such as Germany, Poland and Romania. And how are America's enemies, such as Iran and North Korea, going to behave knowing that Washington needs Moscow's approval to act against them?

Take Romania, for example, a country humbly trying to please the United States and whose soldiers fight and die alongside the Americans in Iraq and Afghanistan. After the Moscow summit, Mircea Geoana, the speaker of the Romanian parliament, a former ambassador to Washington and a strong pro-American politician, stated in the parliament, *"The new American administration seems to be interested beyond Romania...a fact that should make Romania rethink and change its policy toward the East [read Russia]..."* The statement was published by Ziua on July 8th. And in neighboring and troubled Moldova, the weekly publication of the Moldavian Writers Union, Literatura si Arta, had an even gloomier remark. According to its editorial Nr. 27 of July 9th, Moldova's Communist president, Vladimir Voronin, promised Russia that in exchange for its support, if reelected, he will: transform Moldova into a federal republic; adopt Russian as an official language; and, reorient its policy toward Moscow. The publication claims that during this summit, President Obama asked Russia to withdraw its troops from the separatist Moldavian Trans-Dnestr republic. Reportedly, Moscow consented as long as America accepted the transformation of Moldova into a pro-Russian federation. Allegedly, Mr. Obama agreed.

Romania may not be important to America and Moldova may be negligible, but what about Germany, Poland, Turkey, Georgia or Ukraine? For two decades now, Ankara has made sustained efforts to befriend its Muslim kin in the Caspian basin and to secure oil and gas pipelines through its territory for Western use. Moscow, however, outmaneuvered the West and reestablished its domination over many of those huge energy sources. Germany and other European countries also wanted to reduce their dependence on Russian energy, but their efforts failed. As for Poland, a country that has bitter memories of its colossal Russian neighbor, how is it going to react if the U. S. hesitates to install the defensive anti-missile bases on its territory after having publicly agreed to do so?

During President Obama's mission to Moscow, it has become clear what the Kremlin didn't give up. But the question remains, "What did the White House give up?"

Secretary Clinton's Mission to Eastern Europe and the Caucasus. July 23, 2010

Operating within the framework of President Obama's "Reset Button" approach to US-Russia relations, Secretary of State Hillary Rodham Clinton's official visit to five countries in Eastern Europe and the Caucasus – Ukraine, Poland, Azerbaijan, Armenia and Georgia – on a long Fourth of July weekend attempted to alter the impression in the region of American indecision, following 18 months of apparent White House neglect of U.S. strategic interests and the administration's unsuccessful attempt to re-craft policy.

Secretary Clinton's first official visit to these former Soviet republics and Eastern bloc countries became a dire necessity in light of the President's failure in implementing his "community organizer" approach to foreign affairs, specifically with respect to sensitive issues surrounding Armenia-Turkey and Armenia-Azerbaijan relations causing a severe rise in anti-American sentiment in Azerbaijan, a now faltering but strategic U.S. ally. In Ukraine and Georgia, events had overtaken

U.S. policy. While in Poland, the President retreated on U.S. missile defense commitments for Europe.

Ukraine: NATO Accession Out of the Picture

Clinton's first stopover in Kiev on July 1 was significant. A series of political events in Ukraine, since President Obama took office on January 20, 2009, have brought about a dramatic change in US-Ukraine relations. The election of Viktor Yanukovych in February has altered the political landscape for America and its allies in the region, particularly with respect to Moscow. The avowedly pro-Russia Yanukovych displaced both pro-Western candidates, President Viktor Yushchenko and Prime Minister Yulia Tymoshenko, during two heated rounds of voting. Yuschenko and Tymoshenko led the pro-democracy movement dubbed the Orange Revolution in 2004 defeating Moscow's then-choice apparent, Viktor Yanukovych.

Relations between Moscow and Kiev, under Yuschenko's administration, rapidly deteriorated and became so bad the two presidents were not even on talking terms. Yuschenko's position to deprive Moscow of a renewed basing agreement for the Russian Black Sea Fleet in the Crimea at Savastopol due to expire in 2017 was a serious irritant to then-Russian President Vladimir Putin. Subsequent natural gas cut-offs by Moscow through Ukraine's transit pipelines leading to Europe in January 2006 and 2009 over large price increases placed added pressure on the pro-Western Yuschenko government during his years in office.

Upon her arrival in Kiev, Secretary Clinton was greeted with the news that Ukraine's parliament, just the night before, had voted to pursue a "non-aligned" status effectively excluding Ukraine from future NATO membership consideration, as Yanukovych's predecessor had ardently pursued. Although, the parliament did agree to continue Ukraine's Partnership with NATO, the potential cooperation with the Western alliance is subject to hundreds of amendments. Immediately after his election, Yanukovych moved rapidly to secure Russian gas supplies in return for extending the Savastopol lease for 25 years, following numerous meetings in Moscow. Interestingly, as president, Yanukovych's first official trip abroad was to Brussels, the European

Union headquarters, declaring his government's intent to pursue EU integration. The EU has become Ukraine's largest trading partner, while Russia remains its single biggest trading partner.

In a joint press conference with President Yanukovych on July 2, Secretary Clinton sidestepped the NATO accession issue by acknowledging Ukraine's participation in Afghanistan and to the previously scheduled US-Ukraine NATO military exercises, saying, *"And we also support a relationship with Russia that is in Ukraine's interest that helps to further what President Obama has called the resetting of relations with Russia."*

It remains to be seen whether freedom of the press along with these newer and fledgling democracies in the region, Ukraine and Georgia among them, will be sacrificed on the alter of President Obama's so-called "reset" policy with the government rather than the Russian people.

Poland: Missile Defense Shield Climb-Down

On August 20, 2008, Poland's Foreign Minister Radoslaw Sikorski sat with his American counterpart, Secretary of State Condoleezza Rice, at a ceremony in Warsaw to sign the *"Ballistic Missile Defense Agreement Concerning the Deployment of Ground-Based Ballistic Missile Defense Interceptors in the Territory of the Republic of Poland."* Nearly two years later on July 3, 2010, Foreign Minister Sikorski, this time, stood with Secretary of State Clinton in a ceremony in Krakow watching as their respective representatives signed an amendment to the Ballistic Missile Defense Agreement, effectively killing the missile defense shield.

Not long in office, President Barrack Obama sent a secret letter to Russian President Dmitry Medvedev that "was hand-delivered in Moscow by top administration officials three weeks ago," the *New York Times* reported on March 2, 2009. Followed by a series of meetings between Clinton and her counterpart Foreign Minister Sergei Lavrov on March 6 in Geneva and Obama and Medvedev on April 2 in London, the Obama administration announced on September 17, 2009 that it would cancel the BMD program negotiated by the Bush administration.

This unilateral cancellation of the BMD missile shield, which was intended *"to protect Europe and the United States against longer-range ballistic missiles launched from the Middle East, and...linked to other U.S. missile defense facilities in Europe and the United States,"* came at considerable cost in Polish political capital in view of Polish public opinion, particularly in the face of strenuous Russian opposition to this ballistic missile defense system. In fact, in 2007, when President Bush proposed the idea, President Vladimir Putin accused the United States of an arms race and threatened to aim nuclear weapons at European targets from Kaliningrad, the Russian Cold War-era enclave on the Baltic Sea; so much for Russian diplomacy. At the Krakow ceremony on July 3, Secretary Clinton stated, *"Today, by signing an amendment to the ballistic missile defense agreement, we are reinforcing this commitment [to Poland's security and sovereignty]. The amendment will allow us to move forward with Polish participation in hosting elements of the phased adaptive approach to missile defense in Europe. It will help protect the Polish people and all of Europe, our allies, and others from evolving threats like that posed by Iran."*

The BMD system, comprised of 10 land-based interceptor missiles, was to have been located in Poland and was supposed to be completed by 2013. The system, as well as a missile defense radar site in the Czech Republic, was replaced with a Phased Adaptive Approach (PAA) to be completed in four phases by 2020. This project, consisting of a mobile defensive Patriot missile system, was also opposed by Moscow. At a press availability, Secretary Clinton directed her comments at Moscow, overly sensitive to any NATO deployment in the region, when she reassuringly stated, *"With respect to Russia, this is purely a defensive system. It is not directed at Russia. It does not threaten Russia. It is a defensive system to protect our friends and allies and our deployed forces,"* from any of Tehran's missile threats.

Critics in Poland viewed this unilateral BMD cancellation by the United States as a climb-down and an appeasement to Moscow.

Azerbaijan-Armenia: The High Risk Gamble

The geopolitical importance of the Caucasus can be best understood when viewed as the land bridge between the Black Sea and the Caspian Sea, where Russia, Iran and Turkey converge. This volatile area is delineated by the Greater Caucasus Mountains which serve as the southern protective wall between Russia and the region populated primarily by Georgia, Azerbaijan and Armenia.

During his campaign for president, Barack Obama established a strong record of Armenian Genocide recognition. On January 19, 2008, Obama pledged: *"As President, I will maintain our assistance to Armenia, which has been a reliable partner in the fight against terrorism and extremism. I will promote Armenian security by seeking an end to the Turkish and Azerbaijani blockades, and by working for a lasting and durable settlement of the Nagorno-Karabakh conflict that is agreeable to all parties, and based upon America's founding commitment to the principles of democracy and self-determination."*

Obama further noted, "As a U.S. Senator, I have stood with the Armenian-American community in calling for Turkey's acknowledgement of the Armenian Genocide."

However, President Obama's failure to successfully implement this "community organizer" approach to foreign affairs in the Caucasus region has become acutely evident in the collapse of his attempted Turkey-Armenia "reconciliation" in dealing with the decades-long issue over the Ottoman Turkish empire's relocation and massacre of 1.5 million Armenians beginning in 1915 through 1923. The Armenian-American community is large, wealthy and politically active having been credited with delivering large blocs of votes in states critical to Obama's 2008 election victory.

The Armenian National Committee of America, which was highly critical of Obama following his remarks before the Turkish Parliament and at his press conference with President Abdullah Gul, issued a statement on April 6, 2009. In part, the statement read: *"In his remarks today in Ankara, President Obama missed a valuable opportunity to honor his public pledge to recognize the Armenian Genocide."*

In pursuing this approach to U.S. foreign policy over an 18-month period in office, the White House slighted Azerbaijan, a Caspian strategic ally in the region, in a number of ways, including:

1) Outright ignoring Baku throughout the Armenian-Turkish attempt at reconciliation;

2) Excluding Baku from the Nuclear Security Summit held in Washington on April 12-13, while inviting Azerbaijan's nemesis, Armenia, to attend; and,

3) Leaving the position of U.S. ambassador to Baku vacant.

Consequently, Azerbaijan began to reconsider its strategic relationship with Washington announcing on April 19 that it had accepted Iranian mediation of the Nagorno-Karabakh territorial dispute between Armenia and Azerbaijan following years of official mediation by the OSCE's Minsk Group co-chaired by France, Russia and the United States. Simultaneously, Baku cancelled the scheduled US-Azerbaijan military exercises. The Obama administration has put at risk the proposed Nabucco natural gas pipeline from Baku located at the tip of the oil rich Caspian Sea Basin, which is to be routed through Georgia and Turkey, bypassing Russia. In the meantime, Ankara backed away from normalizing relations with Armenia, including opening their border and developing trade relations after 16 years, in the wake of the Armenia-Azerbaijan war over Ngorno-Karabakh.

It was with this backdrop on July 4 that Secretary of State Clinton met with President Aliyev of Azerbaijan in Baku and subsequently with President Sarkisyan in Yerevan, Armenia. These two countries of the Caucasus pose very different problems for the United States and in different ways both are important to Washington. Armenia, with a large Armenian-American community, has Western aspirations and affinities, while for historic and security reasons, has aligned itself with Moscow. Azerbaijan, on the other hand, with its enormous oil and gas reserves is economically and strategically important to the United States. Yet, the two countries are deeply split because of the ethnic Armenian landlocked enclave of Nagorno-Karabakh located in Azerbaijan. With Russian support during the 1992-94 war, Armenian forces occupied and practically annexed the territory. The issue surfaced quickly in Mrs. Clinton's Baku meeting with President Aliyev when he demanded bluntly the withdrawal of Armenian troops from Azerbaijan's territory.

On the other hand, in his Yerevan speech, President Sarkisyan of Armenia approached with greater confidence the problem of the disputed region. He spoke of the right of the people of Nagorno-Karabakh to self-determination as one of the most fundamental principles of international law; in his opinion, this principle has been at the basis of independence for most countries in the world. And he thanked America for the support it offered Armenia on the Nagorno-Karabakh conflict, thus tacitly implying that Washington is on Yerevan's side. Not surprisingly, Sarkisyan's reference to international law echoed Moscow's new foreign policy position of "privileged interests" or "sphere of interests" as set forth by Russian President Dmitry Medvedev on August 31, 2008, following the Russian invasion of Georgia. These interests are backed by Moscow's pledge to use force in countries and regions where Russia has "special historical relations."

At a joint press conference with Azerbaijani Foreign Minister Mammadyarov, Secretary Clinton responded diplomatically to these contentious issues by saying, *"we are very committed to trying to bring the parties together to resolve the conflict in Nagorno-Karabakh, and reach a durable peace settlement. We understand that there was a lot of activity over the past year, both with respect to Nagorno-Karabakh and on the Turkey-Armenia normalization track. And unfortunately, we haven't seen the breakthrough that we want to see."* As President Obama continues to carry out his brand of foreign policy in this region, the U.S. has the most to lose, while Russia has the most to gain, especially with American diplomacy in deep disarray in what is likely to become a zero-sum game.

Georgia: Another Strategic American Ally at Risk

The August 2008 Russian invasion of Georgia has left lasting scars in the region not only on the state of Georgian sovereignty, where the two breakaway provinces of South Ossetia and Abkhazia remain Russian occupied, but on the balance of power, which has shifted dramatically in favor of Moscow. That shift actually occurred at the NATO summit held in Bucharest, Romania, April 2-4, 2008, and it became a reality on the morning of August 8, 2008, when Russian forces crossed into South Ossetia through the Roki Tunnel. In Bucharest, the

Bush administration initiative was blocked primarily by Germany and France, fearing the negative reaction from Moscow. Consequently, Georgia and Ukraine were not invited into the Membership Action Plan (MAP), the next logical step toward NATO enlargement, which Russia vehemently opposed. Arguably, had the Atlantic Alliance moved more decisively in that direction, it is unlikely that Russia would have invaded Georgia.

Events in Georgia changed immediately after the Obama administration took office on January 20, 2009, beginning with the Russian news agencies reporting on January 26 of Moscow's intent to construct a naval base on the Black Sea in Abkhazia, an air force base in Abkhazia and a military base in South Ossetia. Since the August 12, 2008 ceasefire, Russia has occupied both Georgian provinces.

Although Georgian troops participate with NATO and U.S. forces in Iraq and Afghanistan, the Obama administration has yet to make good on the US-Georgian Strategic Partnership of January 9, 2009 regarding Defense and Security Cooperation. However, Secretary Clinton was firm in her position saying: *"We continue to call for Russia to abide by the August 2008 cease fire commitment signed by President Saakashvili and President Medvedev, including ending the occupation and withdrawing Russian troops from South Ossetia and Abkhazia to their pre-conflict positions. We also stressed the need for humanitarian access to the territories."*

Secretary Clinton was unequivocal when she stated, *"The United States is steadfast in its commitment to Georgia's sovereignty and territorial integrity."* She stood by Georgia and its "Rose Revolution" suggesting the "reset" policy was working when responding to press questions in Tbilisi on July 5 while referring to Russia's "invasion" and "occupation" of Georgian territory, language that had not been used during the Bush administration. She said she had told President Saakashvili that *"President Obama and I and other American officials raise our concerns about the invasion and occupation with Russian counterparts on a consistent basis."*

President Bush and then-Secretary of State Condoleezza Rice showed resolute support for Georgia in the wake of the 2008 Russian military invasion and that has continued in large part with the trip to Tbilisi in 2009 by Vice President Joe Biden, along with Secretary Clinton's visit. Congressional support for Georgia is bipartisan, perhaps one reason Georgian President Mikhail Saakashvili has not been overthrown by pro-Russian forces.

Secretary of State Clinton's mission to Poland, Ukraine and the Caucasus is intended to reassure America's allies they are as important to Washington now as before President Obama's "reset" policy with Russia. Arguably, America's foreign policy with Russia would be far stronger if the "reset" was with the Russian people rather than with the Kremlin.

Biden's Moldova Visit. March 21, 2011

Vice President Joseph Biden's trip to the Eastern European country of Moldova on March 11 helped to mark the occasion of the 20th anniversary of Moldovan independence. Biden is the highest ranking U.S. government official to visit this former Soviet republic, following stops in Finland and Russia. Prime Minister Vlad Filat called Biden's stop an "historic day." *"And here – here in this region, it has been over 20 years since the collapse of the Soviet Union and the United States has worked with you for a Europe that is whole, free and at peace," said Biden speaking in Chisinau's Opera Square, once the center of the anti-communist protests. "I am here today to congratulate you, not only on the 20th anniversary of your independence...but also for the powerful message your journey toward democracy has sent to millions of people beyond your border."*

In a similar visit to Kiev in July 2009, Biden voiced his support for Ukraine's European integration strongly rejecting "any sphere of influence" in the region, a clear reference to Russian intentions.

Moldova has become a battleground between Russia and the West. Securing its influence once again in the Ukraine, Moscow is now reasserting itself from Moldova to Georgia. However, the United States could not remain indifferent. Indeed, on February 8 the Senate Foreign Relations Committee issued a detailed report regarding the U.S., Moldova and its break-away region of Transnistria (Transdnestr Republic). Then, on March 11 Vice President Joseph Biden stressed

America's support for Filat's new pro-Western Alliance for European Integration led by his Liberal Democrats. Why this sudden surge of interest? What could and what should America do?

Washington could help Moldova regain full control over all its territory. By doing so it would stabilize the region and promote America's security interests in southeastern Europe. But there is an additional problem. Moldova is historically a Romanian land. Why is Washington ignoring this essential fact?

To understand the difficulties confronting Moldova, a few points should be clarified:

1) Moldova cannot be considered a fully sovereign and independent country as long as it does not control its territory;

2) It is hardly possible to understand Moldova outside its Romanian past;

3) Moldova, and especially Transnistria, is an important Russian geo-political pivot in southeastern Europe; and,

4) With Romania a NATO member and Ukraine once again firmly within the Russian sphere of influence, Moldova has become very important strategically. And the chief problem is Transnistria, the region located mostly on the left bank of the Nistru River and which declared its own independence. Actually, Moscow has never relinquished its grasp on this region. By controlling it, Russia encircles Ukraine and it keeps a foothold near the Balkans. Transnistria is thus a destabilizing factor on NATO's eastern flank and an obstacle in America's policy toward the Middle East.

The official Western policy toward Moldova for some 20 years now has been to recognize it as a legitimate state and to aim at integrating it into the structures of the European Union. However, Moscow has done everything to prevent this. First, it divided Moldova politically, weakened it economically, and made it impossible for Chisinau to adopt a clear pro-Western attitude. And second, Russia has rejected any solution regarding the Transnistria territorial conflict.

The Jamestown Foundation recently published two articles explaining the background and importance of Moldova and Transnistria. (*The Eurasia Daily Monitor*, February 15 and 16, 2011). This area took the first steps to split from Moldova even before Chisinau declared its independence. The split was planned by Moscow in anticipation of the Soviet disintegration and led to a short but costly war between Chisinau and Tiraspol, the capital of the split region. After the war, the two parts assisted by various mediators, engaged in on-and-off negotiations. Eventually, they settled on a 5 plus 2 formula that included Russia, Ukraine, OSCE, EU and the U.S., plus Chisinau and Tiraspol, but the process bogged down in 2006. Then, Germany tried to induce Russia to cooperate on this territorial conflict offering Moscow its mediation for the establishment of an EU-Russia political and security committee. Moscow agreed in principle, but only on its own terms. This year, the pressure to re-start the negotiations has intensified, but the results have been modest. Russia wants better relations with the European Union, but without linking them to the Transnistria conflict.

Moscow and Tiraspol "seem intent on stonewalling the negotiations indefinitely" writes Socor, adding that the authorities of Transnistria came up with "five or six counter-arguments and preconditions" against a resumption of negotiations. Tiraspol wants only a confederated link with Chisinau; it wants international guarantees with Russia and Ukraine as guarantors; and it asks that any solution must include the right to a referendum for Transnistria's "independence and with its subsequent integration with the Russian Federation."

This land with roughly 500,000 inhabitants that runs along Moldova's border with Ukraine 'is the Russian empire's frontier'," wrote Gordon Fairclough on March 11 in the Wall Street Journal. And he stressed that Transnistria's president, Igor Smirnov, declared without equivocation that this territory "will always be with Russia." Moscow and Tiraspol also cite the case of Kosovo to justify the existence of Transnistria. In this vein, they ask: If the West recognized the independence of Kosovo, why apply different standards for Transnistria and the Georgian breakaway provinces of Abkhazia and South Ossetia?

Richard Lugar, former chairman of the powerful Senate Committee on Foreign Relations and currently its ranking Republican member, understands the importance of Moldova and has asked for a more active American policy in the region. The February 8 report on

Moldova and Transnistria commissioned by Senator Lugar stresses specifically: *"Recent events should provide the United States with an opportunity to renew high-level engagement in support of forging a solution to this conflict."* And then, it also recommends that *"The United States should strongly support European efforts to resolve the conflict and thereby assist Moldova in advancing its Euro-Atlantic aspirations. A resolute U.S. commitment to this cause will ensure that we do not cede influence in a region of paramount importance to U.S. foreign policy,"* the report concluded.

Biden's visit was highlighted in the *Stratfor Global Intelligence* report as well as in all newspapers of Moldova. Stratfor stressed the obvious: *"Moldova has been kept in a state of political paralysis that has worked in favor of Russia's interest...Biden's visit is meant to reassure the tiny but strategic country that the United States is interested in building relations and that the West has not abandoned Chisinau."* The journal also stressed that *"Moscow has engineered Moldova's political deadlock...and that Russia has substantial levers in the country, the most significant being the allegiance of Moldova's breakaway territory of Transdniestria, where 1,000 Russian military personnel are stationed."* A throwback to the Cold War era in a remnant of the old Soviet empire.

According to the Moldovan newspaper Timpul of March 12, during his brief visit Mr. Biden expressed the official attitude of Washington. He stated clearly that Moldova "must be part, and should be part, of Europe." As for Transnistria, he declared that "the United States will support any effort which should resolve the conflict respecting the sovereignty and territorial integrity of Moldova."

Actually, Stratfor points out that Moldova is not currently a top issue between Russia and the West, but in the future it could emerge as a strategic battleground. Washington knows that at the moment Moldova is in Russia's sphere of influence. In a way, Moldova, Ukraine and Belarus are now in the situation of Eastern Europe before 1989. It will probably take an earth-shaking event to change the status quo. Such an event may happen and history could repeat itself catching America unprepared.

Before drawing a conclusion, the readers should know a few facts about Moldova. According to the latest 2004 Census, Moldova has a population of about 3.4 million inhabitants as compared to about 3.7 million in 1989. The roughly 275,000 fewer people can be explained through emigration. Consequently, the proportion of Romanian-speaking Moldovans increased from 65 percent in 1989 to over 72 percent in 2004. In addition, given the lack of local economic opportunities, it has been estimated that between 10 and 20 percent of the population has left the country in search of work, to pursue their studies, or to try to relocate permanently. The figure is imprecise because many people have left Moldova without proper documentation. An ever increasing number of Moldovans have obtained Romanian citizenship and passports.

During the Soviet era, the Moldovans were coerced under punishment of law to hide their Romanian identity and to declare themselves "Moldovans." They were also forced to use the Cyrillic alphabet instead of the Latin one. However, in 1989 Moldova reverted to the Latin alphabet and began to teach their students about their true identity. As a result, a younger generation of Moldovans has rediscovered and reaffirmed its Romanian roots.

There are a few thousand "Moldovans" who are working or studying, or who have settled recently in the United States. On March 5 those living in the Washington, DC, area organized the well-known Romanian spring holiday celebration called "*Martisor*." Several hundred attendees, many of them dressed in folk costumes, speaking Romanian and singing traditional Romanian folk songs, made their identity known. Nothing can prevent the present generation from wanting to rejoin Romania. And this is the problem. America ought to know it. But Washington prefers to pretend that it does not.

U.S. policy makers should take a hard look at Moldova and place it in its natural Romanian context. Romania is now a member of the EU and NATO and a loyal ally of the United States. While the State Department is befriending the Bucharest government and now the government in Chisinau, it is ignoring the feelings of the Romanian people. It would be a good idea if Washington started at least to consider the possibility of a future reunification of Moldova with Romania.

Russia's Geopolitical Challenge to NATO. August 22, 2011

In the 1990's post-Cold War period following the dissolution of the Soviet Union, the groundwork was laid for the creation of the NATO-Russia Council (NRC) in 2002, where the Kremlin received a virtual seat at the NATO table. Opposition to NATO expansion has never ceased to be Moscow's goal. For example, in April 2008 it exercised its de facto veto over the Ukraine and Georgia's path to NATO accession. Then, in August 2008, Russia invaded sovereign Georgian territory and occupied South Ossetia and Abkhazia.

An Economist article in July 2010 asked the question: Could Russia join NATO? *"Joining NATO,"* it stated, *"means quite deep internal changes. Russia would have to reach, say, Turkish standards of political contestability and the rule of law in order for discussion of eventual membership to make sense."* Russia today continues to consider NATO a "threat" and a "danger" according to its strategic documents.

Russia's record of expansionism is represented by a strong historical and cultural identity, while its geographic identity is rather vague. From Moscow's point of view, Belarus and Ukraine remain part of Russia. Further west and south from the Baltic Sea to Moldova and from there to Georgia by the Black Sea, the area is seen as a Russian sphere of influence. Beyond that, the West is seen as a world dominated by NATO and America and cannot be trusted. Actually, for Moscow the United States continues to be the main enemy. Consequently, relations with post-Soviet Russia remain uneasy and the recent "resetting" of relations by the Obama administration only encourages Russia's geopolitical ambitions.

Could Moscow join NATO and the European Union to defuse the existing geopolitical stalemate? For numerous reasons, the short answer is No! First and foremost, NATO membership presupposes Moscow's recognition of the territorial integrity of the European nations, including Georgia.

Russia of the last 500 years that the world has known would no longer be itself if submitting to a center other than Moscow. Actually, by adopting the socio-political arrangements and behavior of the West, Russia could even disintegrate. For the current generation of Russians, Russia must keep to itself and must be wary of the Chinese multitude to the east and of the European influences to the west. Yet, in this era of interdependence, Moscow can no longer develop in isolation and for this reason its attitude is ambiguous.

Moscow envies Europe's and America's level of development and prosperity and would like to enjoy the fruits of their status, but without changing its own socio-political system. While trying to emulate some aspects of Western culture and technology, Russia has established economic bridges with the larger European countries, such as Germany and France. However, Moscow continues to fear NATO's eastern expansion and America's global reach and dominance. And there is nothing more that Moscow would like to see than the decoupling of Western Europe from Washington. Thus, in order to strengthen its position, the Kremlin has put its foot down in Belarus and Ukraine and has created a three-legged geopolitical stand in Europe. The three legs are: 1) The Kaliningrad enclave, or oblast, to the Baltic Sea; 2) The Trans-Dniester "republic" in southeast Europe; and, 3) Abkhazia by the Black Sea in the Caucasus.

Kaliningrad

Kaliningrad, formerly East Prussia, is a Russian militarized enclave located between Poland and Lithuania but now without a contiguous Russian border. Yet, Kaliningrad has been part of the Russian Federation ever since the end of WWII. Also, since the war, Russia has maintained important military installations in the area, which were obviously directed against NATO's northern flank. According to the article "Kaliningrad Oblast-Military," one of many articles on this subject available in *Wikipedia*, after the fall of the Soviet Union, the *"Kaliningrad Oblast was one of the most militarized areas of the Russian Federation, and the density of military installations was the highest in Europe."* Actually, Russia has continued to keep ground troops in the oblast, as well as naval and air force personnel. The *Washington Times*, of January 3, 2001, cited anonymous intelligence reports and claimed that for the first time since the Cold War ended Russia had transferred tactical nuclear weapons into a military base in Kaliningrad. In order to maintain a regional balance of power, the previous American administration under President George W. Bush decided to deploy a new anti-missile defense system in Poland and the Czech Republic. However, on November 5, 2008, Russian President Medvedev declared that Russia would deploy modern Iskander missiles in the oblast as a response to U.S. plans for basing missiles in Poland. A few months later on January 28, 2009, a Russian official stated that the deployment of short-range missiles in the Kaliningrad area would be reconsidered due to perceived changes in the attitude of the United States towards Russia following the election of President Barak Obama.

While the previous Republican administration proved to be firm and was ready to install the new missile system, the new Democrat administration, under Barack Obama, changed course. By pursuing a policy of accommodation the new administration caved in to the Kremlin's demands and renounced the already agreed-upon missile defense plan. Eastern Europe reacted with disbelief and had a hard time accepting the new American attitude. It appears that for the first time, since the end of the Cold War, the United States blinked.

Trans-Dniester

The self-proclaimed Trans-Dniester republic split from Moldova by the time Moldova itself became independent and few people remember the 1992 war between the Moldovan forces and those of this region. With Russian military and financial help, the Trans-Dniester region has kept its de facto independence ever since and has become a hub of arms trafficking and illegal activities. On December 7, 2003, The *Washington Post* wrote that this enclave was being led by mafia-style leaders and remained an extremely dangerous place for black marketeering. The paper noted that the area had small remnants of the Russian 14th Army, but with huge quantities of shells, mines, rockets, dirty warheads and possibly other weapons ready to be sold to whoever had the cash to buy them. The situation has not changed over the last eight years and indeed the area continues to represent an unending source of friction in southeast Europe.

In fact, Moscow is using this region against Ukraine, should this country try to pursue a pro-Western policy, as well as against Romania and the south-eastern flank of NATO. (See Nicholas Dima, "The Moldovan-Dnestr Republic: A Geopolitical Game," *The Journal for Social, Political and Economic Studies*, Spring 1999). While it is taken for granted that the Kaliningrad enclave is a Russian territory, and since Moldova has been very much forgotten, Georgia is still fresh in the West's memory.

Abkhazia by the Black Sea in the Caucasus

After the dissolution of the Soviet Union, to secure its position in the geopolitically important Caucasian region, Moscow instigated several local minorities to act as proxies for its own interests. The Nagorno-Karabakh region of Azerbaijan, for example, inhabited mainly by Armenians, waged a war against Baku and linked itself to Armenia. The area is now controlled by the government of Armenia, which itself is the only Russian ally in the region. Then, when Georgia proclaimed its independence and expressed its intention to join NATO and the West,

Moscow helped Abkhazia and South Ossetia break away and declare their own separate independence.

Of these two Georgian areas, Abkhazia is more important geopolitically for Russia because of its location by the Black Sea close to Turkey, an American ally and a NATO member. Three years ago the two areas triggered a bitter war between local forces helped by Russia and Georgia. America and the West protested against the Russian military interventions, but to no avail. To this day these areas have maintained an ongoing feud over the Russian occupation of Abkhazia and South Ossetia. Russia's prime minister, Vladimir Putin, recently referred to the "artificial borders" of South and North Ossetia (which belongs to the Russian Federation) alluding to the possible annexation of South Ossetia, a move that would not be surprising but would alarm NATO and the West.

Abkhazia, however, represents the third leg of Russia's geopolitical strategy against NATO and America. Granted the geopolitical significance of the Caucasus region, its proximity to oil-rich South Central Asia and the Caspian basin, and also its proximity to Israel and the troubled Middle East, the situation of Abkhazia and Georgia deserves special attention.

The recent "reset" of America's relations with Russia pursued under President Obama and Secretary of State Hillary Clinton has been a one way street in favor of Russia. Since the resetting, the United States caved in to Moscow's opposition to Europe's anti-missile shield and practically stopped pressuring Moscow to withdraw its military from the Trans-Dniester area of Moldova. With regard to Georgia and the Caucasus, however, Russia is actually pushing America around.

In this vein, Ely Lake from the *Washington Times* wrote on August 4, 2011: "Russia uses dirty tricks despite U.S. reset." At the same time, the former Senator Christopher Bond, who served as the vice chairman of the Senate Select Committee on Intelligence between 2007 and 2010, said: "We are concerned about the acts of intimidation as well as their record on previous agreements and other activities. It's a real concern, I've raised it. It's not the intelligence committee that fails to understand the problem. It's the Obama administration," concluded the former senator as he referred to Russia's current policy.

NATO itself recognizes what it calls "political differences" remaining on some high-level issues – such as "Russia's suspended implementation of the Treaty on Conventional Armed Forces in Europe (CFE) and issues related to Georgia."

For the time being, the situation of Georgia remains at the forefront of the U.S.-Russian controversy. Moscow perceives Washington as weak and indecisive, while pursuing a policy of challenges and even intimidation. Among other things, The *Washington Post* reported recently that the U.S. intelligence agencies concluded Russia's military intelligence was responsible for a bomb blast that occurred last September at an exterior wall of the U.S. Embassy in Tbilisi. The problem is that weakness and the perception of weakness is provocative.

Given the volatility of the area from Libya to Syria and from Israel to Iran, the United States must demonstrate a clear position of strength not only toward the smaller countries of the region, but also toward an unrestrained Russia. Recent reports show that at home the current Russian leaders have resorted to the old policy of authoritarian control. On the other hand, internationally, prominent Russian circles aim at recreating the former union under the Eurasian banner. And indeed, they are reasserting Russian goals by challenging American interests.

Is the current administration in the White House up to the new challenges? The State Department continues to make rhetorical statements favorable to Georgia and Moldova, but Moscow is ignoring Washington and is rapidly advancing its own agenda under the cover of the NATO Russia Council.

German Chancellor Angela Merkel Visits Moldova.
August 28, 2012

German Chancellor Angela Merkel is the most powerful woman in the world according to a *Reuters* report cited by *Forbes* magazine. The question is why did the most powerful leader of Europe visit Moldova, the poorest country of the continent?

On Wednesday, August 22, Chancellor Merkel paid a short visit to Chisinau allegedly to discuss the problems of the secessionist region of Transnestr and Moldova's intention to accede to the European Union.

Moldova became independent at the breakup of the USSR, but ethnically, Moldova is attracted to Romania where it belonged for most of its history. Realizing that Russia opposes the reunification with Romania, the current pro-Western government in Chisinau is seeking to join the European Union. As it is well-known, Moscow was not pleased with the dismemberment of the FSU and has tried hard to keep its former territory. Consequently, Moscow managed to retain control over Belarus and Ukraine, to dismember Georgia, and to exercise a strong influence over Moldova. A short reminder of the recent past of Moldova is in order here.

Allegedly, when Mikhail Gorbachev agreed to let Germany reunite, the two countries also decided on a number of significant East European issues and apparently Moldova remained under Russia. After the dissolution of the USSR, knowing that the Moldovans wanted to reunite with Romania, Moscow used the proverbial carrot and the stick approach. On the one hand, it promised Bucharest to allow the reunification on the condition that Romania would not join NATO. On the other hand, to blackmail Chisinau, in September 1992 Moscow helped the Transnestr area declare its own independence – the Kremlin, always the mischief maker. Ever since, Moldova has remained in limbo between Moscow's geopolitical interests and its pro-Romanian and pro-Western aspirations. (For details see Dima's books).

For over 22 years, the so-called Transnestr "republic" has remained a bone of contention representing one of the unresolved conflicts of the East. Despite various proposals, local Russian leaders and Moscow have refused any solution. Consequently, there are two political trends happening these days in Moldova. At a governmental level, Moldova is conducting negotiations to adhere to the EU. In this regard, on August 22 *Romanian Global News (RGN)* wrote that Graham Watson, British member of the European Parliament and reporter for the *Accord of Association of Moldova to the EU*, just ended his own visit to Chisinau and declared that "the integration in the EU is Moldova's sole option."

On the other hand, the unionist movement is growing and is increasingly vocal. Nevertheless, following recent manifestations in the city of Balti, the Russians threatened to break up Moldova's territory even further. Moscow's vehemence against the reunification with Romania, against NATO, and against the new American anti-missiles shield located in Romania, is beyond imagination. Moscow certainly remembers that in 1941 Germany attacked the USSR from Poland and Romania, but it refuses to admit that the only reason Romania joined Germany was to recuperate Bessarabia. Since the province was last ceded to Russia by Germany in 1940, some Moldovan journalists questioned the meaning of Ms. Merkel's visit.

Prior to the visit, the Moldovan press stressed the huge interest of the people for the event and emphasized that many Moldovans had high hopes and expectations. The journalists even called the visit an historic event. Indeed, Ms. Merkel's visit received ample coverage. The Moldovan paper *Timpul* of 23 August described in detail the meetings of Ms. Merkel with President Nicolae Timofti and with Prime Minister Vlad Filat. The Moldovan President thanked Ms. Merkel for her visit and spoke among other things of Moldova's decision to join the EU. Ms. Merkel comments were evasive, but promised Germany's support. Then, she asked about Moldova's position regarding the Russian troops stationed in the Transnestr region. The President answered that the mission of these troops as a "peace maintaining force" had expired and that they should be withdrawn. The perspective of Moldova's plea to join the European Union was also discussed with Prime Minister Filat. According to Agence France Presse (AFP) and as reported by *Mediafax* of 23 August, "Ms. Merkel's position was not very encouraging. She recommended patience, further reforms, and a step by step approach."

The German press was skeptical with regard to the timing and purpose of the visit. *Die Welt*, for example, downplayed its importance and called it an "excursion." The publication stressed that if the visit could have solved the (Transnestr) conflict, or could have helped improve the lot of the Moldovan people, then it would have been justified. In addition, *Die Welt* added that the current Moldovan Prime

Minister is pro-Russian and he wants to keep Moldova in the Russian sphere.

At the same time, the chief of the Communist Party of Moldova, former President Vladimir Voronin, was denied a private meeting with Ms. Merkel, but he met her together with a group of Moldovan leaders. Voronin also played down the importance of the visit and sent Ms. Merkel a long letter. Among others, he expressed his fear of a possible reunification of Moldova with Romania which, in his opinion, would lose the constitutional neutrality of Moldova. (*Timpul*, 22 August).

In the end, Ms. Merkel visit did not offer any concrete solutions to Moldova's pleas. According to a number of publications (*www.moldova.org, romanialibera.ro, RGN, and Stratfor global news*) she only recommended patience. Actually, following the visit, Stratfor of 23 August made some pertinent comments:

"Merkel's visit did not lead to the breakthrough that many had expected. Instead of announcing a deal on Transdniestria, Merkel simply said that negotiations on the issue should continue in their current format. This should not have come as a surprise to any serious observer of Moldovan or post-Soviet Russian affairs. Russia typically does not remove its troops from a former Soviet country voluntarily as a result of diplomatic pressure; given Transdniestria's strategic location on the Bessarabian gap and Russia's relatively strong position there, Moscow's stance on the issue is unlikely to change any time soon."

Under these circumstances, the media stressed that the Moldovan population was disappointed with the visit. None of their problems were solved. Some journalists and leaders even concluded that seeking to join the European Union is the wrong path. And they wrote that reunification with Romania is Moldova's sole option. Yet, the visit was symbolically important as a sign that the West has not forgotten the area. (RGN, 23 August).

And there is one more small, but symbolic element. Ms. Merkel visited Chisinau was on 22 August and the next day, 23 August, she went to meet the Baltic leaders. The Ribbentrop-Molotov Pact was signed on 23 August (1939); perhaps, she was trying to undo a past injustice.

Chapter 3
Post-Soviet Russian Federation

Twenty Years since the Fall of the Berlin Wall.
December 10, 2009

For several decades the Berlin Wall was the emblematic symbol of a world divided. On the one hand there was the communist camp with its imprisoned people and on the other the West with its own problems, but free and democratic. Hundreds of years ago, China had also built a wall but to keep the barbarian invaders out. The communists built the wall to keep in their own people. Indeed, if the Berlin Wall and the barbed wire that surrounded the entire communist world had not existed, a great many people would have fled their countries. In the heart of Europe the Berlin Wall kept communism in control, but it could not guarantee its survival. And the human toll caused by those regimes that relied on walls, barbed wire and force was enormous. Hundreds of people were killed during their attempts to escape to freedom; thousands were imprisoned; hundreds of thousands died behind the Iron Curtain. A few fortunate men survived the ordeal and managed to tell their stories. Among them is this author, who was caught at the Romanian-Yugoslav border in the 1950's and who subsequently spent three and a half years in communist prisons and labor camps. However, questions remain. Why was the Berlin Wall built and why did it come down so suddenly almost three decades later? What lessons can we learn from the Wall now 20 years after its demise?

World War II was essentially caused by two fanatical ideologies – Nazism and Communism. The United States entered the war after Japan attacked Pearl Harbor, fought the Axis forces alongside the Western Allies, and won the war. Inadvertently, however, the war also helped the rise of the Soviet Union and its communist camp. Soon thereafter a cold war ensued between the two remaining superpowers; this war consumed an extraordinary number of human lives and a tremendous amount of material resources. Communism threatened the entire world with tyranny and nuclear destruction and only a strong American commitment to freedom and democracy saved the West.

For over four decades the United States and the Union of Soviet Socialist Republics (USSR) confronted each other head-on in post-World War II Germany. Berlin became the capital of East Germany, but it was a city divided. Driven by ideology and controlled by Moscow, East Germany, misleadingly called the German Democratic Republic (DDR), could not offer its people either political freedom or economic prosperity. Hundreds of thousands of East Germans fled and left everything behind crossing into the West. East Germany risked losing its population and legitimacy and was faced with the specter of collapse. These reasons convinced Moscow and East Berlin that the only way to keep their people in was to imprison them at the point of a gun behind a highly guarded wall. As a result, the Berlin Wall was erected in 1961 and became a worldwide symbol of oppression.

While the Soviet Union was seeking global expansion, America resorted to containment. This policy worked in Western Europe for over four decades. However, Eastern Europe became a prison of nations that never accepted their fate. The Berlin Wall separated two vastly different worlds and became such a fixture that many people thought it would be there forever. Personally, I had a hard time convincing my student-officers at the U.S. Army John F. Kennedy Special Warfare Center and School (SWCS) at Fort Bragg, North Carolina, that nothing lasts forever and that one day even the Berlin Wall would be obsolete. Indeed, economic, technological, ethno-demographic and socio-political forces conspired from within and from without to finally bring down the wall.

Facts and Figures

The Berlin Wall was a concrete barrier built to enclose the West Berlin enclave completely and to separate it from East Berlin. This wall ran 96 miles in length surrounding West Berlin. At the end of World War II, Berlin was divided among the Soviet zone and the three Western zones – American, British and French – which later unified as West Berlin. Shortly after the Cold War started, Berlin became one of the major Soviet-American flash points. Between June 1948 and May 1949, for example, the Soviets blockaded the city hoping to eventually bring it to its knees and ultimately under their control. Only America's determination and the Berlin airlift it organized to provision the city saved it from Soviet domination. However, Berlin was the main portal for East Germans to flee their country. Before the Berlin Wall was constructed about 3.5 million East Germans escaped to the West and the majority of them escaped through West Berlin. The only way the communist authorities could keep people inside was to contain them within a wall. In addition to the infamous Berlin Wall, East Germany surrounded itself with a long and dreaded wall that extended through its entire border with West Germany.

The Berlin Wall included watch towers placed along large concrete walls, an inner forbidden and mined zone known as the "death strip," anti-vehicle trenches, and other deadly defenses. Yet, against such odds, during its existence from 1961 to 1989 around 5,000 people attempted to escape over and under the Wall. Most of them were arrested, some managed to cross it, and between 100 and 200 were killed trying to escape to freedom. The Berlin Wall succeeded in making the German people prisoners in their own country, but it failed to imprison their spirit.

By the late 1980s, the Soviet bloc was economically and morally bankrupt and Moscow was confronted with a huge dilemma: Either attempt to again suppress the revolutionary movements that were sweeping Eastern Europe and risk the implosion of the system from within, or let communism go and adjust to a new era. International circumstances and dire internal conditions made the last Soviet leader, Mikhail Gorbachev (1985-1991), opt for Glasnost (openness in government) and Perestroika (restructuring government), and a few years later, on December 31, 1991, the Soviet Union collapsed.

In the end, Soviet communism was brought down by its own failures, by the masses who rejected their system of brutality and corruption, and by the American determination to oppose and defeat it.

Many world leaders, from the West and the East, contributed to the USSR's demise. No one can forget Poland's Solidarity movement and its leader Lech Walesa. Nobody could ignore the contribution of such dissidents as Vaclav Havel of the former Czechoslovakia. And no one can forget the paramount contributions of Pope John Paul II, himself from Poland, and British Prime Minister Margaret Thatcher. From a moral and political point of view, one great Western leader, the former American president, Ronald Reagan, stands out. It is difficult to imagine the defeat of Soviet communism without the crusading zeal and support of President Reagan.

Ronald Reagan and the Berlin Wall

The former conservative Republican President of the United States was a true believer of liberty and freedom and fully understood the communist system and disdained it unreservedly. Looking back, it appears that Reagan had set as a priority for his life to bring down the Soviet communist system. He demanded the dismantling of the Berlin Wall on several occasions prior to becoming president. Having visited Berlin in November 1978, he saw for himself the dreaded Berlin Wall and the 'death strip' on the communist side. He even visited East Berlin and convinced himself once more of the immorality and injustice of such a barrier to freedom. According to the *American Spectator* of December 2009, on that occasion he declared to his entourage: "We've got to find a way to knock this thing down." Bringing down Soviet communism and the Berlin Wall truly became a crusade for the future president. Actually, author Paul Kengor dedicated many pages of his book, *Crusader – Ronald Reagan and the Fall of Communism*, to Reagan's tireless efforts to bring down the Wall. Reagan's intent was clear, writes Kengor. He wanted "an end to totalitarianism and the liberation of the communist peoples."

During the years of uncertainty before the collapse of communism, when Moscow still hoped to save the Soviet regime and keep Eastern Europe under its control, it was President Reagan who stood fast and vehemently condemned the Soviet Union as the "evil empire." Standing within feet of the Wall by the Brandenburg Gate, while visiting West Berlin on June 12, 1987, Mr. Reagan declared with conviction: *"There is one sign the Soviets can make that would be unmistakable, that would advance dramatically the cause of freedom and peace,"* and then he addressed the Soviet leader personally: *"General Secretary Gorbachev, if you seek peace, if you seek prosperity for the Soviet Union and Eastern Europe, if you seek liberalization, come here to this gate. Mr. Gorbachev, open this gate. Mr. Gorbachev, tear down this wall!"*

The Soviet leader, however, did not rush to tear the Wall down, but he, the Soviet empire, and the entire world paid attention to President Reagan's words. Gradually, with the domino-like collapse of the Soviet satellites and the increasing demonstrations for reform in East Germany, Moscow finally conceded and the fate of the dreaded Berlin Wall was sealed. The demolition of the Wall began to happen on November 9, 1989 just after weeks of civil unrest. Unable to control the people anymore and without Moscow's support, the East German government announced that all its citizens could freely visit West Germany and West Berlin. Immediately, thousands of people crossed into the West and began to chip at the Wall and eventually to tear it down. Less than a year later, on October 3, 1990, reunification took place and East Germany ceased to exist. Today only a few remaining sections of the Berlin Wall remain standing mostly as an art object and as a reminder of the very dark past.

Anniversary and Consequences

The 20th anniversary of the fall of the Berlin Wall was celebrated in 2009 with special events and public rallies. The celebrations climaxed on the date of the anniversary, November 9th, with a grand party at the historic Brandenburg Gate. In 1989 the imposing gate that had been a symbol of separation for all those Cold War years became an emblem of union for a new nation in a new era. Among the participating leaders were the German Chancellor Angela Merkel, herself from the eastern part of the country, former Soviet leader Mikhail Gorbachev, Secretary of State Hillary Clinton, and leaders of all 27 European Union countries. In her speech and as reported by the Associated Press, Chancellor Merkel declared: "Freedom is not self evident. Freedom must be fought for. Freedom must be defended time and again." Indeed, freedom is both an end and a process that must be continuously nourished and defended. And what does the fall of the Berlin Wall mean 20 years later for the present and future generation of Europeans?

The tearing down of the Berlin Wall and the collapse of Soviet communism in Eastern Europe were days of euphoric joy and exuberant expectations. The passage of time, however, has tempered the enthusiasm and has brought about a degree of cynicism. Nevertheless, the balance sheet is positive. There is freedom now in most East European countries; freedom of expression, freedom of movement, freedom of religion. There is also democracy, but a peculiar kind of democracy. Unfortunately, many of the former communists have robbed the wealth of their countries and used their new found freedom and democracy for the advancement of their own interests. The oligarchs of Russia are a good example. While a certain segment of the population enjoys the fruits of freedom, a larger segment has been marginalized and continues to be stuck in poverty. Equal opportunity, the rule of law and free market principles elude them. In this regard, a disappointed Muscovite woman who has been through this entire change made a saddening statement: "The children of our former masters are now the masters of our children." The East European societies are now more polarized than ever with another small but different elite in control of various state capitalist systems. These nouveau rich made up overwhelmingly of the former Communist Party *nomenklatura* and secret police officers are now multimillionaires and a few are even billionaires in control of vast natural resources. At the same time, their countries are indebted scores of billions of dollars, some of them owing more than their national GDPs.

Geopolitically, the paradigm shift has been dramatic, but some old interests have remained. Russia, for example, has renounced her old global aspirations, but is stubbornly clinging to new regional ambitions. Thus, Moscow aggressively seeks to carve out its sphere of influence in areas of the former Soviet Union such as the Caucasus, Ukraine, and in other regions as well. On the other hand, many former Soviet satellites have sought security under the NATO umbrella and within the European

Union, which in turn has sought enlargement from the Atlantic Ocean to the Baltic and Black Seas. But these newly integrated countries look again more like satellites than equal partners. In addition, they are losing their sovereignty to a new ideological bureaucracy in Brussels. Many new and old EU members are complaining about this situation. Recently, for example, the Czech President, Vaclav Klaus a Eurosceptic, only reluctantly endorsed the Lisbon Treaty stating: "I cannot agree with its contents because once the Lisbon Treaty will come into effect, the Czech Republic will cease to be a sovereign state." The Lisbon Treaty amended the previous EU founding treaties, the two Treaties of Rome (1957) and the Maastricht Treaty (1993), to complete the economic and political integration of Europe.

On the other hand, it appears that while Moscow renounced communism, the European Union has embraced socialism. In fact, the very man who reigned over the fall of the Berlin Wall, Mikhail Gorbachev, described the EU as "the new European Soviet." And the renowned Russian dissident Vladimir Bukovsky took the idea one step further and observed that "the EU is the old Soviet model, presented in Western guise." In what direction is the European Union now marching? Unfortunately, America itself seems to be drifting these days and instead of being an active player in European affairs it seems to be more and more a spectator. The Berlin Wall and the old Iron Curtain are gone, but democracy, freedom, and prosperity must indeed be nurtured and "defended time and again."

Moscow's Victory Day Military Parades. May 28, 2010

What would Reagan do? President Ronald Reagan, who helped bring an end to the Cold War with the Soviet Union symbolized by his call for Mikhail Gorbechev to tear down the Berlin Wall, would roll over in his grave at the sight of American soldiers marching under the Soviet banner in Moscow's Red Square, where the body of Vladimir Ilyich Lenin, founder of the Soviet Union, is entombed. "Well," as the Gipper would say, that's exactly what happened, on May 9, 2010, when in an unprecedented event members of the U.S. Army stationed with NATO in Europe marched alongside contingents of British, French, Polish and

10,000 Russian troops in the Victory Day Parade. The parade commemorated the 65th anniversary of the defeat of Nazi Germany and the end of World War II in Europe.

Under his watch, America's Commander-and-Chief, Barack Obama, did not attend the Great Patriotic War celebration in Moscow. But, imagine the photo op in this digital age of the president of the United States saluting the U.S. Army marching in Red Square while standing alongside Russian Prime Minister Vladimir Putin, Russian President Dmitry Medvedev and Chinese President Hu Jintao. And all these under the symbol of worldwide communist oppression, the hammer and sickle, as a Russian honor guard carried the Red Army flag, Russian military jets performed a fly over and Russian tanks and intercontinental ballistic missile launchers paraded through Red Square. Not exactly a picture of an American-style Memorial Day of parades and picnics or a even a Fourth of July, Independence Day, celebration of freedom and liberty.

Previously, on May 8, President Obama, through the White House Office of the Press Secretary, issued a statement marking the end of World War II for the Soviet Union: *"On May 9, the Russian Federation will host a commemoration of one of the most important events in human history – the defeat of fascism in World War II. This achievement was won only by the extraordinary sacrifices made by many people, including Americans and Russians, and those sacrifices will be honored by the presence of troops from the many nations that came together to defend our common security and human dignity in an hour of maximum peril. In marking this occasion, President Medvedev has shown remarkable leadership in honoring the sacrifices of those who came before us, and in speaking so candidly about the Soviet Union's suppression of 'elementary rights and freedoms.' His words remind us that we must all work together on behalf of a world in which the fundamental human rights that all people deserve are protected."*

Never mind "suppression," Mr. Obama, tens-of-thousands of political prisoners and millions of families were sentenced to an empty existence for decades-on-end under the Soviet Union's "tyranny and oppression" established behind the Iron Curtain that befell Eastern

Europe following the World War II-era signing of the Yalta Agreement in Crimea, Ukraine.

After several years of disorientation following the official collapse and dismemberment of the Union of Soviet Socialist Republics (USSR) on December 31, 1991, and after searching for a new policy toward its former empire and the West, a resurgent Russia is now attempting to reposition itself geopolitically while simultaneously flexing its muscles once again over the "near abroad" or the former Soviet republics. The victory parades organized in Moscow, throughout Russia and for the first time in four Ukrainian cities this year, especially following the election victory of Viktor Yanukovich, helped to enhance Moscow's image at home. Yet, the Moscow event in particular revealed old resurfacing controversies and new hard to resolve political problems.

The Moscow commemoration was organized to last four days and to culminate with the military parade in Red Square on May 9 in front of the Kremlin. At the same time, to make sure that the leaders of the former Soviet republics, some of them now members of the Community of Independent states (CIS), would attend the celebration, they were also called for a special meeting in Moscow of the Collective Security Treaty Organization (CSTO), the Kremlin's version of NATO, organized among the former Soviet Socialist Republics. The meetings were held just one day before the parade on May 8 ensuring a larger Victory Day attendance.

However, despite all the measures taken by Russia to impress the world with its new found self-assurance, the results were lukewarm. The American, Western European and Eastern European mainstream media barely mentioned the grand event. Compared to Moscow's 50th anniversary celebration and parade in 1995 commemorating the end of World War II in Europe, attended by numerous world leaders including then-President Bill Clinton assembled in Boris Yeltsin's Russia, only 21 countries participated in the 65th anniversary parade on Sunday, May 9, 2010. Of significance, only Germany's Angela Merkel attended this time around. British Prime Minister Gordon Brown, Nicolas Sarkozy of France, Silvio Burlesconi of Italy and Barack Obama of the United States were notably absent. In fact, Moscow, in a diplomatic affront, refused to accept country representatives including Vice President Joe Biden and England's Prince Charles. Instead, the big names on Vladimir Putin's stage included such leaders as Sergai Bogapsh and Eduard Kokoity, the separatist Georgian leaders of Abkhazia and South Ossetia, respectively, along with Georgian opposition leaders with whom Moscow expects to take over in Tbilisi, if Putin succeeds in his ongoing efforts to overthrow the pro-Western Georgian president, Mikheil Saakashvilli. Also attending from the post-Soviet sphere of influence were the leaders of all the CIS states, except for Uzbekistan and the Baltic states.

After the collapse of Soviet Communism, many Russians tried to explain and understand the catastrophe brought upon them by the greatest war of all. World War II was both a huge victory for Russia and, at the same time, a tremendous defeat for the Soviet system. Putin and the new president, Dmitry Medvedev, intervened and put an end to the debate declaring the war a heroic Russian victory. And it was Putin, the former KGB colonel, who set Russia on a new course aimed at reestablishing the former Soviet superiority.

As president, Vladimir Putin readopted the former Soviet national anthem, resorted to a strong-arm policy, pacified Chechnya in a brutal way, and restored the prestige of Russia in the eyes of the people. Ruling over a lucky period when the price of oil skyrocketed, Putin had enough money to secure internal tranquility, to improve the lots of the average citizens, and to start to rebuild Russia's deteriorated military. When time came to retire after two four year terms, Putin found a pliant man to replace him as president, and he assumed the power behind the throne as prime minister in March 2008. His policies of restoring Russia as a superpower continued.

Under Putin as prime minister and Dmitry Medvedev as president, Russia regained partial control of Georgia and most of the Caucasus and brought Ukraine back into Moscow's orbit. At the same time, Russia began to improve relations with the United States, signed a nuclear arms reduction treaty with President Obama, and continued to court Western Europe. The recent parade in Moscow was meant to celebrate more than a victory; it was meant to show the world a new, self-assured and resurgent Russia. The anniversary reminded many observers of Beijing's organizing of the 2008 Summer Olympic Games showing the world a new magnificent China, except for Russia there wasn't anything tangible like Olympic stadiums or new infrastructure; Victory Day 2010 was purely political and for internal consumption.

That thought gives rise to the upcoming 2014 Winter Olympics to be held from February 7 to February 23, 2014 in Sochi, Russia located on the Black Sea just northeast of Abkhazia, Georgia and only some 20 miles from the Georgian border. Sochi was selected on July 4, 2007 just 11 months prior to Russia's brutal invasion of Georgia on August 8, 2008. Not since the 1980 Summer Games in Moscow during the Soviet era has Russia been the site for the Olympics. Athletes from the U.S. and 64 countries boycotted the games in protest of the 1979 Soviet invasion of Afghanistan. That actually begs the question as to whether there should be a boycott of the 2014 Winter Games in Sochi unless Georgian sovereignty is immediately restored for the two breakaway provinces of Abkhazia and Ossetia presently controlled and occupied by Russia.

The Russian success of Victory Day, however, was fleeting and marred by problems. The Europe of 2010 is very different than the Europe ravaged by World War II in 1945. Most Europeans have left the past behind and are trying to solve now their current economic problems with the European Union and to look for a better future. Although Moscow invited many heads of states, only some of them accepted the invitation. The leaders of the most important allies of Moscow during the war, the United States and Great Britain, did not attend the anniversary.

The only Western leader attending the Moscow event was German Chancellor Angela Merkel. Currently, Russia is courting Germany and France with favorable commercial deals. Germany is dependent on Russian energy deliveries, while France has just concluded a deal to modernize the Russian Black Sea Fleet in Sevastopol, Ukraine. On May 10, immediately after the military parade, the German Missions in the United States posted a brief news release announcing that "On Sunday, Chancellor Angela Merkel attended the memorial service to mark the 65th anniversary of the end of the Second World War in Moscow."

The attitude of Eastern Europe, which after the war was actually victimized for over 40 years by Moscow, ranged from cool to hostile. The three Baltic republics, Estonia, Latvia and Lithuania, simply refused to attend the anniversary spectacle. Georgia, mutilated by Russia after the fall of communism, also refused to go to Moscow for Victory Day. Romania, whose eastern province of Bessarabia, part of it now the Republic of Moldova, was not even invited. As for the Republic of Moldova, before the ceremony, its interim president Mihai Ghimpu, declared: *"I cannot attend an event that celebrates the bringing of communism to my country, the bringing of organized famines, the massive deportations of our people to Siberia, the breaking up of my country, and the artificial separation of my nation."*

As a result, Mr. Ghimpu went to Moscow for the May 8 CIS meeting, met President Medvedev shortly, and departed immediately without attending the May 9 parade. Upon his return to Chisinau he explained to Unimedia his decision and said that in his brief discussion with President Medvedev he raised the question of the continued Russian military presence in the Moldovan Trans-Dnestr break-away region. His attitude and comments were amply reported by the Moldovan newspapers such as Timpul, by the Romanian press, and by Radio Free Europe/Radio Liberty.

Another dramatic Eastern European case-in-point is that of Poland. The Poles fought alongside the Allies during the war against Germany, but the Soviet treatment of Poland and the Katyn massacre marred any real post-war reconciliation between Moscow and Warsaw. And, of course, the recent death of Polish President Lech Kaczynski, his wife, and 94 other high ranking Polish dignitaries at the former Soviet military base at Smolensk airport in Belarus as a result of an "accidental" air crash en route to a Katyn commemoration with Russian leaders on April 10 did not do anything to reconcile the two sides. According to some sources, President Kaczynski had not planned to attend Moscow's World War II ceremonies…

Slowly, gradually, and with ever so calculated chess moves, Moscow is flexing its political and military muscles once again. Russia is also pursuing a plan to revamp and modernize its military by 2020. On this subject, President Medvedev declared at the Moscow ceremony that "a global military conflict is still possible and Russia must be prepared." As reported by RFE/RL, he told Izvestia and the government controlled RIA news agency that "one efficient way to protect national interests is to strengthen our military and our nuclear capacity." Previously, however, as reported by Newsweek of May 17, Medvedev had deplored the dire economic situation of Russia and its "humiliating" dependency on oil and gas exports on the one hand, and on imported Western technology on the other. How is this dire state of affairs going to be changed? The Russian economy is stagnating and once again, since the fall of the USSR, requires Western technology and foreign investment. At the same time, the Russian population is declining, the ethnic minorities are still increasing and restless, especially at the fringe of the Russian Federation and Eastern Siberia is slowly falling under the Chinese sphere of influence. The May 9 celebrations in Moscow may well turn into a May Day call for the Russian Federation, which may very well be on the same course pursued in the past by the former Soviet Union.

The Dismemberment of the Soviet Union. Part 1.
August 31, 2011

Russia, which extends over eleven time zones, is the largest country on earth. During the Soviet years, Moscow enjoyed its greatest geographic reach and had aspirations of even greater expansion. Moscow's dreams of being an embryonic world state died in Afghanistan in a war that exhausted an already weakened Soviet system. The perpetual crises of the Soviet state were an indication of a fatal flaw brought on by the absence of a unifying factor that could overcome the vast differences among the fifteen Soviet republics. While Mikhail Gorbachev, the last Soviet Communist Party General Secretary, resorted to *glasnost* and *perestroika* in an attempt to reform the system, his efforts hastened the collapse of the USSR on December 25, 1991.

The dissolution of this multinational empire has generated new questions which must be addressed in order to understand those historic events of 1991. Today, we need to know if the Russian Federation has achieved a new national identity and if the post-Soviet citizens have benefitted from the Soviet collapse. In looking at Moscow's international standing, it is essential to determine if it renounced its expansionist geopolitical goals? To answer these questions, it is necessary to examine: 1) the evolution of the new socio-political system; 2) the status of Russia's economy; and, 3) the ethnic factors that will shape this new national community.

Twenty Years Later

Twenty years after the collapse of the Soviet Union, an article entitled "End of the USSR," appeared in London's *Guardian* (August 17, 2011). In compiling statistics about the former USSR, the *Guardian* data team asked if the changes made life better or worse for the former Soviet citizens. Numerous accounts document that condition of Soviet life in the throes of the regime's final years. The country was morally corrupt, politically ossified, and economically bankrupt. This disastrous condition became clear to me in 1989 when, as a Voice of America reporter, I was assigned to the USSR for just over a month.

The official exchange rate at the time was 0.7 rubles to one U.S. dollar but the unofficial rate was 10 rubles to a dollar. With the official rate I would have starved, but luckily I happened to come across a bus load of American tourists on their way back home and they gave me all their remaining rubles at a black market exchange rate. Suddenly I felt rich. In Kiev I hired a "private" cab just for myself though no private cabs were supposed to exist at the time.

The driver took me wherever I wanted, but I had a hard time seeing through the windshield, which was cracked in a hundred places. I asked him how much a new one would cost, and when I found that it was only 90 rubles I offered to buy him one. But he laughed. "This is the official price," he answered, "but to get it you have to bribe the store manager with about 1,000 rubles." Then, we were stopped by a militiaman for the cracked window, though the militiaman knew that there were not enough windshields in the stores to replace the broken ones. Without saying practically anything, the driver passed him a handful of rubles and he let us go. Later, in Chisinau, I hired another driver. One day we went to a restaurant to eat, but the line to get in was very long. The driver talked to a doorman, gave him his due, and he let us in telling the waiting people that we were on official business. However, when we wanted to leave the restaurant, the door was locked and another doorman was guarding it. He would not let us out because we had intruded, forcefully, he said. Another bribe opened the door.

I was escorted by "Inturist" people, the official Soviet tourist agency, almost everywhere at the time and when I was not escorted I was tailed by the KGB. Yet, it was in Chisinau, where I had to report on the Moldovan Popular Front, that I really felt the KGB's long hand. One night, all four tires of the car that was taking me around were punctured. The very next day, the chief manager of my hotel told me in a grave note that I had an appointment with two officials at 11o'clock in his office. When I argued that I had other plans that morning, he was almost shaking. The two officials were the Minister of Internal Affairs of Moldova, General Munteanu, and the Minister of Tourism, whose name I forgot. Anyway, they arrived accompanied by a translator who knew Russian, English and Romanian. The two hour discussion was vague, tortuous, and even puzzling. In the end, they wanted to know who was paying me to try to destabilize the Soviet Union. At the end they convinced me "to rent" an official car which would come with a driver and a translator. Instead of being followed by the KGB now I had to follow the KGB. That was the Soviet Union that I encountered. The USSR was at a standstill.

Mikhail Gorbachev became the General Secretary of the Soviet Communist Party in 1985. Rising to the highest position in the Kremlin and realizing that the Soviet Union was collapsing from within, he launched a policy of structural changes. He named his plans *Glasnost* (openness) and *Perestroika* (restructuring). While his intention was to save the country through political and economic reforms, once started, the process could no longer be halted or reversed. Recollecting those "earth-shaking" events, the German magazine *Der Spiegel* interviewed Mr. Gorbachev and on August 16, 2011 published a lengthy article. The magazine asked him if he had a plan for transforming the Soviet system and if the party leadership was on his side. Gorbachev's answer was equally shaky: *"The party establishment didn't need perestroika. Each of them had it made. The district party leader was the king in his district, the regional leader was a czar and the general secretary was practically God's equal. That's why we needed glasnost first. It was the path to freedom. We later conducted the first free elections in Russia in 1,000 years,"* Gorbachev explained.

The introduction of *Glasnost* and *Perestroika* was a gamble based on the assumption that the Soviet system enjoyed fundamental stability. The prospect of success was balanced by the danger of violence and a complete systemic collapse. Recognizing this, those elements of the "old guard" who enjoyed the full benefits of socialism were skeptical, while younger leaders recognized the need for structural reform. The extremely diverse Soviet population was also divided based on ethnicity. Most Soviet citizens wanted significant improvements but not the dismemberment of the USSR. Gorbachev's reforms tested the system in a way that resulted in convulsions that threatened the very foundations of the all powerful Soviet state.

In August 1991, Mikhail Gorbachev was vacationing in Crimea, when elements of the old guard staged a coup to prevent further implementation of these reforms. The upheavals ushered in by the abortive coup set the stage for Russia to become a representative system under Boris Yeltsin. As the outspoken president of the Russian Federation, Yeltsin enjoyed the support of the Army as well as millions of citizens. On August 20, 2011, *The Wall Street Journal*, published an article entitled, "A Cold Warrior at Peace" by Nancy Dewolf- Smith. In the article, she gave an account of an interview with America's prominent Russian scholar, Richard Pipes. Here is how Mr. Pipes described the final days of the Soviet Union:

"The August putsch began as an effort by Communist Party hard-liners to overthrow President Mikhail Gorbachev and stop his reforms, including efforts to give the Soviet republics more freedom from the center. Civilian resistance in Moscow and other cities, aided by military units who refused to move against the protesters, effectively foiled the plot and made a popular democratic hero of Russian Federation President Boris Yeltsin. By the time Mr. Gorbachev resigned and Mr. Yeltsin took power over Russia, most of the republics had declared independence and Soviet Communism was dead."

Reflecting on the same events from a Russian perspective, Boris Nemtsov, a leading reformist and a member of the Russian parliament, declared on Radio Free Europe/Radio Liberty: *"I was a deputy of the Russian parliament and I was with Russian President Boris Yeltsin... Really, those were very dramatic days... I was not far from Yeltsin when he proclaimed his historic speech from a tank. And he said that this (coup against parliament) was completely illegal, unconstitutional, and anti-Russian..."*

When questioned about his expectation at that time, Nemtsov's answer was thoughtful: *"I understood at the time that those were very important days for my country. And really it was the death of communism. We believed that the way to freedom and successful life would be much shorter...We were very naïve. Not only me, but Yeltsin and all of our team..."* ("We were romantic." RFE/RL, September 12, 2011).

Valery Vyzhutovich, another Russian insider and a commentator for *Rossiyskaya Gazeta*, wrote that *"August 1991 marked the beginning of the Yeltsin era. Now this era is called simply the 1990s, and it was replaced by the era of Putin – the era of stability."* Vyzhutovich described the Putin era as, *"The end of the hopes and illusions of the first post-Soviet years; the crisis of ideology and persistent yet futile attempts to find a national idea; the strengthening of the state and all its institutions by the creation of the vertical power; the increase in nationalism and xenophobia.... Indeed, Putin and his men put an end to Russia's hopes for democratization."*

In explaining how this change happened and why Vladimir Putin managed to rise so quickly to power, Boris Nemtsov observed, *"For many in Russia, the collapse of the Soviet Union marked a significant loss of status and prestige. Prime Minister Vladimir Putin has stated bluntly that the collapse of the Soviet Union was the greatest geopolitical tragedy of the 20th century. As a result, it has been harder for many Russians to imagine a future that is more attractive than the country's past, and leaders like Putin have exploited such nostalgia to restore authoritarianism at home and to exert influence in what Moscow sees as its sphere of privileged interests."* (The Loss of Empire, RFE/RL, August 18, 2011).

President Yeltsin brought former KGB colonel Vladimir Putin to Moscow in the expectation that Putin would strengthen his position. Eventually, Putin made his way to the senior leadership level. Later, as president, Putin enlisted other former KGB officers, who took over the vast economic resources of Russia. Shortly thereafter, he restored Moscow's dictatorial policies and reasserted control over Eurasia's periphery. Those who opposed his policy were arrested or in some other way brutally suppressed.

Mikhail Khodorkovsky, who made a fortune during the first years after the dissolution of the Soviet Union, was among those imprisoned. Khodorkovsky had acquired Yukos, the Russian oil giant. His wealth did not protect him from being arrested because of his opposition to Putin. Khodorkovsky was charged with fraud and in 2005 was sentenced to eight years in prison. Many articles, such as "Khodorkovsky: An oligarch undone" (*BBC News*, 31 May 2005) and "Russian oligarch Mikhail Khodorkovsky goes on trial for second time" (*The Telegraph*, March 3, 2009) have outlined his case. Clearly, under Putin, only those from his inner circle could occupy top political and economic positions.

Other Putin opponents, such as General Alexander Lebed, were also eliminated. Lebed was the commander of Russia's 106th Airborne

Division from 1990 to 1991. At the height of the crisis, the Army was ordered by the coup organizers to surround the Russian parliament. General Lebed sent in his motorized division, but he never took any action against the parliament or against Yeltsin. Later, the general entered politics, ran for Russia's Presidency in 1996 and obtained 14 percent of the vote. He ran on an anti-corruption platform and argued that "preserving the army is the basis for preserving the government." At the same time, Lebed described Chilean General Pinochet as having managed to revive Chile by "putting the army in first place." Putin never forgave him for such allusions. In May 1998, Lebed was elected governor of Krasnoyarsk, Russia's second largest region. However, he died in 2002 in a very suspicious helicopter crash. ("Alexander Lebed— Russian General who applied military toughness to politics," *The Guardian*, April 29, 2002; See also, the *Decline and fall of the Soviet Empire: Forty Years That Shook the World, from Stalin to Yeltsin*, by Fred Coleman).

In the interview cited above, Richard Pipes stressed that by 2000 Putin had launched a war in Chechnya and began to reduce newly acquired freedoms throughout the Russian Federation. He ended popular election of governors, took over television stations and reinstated *"a culture in which free-speaking journalists got murdered."* Mr. Pipes told the *Wall Street Journal* that among Russians, Putin's approval ratings soared. "Russians like strong leaders, autocratic leaders: Ivan the Terrible, Peter the Great, Stalin… They have contempt for weak leaders who don't impose their will but listen to the people," Richard Pipes declared.

A public opinion poll conducted by a Moscow TV station in December 2008 confirmed Mr. Pipes' observation with its findings that Soviet dictator Josef Stalin was among the most respected Russian leaders. The poll itself did not refer to any living leader but Putin and the analysis supported the proposition that Putin had emerged as a popular Russian leader. In 2007, Vladimir Sorokin, a well-known Russian writer, told a German magazine: "We still live in the country that was built by Ivan the Terrible." Douglas Birch, in his article, "Russia's military action rooted in 1,000 year-old empire," wrote that to protect its unique culture, which is neither Asian nor European, Russia had *"adopted a kind of psychological isolation from the rest of the world..."* Thus, twenty years after the dissolution of the USSR, Russia, under Putin and Dmitri Medvedev, is once again an authoritarian state.

Part 2 September 5, 2011

By 1990 the communist regimes in Eastern Europe had collapsed. Meanwhile, the decline of the Soviet economy was accelerating and Soviet citizens were desperate for a dramatic change. While that change did come, it did not bring the anticipated benefits so many had expected. Most Soviets expected economic improvement and the introduction of at least some elements of Western democracy. Instead, they got political and economic corruption and a new class of "oligarchs" who took advantage of Russia's chaotic situation in order to enrich themselves.

There are two factors that contributed greatly to the unsatisfactory evolution of the post-Soviet economic and political environment. The first was the absence of any model for transformation of a socialist economy into a market economy. Such an event was without historical precedent. The second factor was the inability of the West, taken completely by surprise, to assist in such a radical transformation. The West was unprepared.

Whereas, in the aftermath of the Second World War, there was a political consensus in the United States that the reconstruction of war-torn Europe was worth the effort, when the Soviet Union collapsed circumstances did not allow for such a commitment. By contrast, the collapse of the communist systems in Russia and Eastern Europe opened the region to an influx of Western businessmen, the vanguard of the so-called 'Washington Consensus', who had hoped to take advantage of these dramatic events to establish a free market.

A further consideration is that the newly arrived Western businessmen found willing partners among those who had dominated the communist system. While many Russians liked the idea of democracy, they did not want to lose the control over the former Soviet republics. As a result, political democracy advanced half-heartedly, while the economy was left in the hands of those who had already been in charge.

Gradually, the people found themselves controlled by another ruthless system. By 2000, embittered Muscovites would conclude with sadness *"the children of our former masters are now the masters of our children."*

Mikhail Gorbachev, the last Soviet leader, inherited a ruined economy. According to *Der Spiegel*, shortly after assuming office, Gorbachev flew to the automobile-manufacturing city of Tolyatti on the Volga and then to Kuybyshev where, according to his advisers, he would encounter "a sense of hope the likes of which hadn't been seen since the end of the war." Yet, when he visited these places he could not disguise his horror. He compared them with 18th century factories. While there he was informed of the housing shortage, the lack of kindergartens and recreational facilities and the dismal state of the food stores. At the same time, Gorbachev noted that members of the party elite were catered for in special stores and had everything they wanted. His effort to restructure the Soviet society was failing. The German magazine reported: *"Gorbachev had a limited understanding of economics and also failed to enlist the right advisers. Rather than putting an end to central planning and decontrolling prices, he established new super-ministries and continued to subsidize a number of goods... When the oil price fell dramatically, causing problems for the state budget, soap and washing powder were added to the list of rationed goods alongside eggs and butter. But the population was no longer willing to put up with such conditions. The most serious wave of strikes in the history of the Soviet Union broke out – and didn't abate until the country collapsed."* (The Mystery of Mikhail Gorbachev's Ambiguous Legacy, *Der Spiegel*, August 18, 2011).

The economic decline accelerated under Boris Yeltsin's leadership. According to the *Guardian* of August 17, 2011, in this period Russia's GDP fell as much as 50 percent resulting in capital flight, industrial collapse, hyperinflation and widespread tax avoidance. As union republics asserted their independence from Moscow, there was a wave of violence at the periphery of the former empire and a growing popular demand for order and stability. It was in such a climate that

Yeltsin brought Vladimir Putin to Moscow and designated him as his successor.

Vladimir Putin subsequently came to power following the Russian election of March 26, 2000 on a platform calling for economic reform, government reorganization and the eradication of corruption. He took a tough stand against dissident minorities, crushed Chechnya's separatist movement, and promoted his collaborators to positions of leadership. His presidency benefitted from a period of high oil and gas prices, which allowed him to increase the pensions and salaries of government workers. Thus, Putin emerged as a traditional strong leader, while he stabilized the country and asserted his influence not only in the new Russia, but also in the "near abroad" and overseas.

The *Guardian* further notes that Putin managed to reverse Russia's economic decline. However, Russia lost some seven million people due to emigration and life expectancy declined, as drug and alcohol abuse became rampant during this period. In assessing socio-political factors, the *Guardian* placed the new Russia at the bottom of the Global Peace Index, citing rigged elections and the 'vertical' power centered on the Kremlin as being reminiscent of the Soviet era.

After serving two four year terms as president, Putin designated Dmitri Medvedev as his hand-picked successor, while as prime minister he remained the "power behind the throne." By 2011, Putin was already preparing his new presidential campaign for 2012. An August 16, 2011 article posted by Radio Free Europe/Radio Liberty (*RFE/RL*) titled "Vladimir Putin isn't going anywhere," describes how he governs Russia: *"Putin designed a system of managed conflict. There is no competition in public. But he created different clans and groups who are fighting against each other. This is the way Putin keeps control over the system. He is a judge and arbiter who is keeping the balance... Without him, all of these clans would fight each other, like after Stalin's death."*

Kremlin-watchers claim that this system comprises the core of Russia's ruling elite with about thirty key players at the top and an inner circle of about twelve people. It amounts to a new *Central Committee.* The RFE/RL article quotes Nikolai Petrov of the Moscow Carnegie

Center, (as) describing those leaders as "shareholders" who *not only manage Russia "but they also enrich themselves."*

Among the men promoted by Vladimir Putin is Igor Sechin, deputy Prime Minister and one of the new oil "oligarchs." He is also the leader of the Kremlin's lobby known as *Siloviki*. Since July 2004, Sechin has served as chairman of the board of directors of Rosneft, which appropriated the assets of Yukos, Mikhail Khodorkovsky's former company. Khodorkovsky accused Sechin of plotting his arrest to plunder his oil company. (See "Jailed tycoon Mikhail Khodorkovsky framed by key Putin aide," *The Sunday Times* of London, May 18, 2008).

Oil and gas are some of Russia's most lucrative businesses but these fields have been renationalized by the state or appropriated by the new oligarchs. The people working in the oil industry are content to have jobs and to make a decent living.

In light of the prevailing business climate, a number of questions arise including, "Is Russia economically better off today than it was 20 years ago?" And, "Have the Russian's living standards improved?" The answers are complex.

By comparison with the stark days of the USSR, the new Russia appears prosperous. The stores are stocked with merchandise. There is plenty of food in the supermarkets. And big cities like Moscow look like a real metropolis. While some new tycoons have amassed billions of dollars, many Russians still live in poverty and social polarization has become a major concern. By and large, people live better, which also reflects the recent increase in Russia's per capita GNP. People are also free to speak, but they are not free to directly criticize the new system. What is worse for average Russians is that they see the *nouveau riche* as corrupt, callous, dishonest and uncaring. And, there is nothing they can do about it. There is a new apathy and a sense of despair similar to that of the old Soviet times. From this point of view, the title of an article "20 Years later, Hope is lost in Russia," published by the *Washington Post* on August 19, 2011 tells the entire story.

The new Russia also faces many serious demographic problems. While the rate of population growth has been declining since 1959, Russians have experienced a negative growth rate for the first time since

1993 characterized by the country's low fertility and aging population. The Russians are the most numerous European group numbering about 140 million worldwide. Roughly 116 million of them live in Russia and about 16 million more live in the neighboring countries. However, only about 80 percent of the population of the Russian Federation is ethnic Russian and this proportion is decreasing. That trend will create a labor shortage in the future. There are also millions of Russians in the neighboring former Soviet republics. While some of them want to come back home, others provide a reason for the Kremlin to interfere in the "near abroad." Another demographic problem is that the Russian population is increasingly overwhelmed by that of neighboring China. There are currently ten times more Chinese than Russians and in the future this disparity will increase. With millions of Chinese settled legally or illegally in Eastern Siberia, Russia may eventually lose the area to China. Consequently, Russia's demographic future looks quite bleak.

Part 3 September 11, 2011

At his annual address to the parliament on April 25, 2005, Vladimir Putin declared on Russian TV the collapse of the Soviet Union as "the greatest geopolitical catastrophe of the century." And he added: "For the Russian people, it became a real drama. Tens of millions of our citizens and compatriots found themselves outside the Russian Federation..."

Now 20 years after the implosion of the Soviet Union, Russia, under Putin's leadership is attempting to cobble together a Eurasian economic union comprised of the former Soviet states, starting with Belarus and Kazakhstan.

Russia has always been an expansionist colonial empire. First, its goal was the possession of sea ports as Moscow set its sights on the Baltic, Black and Caspian seas and the Arctic and Pacific oceans. Later, its goal was the conquest of the weaker neighbors in Eastern Europe, the Caucasus, Central Asia, and Siberia. After 1917, Russian colonialism was clothed in Marxist terms but its ambitions remained the same. The 1991 collapse of communism cut the USSR down to size and forced the Russians to face a new reality. Consequently, it reverted to its previous historic trends. First, Moscow lost control over Eastern Europe and the Soviet union- republics. Then, the Kremlin was challenged by ethnic minorities within the Russian Federation itself. Eventually, Eastern Europe moved toward NATO and blocked Moscow's western aspirations, while to the east China became a super-power and more than Russia's equal. Yet, there is still a void between the new Russia and the outside world over which Moscow still makes claims.

For a number of years after 1991, Russian politics and geopolitics were turbulent. Westernizers wanted to draw Russia toward the West, while the nationalists insisted on Russia's traditional isolation. As a result, first, Moscow tried to define its geopolitical sphere through the concept of a "Near Abroad" which was based on the assumption that newly independent former Soviet republics were not actually foreign states. Then, after reluctantly accepting the independence of the union republics, Moscow brutally suppressed the trend of independence of its own minorities, notably of Chechnya. Eventually, Russia reasserted its priorities from the Baltic Sea to the Caucasus and to the former Soviet Central Asia. Twenty years after the dismemberment of the USSR, Moscow seems to have settled for a threefold ethnic and geopolitical stand: 1) Strong domestic control of all ethnic minorities; 2) Geostrategic intervention or influence in the Near Abroad; and, 3) Opposition to America's global domination.

However, is the new policy working? The new Russian Federation continues to reflect the organization of the former Soviet Union. It has 21 national republics, meant to be home to a specific ethnic minority, and 5 autonomous areas, which usually have a substantial local ethnic grouping. The country is multi-ethnic with the Russians making up 80 percent of the population and with many ethnic groups living in their historic areas where they feel strongly attached to their land. Notably, many of these minorities, who are Muslim, increase demographically faster than the Russians, and some of them nurture aspirations of independence. The most numerous of these minorities are the Tatars, numbering close to 6 million. They are located in the middle of Russia and have accepted their place in the Russian Federation. Moscow's policy toward minorities involves use of the proverbial carrot and stick, a policy which seems to work for now. Members of various minorities are sent to school, encouraged to assimilate, sometimes are relocated, and often they are promoted. However, if minorities revolt against Moscow, the likely Russian response will be barbaric. This was demonstrated when Chechnya openly defied Moscow's domination.

Chechnya is situated in a strategic locality in the Northern Caucasus next to other Muslim republics and close to the Caspian oil. An important Russian oil pipeline crosses Chechnya, and Grozny, the capital of the republic, is the site of a big oil refinery. This autonomous republic began its drive toward independence under the former Soviet General Djocar Dudaev. The pro-independence movement was strong and dangerous because it aimed at uniting all the Muslim republics of Northern Caucasus into one new free country. The two wars that ensued were very bloody and Moscow eventually won through a policy of extreme brutality promoted by President Putin and aimed at dividing the Chechen people. Moscow found a local leader, Ramzan Kadyrov, who sided with Russia and who, in the name of Islam, installed an awful dictatorship. For example, when bodies of slain women were found dumped by the roadside, Kadyrev declared that they were women of "loose morals rightfully shot by male relatives in honor killing." Such acts violate the Russian constitution, but are accepted when they serve Moscow. And the Russians, who always see themselves as liberators whenever they conquer a new piece of land, admire Putin for having "pacified and stabilized" Chechnya.

From among the former Soviet republics, only Lithuania, Latvia and Estonia made a clear and definitive break with the past. Apparently, Moscow has resigned itself to losing them. It is worth mentioning that "officially" the United States and the West had never recognized the annexation of the three free Baltic republics to the USSR. In fact, culturally, the three countries remained outposts of Western civilization even under the Soviet regime. Now, the new border between the West and the East is between Lithuania, a NATO member, and Belarus, a Stalinist vestige of the Soviet past that wants to reunite with Russia and to recreate the former union.

On August 25, 2011, the newspaper *Romania Libera* published an interesting article describing the new "Iron Curtain" which divides a small former Soviet village. The northern part of the village named Norviliskes now belongs to Lithuania and is part of the European Union. Pizkuny, the southern part of the village, belongs to the last dictator of Europe, Belorussian President Aleksandr Lukasenko, and is indirectly controlled by Moscow. Relatives and friends are again separated by a fence as they were under the previous and very real Iron Curtain. Nobody can cross this border without permission. In reality, the curtain is separating two different political systems, two civilizations, and two entirely different mentalities.

Moscow continues to control Belarus, it keeps military units in Moldova, and it has reasserted itself over Ukraine. In April 2010, it managed to convince the new pro-Russian Kiev government to renew the lease of Sevastopol's harbor for Russia's Black Sea Fleet. Actually, it seems that Moscow is trying to once again swallow more than it can chew. Nobel Prize winner Alexander Solzhenitsyn, author of the *Gulag Archipelago*, once advised Moscow to retain only Ukraine, Belarus and Northern Kazakhstan, to give up the rest, and to concentrate on internal affairs. After returning home from exile, Solzhenitsyn restated his position, but Moscow would not listen. Interestingly, Solzhenitsyn, who lived many years in the U.S. and had had a taste of democracy, was a supporter of strong man Vladimir Putin. The reality is that the true nature of Russia's "new" policy and geopolitics has changed little, a fact that is best demonstrated by the 2008 war in Georgia.

The 2008 war has reestablished Russia's dominance over the Caucasus allowing it to challenge Western interests in the strategically important Black Sea-Caspian Sea-South Asia region. As for the former Soviet Central Asia, Moscow has a huge say in Kazakhstan, where a large Russian population live. The other four central Asian republics are now under totalitarian regimes of quasi-Stalinist nature and they enjoy good relations with Moscow. In this vein, *Newsweek* of September 15, 2011 mentions, for example, Saparmurat Niyazov, who ruled Turkmenistan from 1990 until his death in 2006. His apparent lunacy was demonstrated when he arbitrarily renamed the months of the year, appointed himself president for life, and for 16 years made himself a god-like figure. However, in order to avoid a deeper split with Washington, Moscow allowed U.S. transshipments of arms through its territory toward Afghanistan and mitigated the extension of a leased American air base in Kyrgyzstan.

Yet, to what degree can Russia impose again its will over the Near Abroad at the beginning of the 21th Century? On the 20th anniversary of the dissolution of the Soviet Union, The *Guardian* of August 17, 2011 examined the performance of the newly independent former Soviet republics. The British paper noted that while some of them are doing well, others are doing very poorly. Under such conditions, one may ask, are these countries better off today and glad to be independent? The question is irrelevant. These countries wanted freedom from Russian control and now they cherish it. In this regard, a better question is: Has Moscow accepted the new status quo? The answer is No. Moscow is pursuing its traditional Eurasian policy, but this time the policy is more nuanced and differentiated from place to place.

During the post-Soviet years, Moscow has been using a number of ploys to interfere in the affairs of the Near Abroad. The supply of energy, for example, has been an effective weapon especially against Belarus, Ukraine and Moldova. In addition, the recent global increase in the price of oil gave Moscow a great advantage over its Western neighbors. However, this ploy did not work in Central Asia because Kazakhstan, Turkmenistan and Azerbaijan have their own oil and gas resources. In fact, the *Guardian* noted that these countries have used their oil to consolidate their dictatorial powers. Yet, Moscow is promoting its interests through other means such as local dictators and ethnic Russians.

An important tactic used effectively, so far, has been for Moscow to intervene to allegedly defend the local ethnic Russians. According to Wikipedia, which cited *Demoscope Weekly*, in 2002, there were 8.3 million Russians living in Ukraine, 3.8 million in Kazakhstan, 785,000 in Belarus, 640,000 in Uzbekistan, 607,000 in Latvia, 420,000 in Kirgizstan, 369,000 in Moldova, 142,000 in Azerbaijan, 67,000 in Georgia, and so on. The number of Russians living in these countries is declining. For example, the Moldovan Census of 2004 specifies that only 201,000 Russians were still living in Moldova. Nevertheless, Moscow claims to have a legitimate right to intervene and defend all ethnic Russians living in the Near Abroad. Yet, while Moscow invokes the rights of those Russians living outside the Russian Federation, millions of ethnic Chinese have settled recently in Eastern Siberia. That made the Russian minister of defense state that "the Chinese are making a peaceful conquest of the Russian Far East." Will this trend give Beijing the right to intervene in Russia at some future time? (Nicholas Dima, *Culture, Religion, and Geopolitics*, Xlibris, 2010).

As for global geopolitics, the trend of Russia's new policy is especially nuanced. Besides reestablishing itself as a regional power, Russia wants to assert its presence and influence internationally. In Europe, for example, it courts Germany with good business deals; it lures France with attractive defense contracts; and, it offers less expensive oil and gas to other Western countries hoping to distance them from Washington. In South Asia, Russia contracted a new and modern radar system with Iran and only strong Western intervention stopped Moscow from delivering it. From Moscow's point of view, this is only a temporary and tactical move. "One step back, two steps forward." These days, Russia is also equipping China with sophisticated weapons to help it oppose even more strongly the so-called American hegemony.

Moscow is also trying to annoy the United States whenever and wherever it can. As one analyst has put it, Russia can no longer threaten America, but it can make its international efforts more difficult. And this is what the new Russia does. Currently, Moscow is strengthening Hugo Chavez militarily, is establishing a bridgehead in Venezuela, and is trying to make its global military presence more visible. For example, in November 2008, the Russian nuclear cruiser *Peter the Great* led a navy squadron in naval exercises with 11 Venezuelan ships. Then, in December, for the first time in many decades, a Russian destroyer crossed the Panama Canal. Yet, according to *Arizona Daily Star* of 15 February 2011, citing the Associated Press, "NATO is not impressed by Russian Military." Yes? Tell this to the Georgians!

Chapter 4
Poland-A Special Case

Intermarium: The Land between the Black and Baltic Seas, Marek Jan Chodakiewicz (A Case for American Leadership in the post-Soviet Sphere): Transaction Publishers, New Brunswick, 2012, March 12, 2013

No other book explains better the background of the land that separates Russia from Europe than *Intermarium*. No recent book prepares the reader to better understand today's Russian attitude and policy toward the "near" and the "far" abroad.

Intermarium (Latin for *In between Seas*) is a well-researched and well-written book; a balanced combination of theoretical insights with good narratives; an objective study of an area full of subjectivities; and, a thorough summary of important historical events. The book also offers an exhaustive bibliography full of valuable quotations and a much needed alphabetical index. Although it took a team to accomplish this exhaustive study and two decades of research, as well as many field trips, personal interviews, translations and interpretations, all these do not diminish the great personal contribution of the author.

Intermarium is defined as the former Polish-Lithuanian Commonwealth of the early modern period (1386-1795) or western Ruthenia of the old "Rus." Currently, the area is made up of the three Baltic republics to the north, Belarus and Ukraine in the center, and to a lesser degree, the republic of Moldova or former Romania Bessarabia, to the south. However, few people associate this vast area with the former Polish-Lithuanian Commonwealth. A more detailed background in this regard would have been welcome.

The work is well organized into four parts: Background and brief history; The Armageddon and its aftermath (the period from 1939 to 1992); the post-Soviet years; and, a short segment dedicated to individual recollections.

By reading the brief historical background of the Muscovy princedom, the reader is surprised to realize how much Russia's behavior of today mirrors the behavior of the old Muscovy of yesteryears. In fact, it appears that the attitude of the new Russia toward the *Intermarium* has changed little over the centuries. By reading, for example, the short chapters "Medieval Ruthenia and the Mongols," along with "The Balts, the Germans, and the Poles," the reader understands better the roots of Moscow's rejection of anything Western, Polish, or of Catholic influence. It appears that the Moscow of today has virtually the same mentality and geopolitical goals as the old Grand Duchy or Grand Principality of Moscow, more commonly referred to as Muscovy.

Intermarium summarizes how Moscow first seized the other "Ruthenian" principalities, while it was still under Tatar domination. Then, Moscow kept expanding westward to the detriment of the Poles and Lithuanians. Eventually, under the banner of Communism, Moscow reached its maximum extension from the Baltic to the Black Sea. This is the *Intermarium* analyzed in the book, representing the "Near Abroad" of today's Russia. It seems that in order to feel secure, Russia must control all the lands around its periphery, as far as nature allows it or to the point when other powers stand up against its inherent expansionism. This is what Moscow has done for over 500 years! And, according to several of the book's chapters, specifically "Transformation," "The Liberation," and "Post-Soviet Continuities and Discontinuities," this is still what Moscow does these days, but in a more subtle and less overt way. While 21st Century Europe is moving toward freedom, democracy and integration, Russia is stuck in the 19th Century geopolitics. Will Russia ever change and become a normal country?

The author, Marek Jan Chodakiewicz, a professor of history, who holds the Kosciuszko Chair of Polish Studies at the Institute of World Politics in Washington, D.C. makes his study mostly through a Polish intellectual prism and with the interests of the United States in mind. Considering the past history of the area, the Polish-centered point of view is quite justified. However, the American interests in the area must be interpreted in light of Washington's past and recent policies and must be balanced against the Russian ones. From this point of view, it is questionable whether the United States would ever challenge Russia in its own backyard. It certainly did not do so at the time of the Russian invasion of Georgia in 2008 during the presidency of George W. Bush. Actually, given the facts offered by the author about the past and recent American and Western ambiguities, it is hard to believe that the United States would necessarily change its position regarding the *Intermarium*.

Among the many case studies, Chodakiewicz's book emphasizes the extremely complicated relations between various social and ethnic groups during the Russian Civil War and during the occupation of the area by Nazi Germany and the Soviet Union during the Second World War. The aspirations of the local people were incompatible with both occupiers, and the invaders would not accept neutrals in the conflict. The suffering of the local people was beyond endurance. Courageously, the author puts the Nazi and the Communist atrocities on an equal footing: *"Mass terror, extermination and deportations were the trade mark of both the Germans and the Soviets."*

According to the study, counting the number of those deported to Siberia by the Soviet authorities is impossible. The author thinks that maybe twice the number of deportees found in official records were actually deported. In my own research on Moldova, by using Soviet official data and by very conservative estimates, I found about 200,000 people missing due to deportations. Local analysts, however, claim a minimum of a half-million victims. Yet, the short section on Moldova is frightening. It is difficult to believe the stubbornness with which Moscow is still clinging, even now, to this small territory.

Intermarium clearly depicts how most people suffered at the hands of both Russia's Communists and Germany's National Socialists, with some ethnic groups suffering more than others. The Poles, for example, fought against both occupiers and as a result were horribly victimized by both. Next to be victimized were the Ukrainians and the people of the Baltic nations. Some ethnic groups also turned against each other. The Jews were victimized by the Nazis, but Communists among them victimized other ethnic groups. Most nationalities were split, but as a general rule they feared the Germans and hated the Russians. The author should be commended for his objectivity and the courage to tell the entire truth.

Based on facts, Chodakiewicz writes that Poland was betrayed by the West during the most critical years covered by this book. Worst still, most of this time the Western historiography accepted Stalin's propaganda; allegedly, that the USSR "liberated" Eastern Europe and brought "democracy" to the region. For much too long, writes the author, America embraced the official Soviet lies. The question is, can he still trust the West knowing its past deceptions and betrayals? Apparently, the author does, but it is not clear if he truly believes it. Given the history of the Roosevelt administration during the Second World War as well as the Obama administration during Washington's "reset" policy, one couldn't blame him if he didn't entirely trust the West.

Eventually, the Intermarium region was liberated in the early 1990s by a combination of internal forces and external factors. In the author's opinion, the true liberation "*started with the offensive unleashed by John Paul II, Ronald Reagan and Margaret Thatcher.*" In this vein, he writes: "*Gradually, the nationalist dream was realized. The nationalists, however, were excluded from its fruits. Ultimately, it was the post-Communists who stole the thunder of the nationalists and emerged victorious in most of the newly independent states of the Intermarium.*" And further, freedom did come, but it was skewed. "*Once the dissolution of the USSR occurred, the former Communist masters continued to exercise power over their former captive peoples.*" In fact, the former Communists morphed into the new capitalists.

From this standpoint, one can understand the author's disillusionment. He writes that the Communist societies have been "transformed," but not really "reformed." And the book also offers a very good analysis of nationalism, which is so much maligned in the West. He writes that the West still fears nationalism, whereas, the former East European and Soviet Communists are fully accepted. As a result, millions of victims have been forgotten and the truth about the

Communist atrocities is carefully avoided by many Western circles. *"Let us forget the past. We were all victims,"* cry the post-Communists rebranded now as Social-Democrats. Here, the author cogently writes, *"It is singularly unhelpful that the postmodernists dominating the historical discourse in the European Union refuse to equate Nazism and Communism, or even acknowledge the crimes of Moscow, for example, the Katyn Forest massacre."* In this regard, Chapter 16, "Contemporary Politics," offers a good analysis of the current left-leaning attitudes of the West and concludes, *"Thus, Communism may be 'dead' but the nefarious leftist ideas which birthed it are well and alive."* And, I may ask then, who really won the Cold War?

On a rather small critical note, despite a comprehensive bibliography, I could not find the source of certain precise data about Moldova that is given in the book. The root of the Polish-Lithuanian friction is not well explained either. In addition, the current sizes of ethnic minorities living in the post-Soviet republics are not given even though the issue of nationalities continues to be important.

In conclusion, *"Russia is angry and wants to reassert itself,"* writes the author, adding: *"The Kremlin's aim is clear: to reimpose its control over the Intermarium in the short run and over the rest of the post-Communist sphere in a long run."* As for the *Intermarium* as a whole, the region is too weak and too fragmented to stand on its own and that is an invitation for Russia and Germany to reenter the area. Indeed, these days Moscow is cozying up to Berlin, a fact that is worrisome to the local people.

And what is America doing? The author writes, *"The United States lacks a coherent geopolitical vision and foreign policy in regard to the post-Soviet sphere, including in Europe."* And further, *"NATO is often perceived as rudderless,"* while *"America has failed to provide appropriate leadership."* The author also warns that dispensing false hope to the people of the area is no longer enough in our age. *"America may no longer take for granted the support of its foreign policy by the nations of the post-Soviet sphere."* Therefore, Washington needs a proactive policy in the Intermarium region of Europe: *"In essence, promoting a pro-American bloc in the middle of Europe, either to complement or counterbalance the increasingly anti-American Western Europe, would be indispensable to return US influence in the old continent.*" The author deftly points out that "*outside the Baltics, Brussels has played a rather ambiguous role in the region.*"

On a positive note, the author recommends objective research and studies, publishing personal recollections, accepting the truth, and starting the process of reconciliation. First, however, Moscow will have to accept its past wrong doings and reconcile itself with the truth. And, as a reviewer, in closing, I am asking a simple question: If Nazism was condemned at the Nuremberg trial, why not a trial of Communism? Why not go to the roots of the evil? And, if I am allowed to answer my own question: it is because the former perpetrators are still there, maybe still pursuing a Marxist ideal; albeit, in a more subtle manner.

Lech Walesa-Vaclav Havel: Lament Rise of Revisionist Russia. July 31, 2009

With a changing of the guard occurring in the U.S. as well as in Central and Eastern Europe comes a growing sense of trepidation in Eastern European capitals among those seemingly timeless dissident leaders like Lech Walesa of Poland and Vaclav Havel of Czechoslovakia, who helped to forge a future for freedom and independence from Soviet domination during the largely bloodless revolutions of 1989.

In the wake of the 20 years since the Velvet revolutions of the former Eastern Bloc states surviving under Communist rule is a new generation coming of age in the Central and Eastern European (CEE) countries. This generation lacks a sufficient connection and understanding of the importance of the American role or for that matter even that of its own leaders in achieving their country's freedom and independence from Soviet Russia. During this critical transition period where new leaders are emerging, the former policy makers and intellectuals of the CEE have issued an Open Letter to President Barack Obama. In part, they point out that the joint successes of U.S. Cold War-era policy have laid a "proper foundation for the transatlantic renaissance we need today." More specifically, they posit: "*Twenty years have passed since the revolutions of 1989. That is a whole generation. We need a new generation to renew the transatlantic partnership. A new program should be launched to identify those young leaders on both sides of the Atlantic who can carry forward the transatlantic project we have spent the last two decades building in Central and Eastern Europe."*

The evolution of this "Open Letter" is most interesting. Under the leadership of the German Marshall Fund (GMF) of the United States, a largely German government supported Washington-based think tank concentrating on transatlantic policy, GMF backed the Central European Task Force consisting of six regional experts who produced a GMF Policy Brief entitled: Why the Obama Administration Should Not Take Central and Eastern Europe for Granted, published July 13th. On July 16th, GMF hosted a CEE roundtable discussion in Washington featuring former Clinton administration Secretary of State Madeleine Albright, who served as commentator. Simultaneously on July 16th, the Open Letter was widely disseminated appearing on the GMF web site, the Polish newspaper Gazeta Wyborcza and Radio Free Europe/Radio Liberty. In fact, the GMF Policy Brief had become the basis for an expanded version of the Open Letter.

The Open Letter iterates at the outset its concerns over the dramatic changes having taken place in the region due to the success of U.S. policy, from those dark days of Cold War subjugation as part of the former Eastern Bloc under Moscow's control, there being no further need for concern. Accordingly, they write: *"As the new Obama Administration sets its foreign policy priorities, our region is one part of the world that Americans have largely stopped worrying about. Indeed, at times we have the impression that U.S. policy was so successful that many American officials have now concluded that our region is fixed once and for all that they could 'check the box' and move on to other more pressing strategic issues. Relations have been so close that many on both sides assume that the region's transatlantic orientation, as well as its stability and prosperity, would last forever."*

In view of the formidable push made by the German Marshall Fund in bringing the region's serious concerns to the forefront, it is easy to comprehend those concerns expressed by the signers of the Open

Letter in light of the November 2008 election of a relatively obscure and inexperienced first term U.S. Senator from Chicago who is raised to the dizzying heights of the presidency of the United States of America. Given President Obama's lack of experience in foreign affairs, the prescience of the GMF was validated during his recent trip to Moscow. It is difficult to evaluate the achievements of the president's trip especially when balanced against the concessions that were made. What concessions did the U.S. president make to Moscow? Apparently, the Russians received an approving nod for strengthening their presence in Central Asia; it is likely they got away with their gains in Georgia; and most likely, they gained the upper hand once again in the Ukraine and Moldova. It seems, however unexpectedly, that Moscow also obtained some concessions in Central and Eastern Europe.

The culmination of Obama's trip was the July 6th signing of a Joint Understanding between the United States and the Russian Federation regarding strategic missiles that would begin a process to replace START (strategic arms reduction treaty) with a new treaty. This agreement for the mutual reduction of nuclear arsenals comes in the midst of continuing tensions over the proposed U.S. installation of a missile defense shield in Poland and the Czech Republic, strenuously opposed by Moscow. Just 10 days after the signing of the Joint Understanding, GMF published the Open Letter to President Barack Obama and held its roundtable discussion.

Among the six critical steps proposed by the Open Letter, the authors describe their third step as the "thorniest" of issues. Of course, this is the missile defense shield to be placed in Poland and the Czech Republic. On July 6th, in an interview given to the Russian newspaper *Novaya Gazeta*, Obama said, "We have not yet decided how we will configure missile defense in Europe. But my sincere hope is that Russia will be a partner in that project." Moscow views this missile defense shield as a threat to its interests and as expressed by Russian President Dimitry Medvedev on July 10th at the G8 Summit, if the U.S. installs the missile shield, Moscow will install the mobile *Iskander-M* ballistic missile system in the Kaliningrad enclave, a result of the accommodative Potsdam Conference of August 1945. The Open Letter clearly and explicitly addresses missile defense in Europe stating: *"Regardless of the military merits of this scheme and what Washington eventually decides to do, the issue has nevertheless also become – at least in some countries – a symbol of America's credibility and commitment to the region. How it is handled could have a significant impact on their future transatlantic orientation. The small number of missiles involved cannot be a threat to Russia's strategic capabilities, and the Kremlin knows this. We should decide the future of the program as allies and based on the strategic plusses and minuses of the different technical and political configurations. The [NATO] Alliance should not allow the issue to be determined by unfounded Russian opposition."*

How to deal with the rise of a revisionist Russia, particularly in Central and Eastern Europe, sets the tone for the entire Open Letter in the context of the transatlantic relationship. Moscow has treated the CEE countries with outright contempt and disrespect for their sovereignty once having been either part of the former Eastern Bloc or the former Soviet Union itself that Moscow today considers its "near abroad" within its sphere of influence. On the issue of how to deal with Russia, the Open Letter explains: *"Our hopes that relations with Russia would improve and that Moscow would finally fully accept our complete sovereignty and independence after joining NATO and the EU have not been fulfilled. Instead Russia is back as a revisionist power pursuing a 19th-century agenda with 21 st-century tactics and methods. At a global level Russia has become, on most issues, a status-quo power. But at a regional level and vis-à-vis our nations, it increasingly acts as a revisionist one. It challenges our claims to our own historical experiences. It asserts a privileged position in determining our security choices. It uses overt and covert means of economic warfare, ranging from energy blockades and politically motivated investments to bribery and media manipulation in order to advance its interests and to challenge the transatlantic orientation of Central and Eastern Europe."*

Moscow has sought a monopoly of energy supplies with the intent of creating a European dependence on natural gas setting high prices to pressure transit and end user countries. Alternatives have included American support for the Baku-Tbilisi-Ceyhan pipeline, which would not have otherwise been built. European energy security includes the recent agreement to build the Nabucco natural gas pipeline project completely bypassing Russia, which was signed in Turkey on July 13th.

Praising America's historic support for liberal democratic values, the authors compare the widely different and unfortunate outcomes when America stood up for those values and how the region suffered when it did not, citing the "reality of Yalta," a reference to the post-World War II division of Europe and the Iron Curtain that descended upon Central and Eastern Europe for nearly 50 years. If the "realist" view had prevailed in the 1990s, they would not be members of NATO or the EU. Similarly, they express the nervousness permeating their capitals today warning of their concern that under the Obama administration the United States and the major European powers might embrace a new contemporary division embodied in what they refer to as the *"Medvedev plan for a 'Concert of Powers' to replace the continent's existing, value-based security structure."* The authors conclude their Open Letter with a very nuanced but prophetic statement: *"We, the authors of this letter, know firsthand how important the relationship with the United States has been. In the 1990s, a large part of getting Europe right was about getting Central and Eastern Europe right. The engagement of the United States was critical to locking in peace and stability from the Baltics to the Black Sea. Today the goal must be to keep Central and Eastern Europe right as a stable, activist, and Atlanticist part of our broader community."*

Without a revisionist Russia and the election of a U.S. president who is young and inexperienced, there would be no need for such an Open Letter from these venerable pro-Western leaders from Central and Eastern Europe. Written and signed in their personal capacities as individuals "who are friends and allies of the United States as well as committed Europeans," this all important missive conveys a desperate sense of need for reassurance from Washington at a very critical time.

The Open Letter was signed by Valdas Adamkus, Martin Butora, Emil Constantinescu, Pavol Demes, Lubos Dobrovsky, Matyas Eorsi, Istvan Gyarmati, Vaclav Havel, Rastislav Kacer, Sandra Kalniete, Karel Schwarzenberg, Michal Kovac, Ivan Krastev, Alexander Kwasniewski,

Mart Laar, Kadri Liik, Janos Martonyi. Janusz Onyszkiewicz, Adam Rotfeld, Vaira Vike-Freiberga, Alexandr Vondra and Lech Walesa.

Katyn Tragedy Redux. April 20, 2010

Background to an Old Tragedy

The aircrash that killed Poland's president, Lech Kaczynski, is set in a background of tragedy dating back to the Nazi-Soviet Pact of August 23, 1939, when the German Army invaded western Poland. Two weeks later, the Soviet Army invaded the eastern part of Poland, and France and Great Britain, which had given security guarantees to Poland, declared war on Germany, leading to the beginning of World War II. The Polish Army fought against the Germans, but not against the Soviet Union. Numerous Polish officers surrendered to the Russians hoping to be well received and together to fight against the Germans. At the time, however, the Soviet Union and Germany were allies; therefore, the Polish officers were placed in concentrations camps. Shortly thereafter, in 1940, the Soviet Union decided to execute them. Some 50,000 young, educated and well-trained Polish officers — Poland's best and brightest – were shot individually KGB-style in the back of the head. The best known case is the massacre in Katyn, a forest in present day Belarus, a former Soviet Socialist Republic, where over 20,000 Polish officers were murdered and interred in a common pit.

For decades, Moscow claimed that the Polish officers were killed by the Germans, but the evidence proved otherwise. Finally, after launching perestroika and glasnost in the late 1980s, President Mikhail Gorbachev admitted on April 13, 1990 this horrific genocide, which was committed in the spring of 1940 by the Soviet secret police in the Katyn Forest. Gorbachev did so when he handed over to then-Polish President Wojciech Jaruzelski boxes of documents proving Soviet involvement in the massacre. Poland accepted with dignity and resignation Moscow's admission of guilt and began to put the abominable act behind it. Poland also built a memorial at Katyn and the Polish people began a tradition of pilgrimage to the place where their sons were murdered. Ever since the fall of the Soviet empire, Polish officials and private citizens have visited the Katyn memorial.

Reality of a New Tragedy

The U.S. Department of State issued the following statement on April 7, 2010, in anticipation of Katyn commemoration ceremonies: *"On April 7 and 10, senior Polish and Russian leaders are participating together in ceremonies commemorating the 70th anniversary of the Katyn massacre. The mass murder in the Katyn forest 70 years ago is a tragic stain on Europe's past. This meeting of the current generation of Polish and Russian leaders is a sign of a much better present and of the hope for an increasingly bright and peaceful future. We welcome the strengthening of the Russian-Polish relationship this mutual tribute symbolizes, and hope that it promises the continued growth of cooperation in Europe. The United States joins Poland and Russia in remembering those who lost their lives in the Katyn forest seventy years ago."*

Saturday, April 10, 2010, on the 70th commemoration of the Katyn massacre, Polish President Lech Kaczynski with his wife and First Lady, Mrs. Maria Kaczynska, led a large delegation for a special ceremony at that memorial. Along with his wife, he was accompanied by 94 Polish high-ranking civilian and military officials, including a dozen members of parliament, the president of the national bank, all the heads of Poland's armed services and the head of the national security bureau. They were supposed to attend a second memorial service. A first one had been held three days earlier, but President Kaczynski was irritated because Russian Prime Minister Vladimir Putin had invited only the Polish Prime Minister, Donald Tusk, and the Russian leader had not mentioned the Polish officers massacred by the KGB. Consequently, Kaczynski wanted a proper ceremony held at Katyn and was on his way to attend it. At the first ceremony Vladimir Putin, himself a former KGB colonel, admitted the Russian hand in the tragic event, which was a step in the right direction. However, he then gave an interview justifying the massacre. As reported by the UK newspaper, The Independent, Vladimir Putin said that Soviet dictator Josef Stalin personally wanted revenge for the alleged deaths in 1920 of about 32,000 Soviet soldiers in Polish prisons and war camps following World War I.

Ironically, President Lech Kaczynski wanted to set the record straight. For the new commemoration, he and his delegation were traveling to Katyn aboard a Soviet-built airplane, a Tupolev-154M, but the plane crashed killing the entire Polish delegation. Later, it was revealed that Moscow had wanted to divert the plane's route, allegedly due to bad weather. The Polish delegation insisted, however, to fly a more direct route to arrive at the ceremony as scheduled, but they never made it, with the plane crashing just 1000 feet short of the runway at Smolensk North Airport, once a Soviet military airbase. It was apparently a grim accident, which instead of helping the reconciliation process reminded the Poles of the other huge tragedy that had split Moscow and Warsaw decades earlier. The terrible accident stunned Poland and raised many eyebrows in Eastern Europe. Most papers admitted that it was an accident, but many people remembered quickly that it was an accident "typical of Russia." Some papers even pointed out what President Franklin Delano Roosevelt once said: "Nothing happens by accident in politics. And if it does, you can bet that it was planned to happen." What can one say when such a tragic accident decimates an entire governmental delegation led by the very president of that nation when visiting a not so friendly country?

President Kaczynski was a Polish patriot and a staunch critic of Vladimir Putin and Russia's efforts to regain control over the former Soviet sphere. As elaborated by Stratfor-Global Intelligence, among others, Mr. Kaczynski even proposed that the EU "impose sanctions on Russia for its economic bullying in Eastern Europe." Also, in a public speech given in June of last year he proposed that the EU show "energetic solidarity" in order to protect the country against "international blackmailing," obviously referring to Moscow. When Russia invaded Georgia and flexed its muscles in Ukraine, he also expressed vigorous support for the integrity of Georgia and for the independence of Ukraine. Moscow was irritated by his statements and attitude. But following the April accident, the Kremlin became more cautious regarding its relations with Warsaw.

To limit any further damage, Moscow ordered a full investigation of the accident. However, the investigation was mostly conducted by the Russians. It revealed that weather conditions were indeed very poor, that the plane flew through dense fog, and that visibility was limited. According to the same Russian sources, the air controllers also complained that the Polish pilots could not express themselves properly in Russian and could not understand good Russian either, which contributed to the problem. The Polish investigators in their turn complained that they did not have immediate access to the scene of the accident and in addition they found some contradictions in the Russian official investigation. Adding to this complex puzzle, it was pointed out that the Tu-154M was not only Soviet-built, but it had been inspected and modernized also by Russia in December 2009. Yet, Moscow blamed the entire accident on the Polish pilots, although they were among the best Polish military pilots.

Furthermore, the Polish Defense Ministry announced that in the past Russia organized military maneuvers with new electromagnetic weapons in the area of the accident and alluded that those weapons could have damaged the jet's electronic equipment. Then, Artur Gorski, a member of the Polish Parliament, accused Russia of direct involvement. As reported by the Associated Press, Mr. Gorski accused Moscow of denying the Poles access to the scene of the crash as well as to the transcript of conversations from the cockpit voice recorder detailing events before the fatal accident.

A huge funeral service was held Sunday, April 18, in Warsaw and later the bodies of the president and his wife were flown to Krakow for burial. As reported by the Associated Press, the interim President, Bronislaw Komorowski, stated at the funeral service that "Our world was crushed down for the second time in the same place," near the forest of Katyn. It seems indeed that not only some of the most prominent members of the Polish elite were buried on that sad Sunday, but also the much needed Russian-Polish reconciliation. In Eastern Europe, for example, as reported by the Romanian press, including the widely circulated daily Romania Libera, the recent resurgence of Russia is not only a fact, but it is a real menace. And all that occurs in a new international climate in which the United States seems to have adopted a policy of accommodation.

The Lie of Katyn. January 17, 2011

Arguably, there is no other country on the face of this earth that has been as victimized during the 20th Century as the Polish nation. Marking the start of World War II with the Nazi and Soviet invasions of 1939, Poland became the first nation to stand against Hitler and Stalin. It withstood the subsequent mass executions of German occupation followed by the Soviet annexation of eastern Poland and post-war re-division. Then in 1989, the Republic of Poland emerged from 45 years of Moscow's oppressive rule and subjugation to become a sovereign, free and independent nation; the Peoples Republic of Poland had become history. Yet, it is the atrocity in the forest of Katyn, shrouded in 50 years of lies that epitomizes this genocide of Poland's national identity.

The Nazi-Soviet rapprochement of August 23, 1939, or so-called Ribbentrop-Molotov non-aggression pact, secretly demarcated their respective "spheres of influence" for Eastern Europe and led to the Nazi invasion of western Poland on September 1, 1939 and the Soviet invasion of eastern Poland on September 17, 1939. In a so-called treaty on friendship and borders between Moscow and Berlin, signed on September 28, 1939, the Soviets had proposed the final liquidation of Poland.

By 1943, Nazi Germany had uncovered the mass graves of the Katyn forest near the city of Smolensk after turning on its former Soviet ally in its advance to Stalingrad (Volgagrad) with hopes of further seizing the Caspian oil fields. Although, Soviet-era propaganda laid blame for the war time crime on Germany and forced the post-war Polish state to do the same. According to Polish film maker, Andrzej Wajda, producer of the haunting 2007 film *Katyn*, "After 1945 the Katyn lie became the basis of the Soviet-Polish friendship."

At the twilight of the USSR in 1990, Mikhail Gorbachev acknowledged Soviet responsibility for the crimes of Katyn that took the lives of some 22,000 members of the Polish elite, including military officers, engineers, diplomats, politicians, writers, artists, college professors, teachers, civil servants, land owners, and factory owners. Further, Russian President Boris Yeltsin ordered a limited number of documents declassified in 1992.

On December 18, 1998, the Polish Parliament established the *Institute of National Remembrance – Commission for the Prosecution of Crimes against the Polish Nation* (IPN) headquartered in Warsaw (www.ipn.gov.pl/). Simply put, its mission is to preserve the memory of the losses incurred at the hands of traitors of the Polish nation, Nazis and the Soviet Communists during World War II.

Upon this background, the Institute of National Remembrance held a press conference on December 1, 2004 announcing the "Decision to Commence Investigation into the Katyn Massacre." In part, IPN press release states: *"On 30 November 2004, the Departmental Commission for the Prosecution of Crimes against the Polish Nation in Warsaw issued a decision to commence investigations, Case No. S 38/04/ZK, into the 'mass murder, by shooting, of not less than 21,768 Polish citizens, for the purpose of liquidating a part of the Polish national group, during the period between 5 March and an unspecified date in 1940 in Moscow, Kharkov, Smolensk, Katyn, Kalinin (now Tver), and other locations on the territory of the Union of Soviet Socialist Republics by its state functionaries acting on instructions from the authorities of their state, which was then allied with the Third Reich...as a result of the implementation of the criminal resolution by the Politburo of the Central Committee of the All-Union Communist Party (Bolsheviks) reached in Moscow on 5 March 1940...'"*

In April of 2010, Russian President Dmitry Medvedev ordered the online publication of these previously declassified documents. Revealed was a key letter marked "Top Secret" dated March 5, 1940 written to Soviet dictator Josef Stalin from his chief of secret police (NKVD- predecessor of the KGB) Lavrenty Beria, a fellow Georgian, recommending the execution of over 20,000 of the more than 250,000 captured Poles, following the invasion of eastern Poland by Soviet forces in 1939. The BBC reported on the release of the Beria letter to Stalin that April publishing excerpts including the following: *"To Comrade Stalin: In prisoner-of-war camps run by the USSR NKVD and in prisons in western Ukraine and Belorussia there is currently a large number of former Polish army officers, former officials of the Polish police and intelligence services, members of Polish nationalist counter-*

revolutionary parties, members of unmasked rebel counter-revolutionary organizations, defectors and others. They are all sworn enemies of Soviet power, filled with hatred towards the Soviet system.....Give special consideration to.....Imposing on them the sentence of capital punishment – execution by shooting."

The letter was signed by "L. Beria" in his capacity of "USSR People's Commissar for Internal Affairs." The first page bore the blue penciled signature of approval by Josef Stalin and regular penciled signatures of Politburo members K. Voroshilov, A. Mikoyan and V. Molotov. Aides to Stalin, Kalinin and Kaganovich signified their approval in the margin, also in blue pencil.

On November 26, 2010, the lower house of the Russian Parliament known as the State Duma debated a resolution regarding the Katyn massacre. The *Moscow Times*, an English language newspaper, wrote: *"this past May, Russia handed over 67 volumes pertaining to the execution of Polish officers to the Polish side. Warsaw had not previously received documents of the criminal case, only archive information."* Two days later the Duma condemned former Soviet dictator Josef Stalin for the 1940 mass execution of nearly 22,000 Polish prisoners including officers and civilians in one of the most heinous atrocities of the 20th Century. According to *Reuters*, the vote was widely seen as a Russian attempt to improve long-strained ties with Poland.

The *Wall Street Journal* article by Richard Boudreaux headlined, *"Russia Admits Stalin Ordered 1940 Massacre of Poles,"* dated November 27-28 reported the State Duma passed a resolution declaring long-classified documents *"showed that the Katyn crime was carried out on direct orders of Stalin and other Soviet officials."* The resolution, backed by 342 of its 450 members, also called for the massacre to be investigated further in order to complete the list of victims, since a 2005 Russian judicial report had only confirmed the execution of 1,803 Poles at Katyn.

The Duma resolution reads: *"Material, kept for many years in secret archives bear witness to the fact that the Katyn crime was carried out under Stalin's orders."* The document mentions that *"the State Duma deputies extend a hand of friendship to the Polish people and hope this will mark a new era of relations between our countries."* The Communist Party members of the Duma denied, once again, any Soviet involvement and voted against the resolution. It has often been said that history repeats itself. So much for the Polish-Russian reconciliation!

Chapter 5
Ukraine, New Challenges

Vladimir Putin Asserts Russia's Regional Power.
October 16, 2013

Something strange is happening in the world this fall of Anno Domini 2013. The United States seems politically deadlocked. Europe is struggling both politically and economically and is not really functioning as a union. The Middle East has just stopped short of a new war. And Russia under the old and new President Vladimir Putin is reasserting itself as an international power.

Important events are in the offing, and Moscow is working feverishly to take full advantage of them. After decrying the dismantling of the Soviet Union and reinstating the Soviet anthem, Putin seems determined to reconstruct the former USSR into a Euro-Asian super state. This Eurasian Customs Union is supposed to stretch from Belarus and Moldova to the Caucasus and Central Asia, thus recovering most of the former Soviet Union. For the time being, Moscow is using the traditional carrot and stick approach to prevent the former Soviet republics from joining the European Union. And the timing is critical because the EU will meet next month for the third Eastern Partnership Summit in Vilnius to possibly grant associate status to several East European countries, as Lithuania, once in the Soviet orbit, presides over the EU.

The *Economist* of September 16 writes that since May of this year when Putin began his third term as President "his declared objective has been to launch a 21st century Russian resurgence." And, he emphasized that "the threat to Russia over the past quarter century has come from the Western world, and specifically the USA. They are our geopolitical opponents." As a consequence, Russia is now modernizing its military machine and is trying to reach for foreign allies. Interestingly, the new Chinese leader, Xi Jinping, made his first international trip in his capacity as General Secretary of the Communist Party of China, to Moscow and, according to the *Economist*, Russia and China participated this past July at the biggest naval exercises the two countries had ever held together in the Pacific.

Putin's vision is a huge free-trade zone with a strong military alliance. The former Soviet republics are reluctant to join the new Russian sphere, but Moscow is hell-bent on bringing them to order. The key is first to co-opt Ukraine, but Kiev received Moscow's plan with great reservations. Heavy handedly, Russia reacted by blocking its imports. The Kremlin's pressure on Ukraine is an ongoing process, but not the only one.

On September 29 the *Washington Post* dedicated an editorial to the efforts of Moldova to join the EU and to Moscow's fierce opposition to sabotage any EU-Moldova accords. For those who know the region and Russia's position, the editorial does not offer many new elements. Yet, the article is important because it brings to the fore the deteriorating relations between Moscow and the West. With U.S. foreign policy in disarray, Putin is pressuring Moldova, Ukraine, Georgia, as well as the former Soviet Central Asia, to join the Eurasian Customs Union. In September, ahead of the Vilnius meeting, Moscow banned the importation of Moldovan wines (its biggest export); it threatened to cut its supply of natural gas; and, it began to harass and deport Moldovan guest workers. Putin's Eurasian Customs Union has already attracted Belarus, Armenia, Kazakhstan, and likely other Central Asian republics. Tajikistan, for example, has already signed an accord to extend for another 30 years an important Russian military base on its territory in exchange for receiving natural gas and a good treatment for its migrant workers in Russia. Moscow's economic pressure is aimed at preventing the former Soviet republics from any form of association with the EU. Such association could later lead to full membership in the EU and eventually to integration into NATO. If Moscow's pressure over the larger and stronger Ukraine is subtle, its pressure over smaller and weaker Moldova is open and much harsher, depicting the tactics of a bully.

According to *Mediafax* and *Romania Libera* of September 26, as a response to Russia's blackmail, the European Commission began to consider opening the EU's market to Moldovan wines. Yet, the Russian news agency *RIA Novotni*, cited by *Romania Libera*, announced that President Putin warned Moldova if it signs an accord with the EU, it should not expect the Eurasian Customs Union will accept its wines. And he stressed that Russia, Ukraine, Belarus and Kazakhstan represent the biggest market for Moldova's wines, therefore, Moldova should join. Furthermore, Russia's Vice-Premier Dmitri Rogozin, came to Chisinau and cautioned Moldova if it signs the association agreement with the EU *"it will lose Trans-Nistria, will freeze in the coming winter, and will become Europe's servant."* All this time, the Russian leadership of the break-away region of Trans-Nistria is increasingly hostile toward the government of Moldova.

The tug-of-war is over control and influence of the six countries – Belarus, Ukraine, Moldova, Georgia, Armenia and Azerbaijan – that comprise the Eastern Partnership. While the EU would like to attract them, Russia is doing everything to integrate them into its own union. Putin's pressure to keep Ukraine under Moscow is more nuanced than in the case of Moldova, but is very firm. He claimed recently that the economic interests of Ukraine would be much better served if Kiev were to join the Eurasian Customs Union. Yet, he threatened Kiev with serious consequences if it signed an agreement with the EU. As a result, Ukraine is hesitant and is facing a dilemma. Its foreign minister declared Ukraine did not want to renounce the present agreements with Russia and expressed his hope that maintaining relations with both systems should be acceptable to all Ukraine's partners. Nevertheless, *Romania Libera* reported on September 13 that the president of the European Commission, José Manuel Barroso, had made it clear that a country cannot belong to two different custom systems.

Then, at the 1,025-th anniversary of Russian Christianity held in Kiev, Putin gathered most of the heads of the Eastern Orthodox Churches and stressed their spiritual unity. The gathering was attended by the leaders of Serbia, Bulgaria, Montenegro and Cyprus, where Russia would like to obtain a naval base, as its warm water Mediterranean port of Tartus in Syria is at risk. Although allegedly a religious gathering, it resembled more of a geopolitical meeting. Interestingly, Romania, primarily an Orthodox country, but a firm NATO member and an American ally, was absent from the meeting. Bucharest cannot possibly forget the past Russian abuses of its lands and the alienation of its former province of Bessarabia, part of what is now the Republic of Moldova.

The big prize in Russia's geopolitical-economic struggle for the domination of Eurasia is Ukraine. This is discussed in the article "Ukraine and Russia-Trading Insults," in the *Economist* of August 24. Putin's chief economic adviser, Sergei Glazyev, warned Kiev without going into details that associating itself with the EU at the coming Vilnius summit, would be "suicidal." While Russia is actively promoting a clear-cut policy choice ahead of the Vilnius summit, Europe seems to be intimidated and has a tepid attitude, while the United States is mired in its own problems and is absent from this important European event.

On September 29, Carl Gershman, president of the National Endowment for Democracy (NED), writing in the *Washington Post* stressed that even the Russian journalists are aware Moscow is trying to blackmail its neighbors to coerce them into the Eurasian Customs Union. Yet, the Russian online newspaper *Gazeta.ru* wrote, *"Blackmail is the worst possible way of advertising economic cooperation."* The journal added, *"Russia's problem is more than tactical. Its post*-communist neighbors prefer the relative dynamism of Europe to Russia's stagnant economy."* And the very title of the articles speaks volumes: *"Former Soviet states stand up to Russia." Will the U.S.?*

The EU's Vilnius Summit and the Ukraine Fiasco.
December 17, 2013

A much anticipated summit was held in Vilnius, Lithuania (Nov. 28-29), to prepare the eastern expansion of the European Union. The big prize was to bring Ukraine closer to Europe. At the same time, three other smaller countries, Moldova, Georgia and Armenia, were expected to sign association agreements with the EU. In reality, the meeting was a geopolitical and eco-political confrontation between Russia and the

West. The United States was absent from the meeting, while the European Union was powerless facing Moscow alone. The result of the summit was that Russia won another important strategic battle. Ukraine, the country-pivot of East Europe, remained, for now, in Moscow's embrace and so did small Armenia located in the Caucasus Mountains. They both succumbed to Moscow's economic and political pressures and rejected any new association with the EU.

Ukraine, by far the most important East European country, was expected to sign an agreement with the EU, and the summit was supposed to be just a formality. However, a week before the meeting, Ukraine backed off as it came under intense Russian pressure to oppose any further association with Europe. On one hand Moscow threatened it economically, and on the other, it offered advantages for not signing a new agreement. And to make good on the threats, just before the summit, Russia restricted several imports from Ukraine worth, in Kiev's opinion, over six billion dollars. Furthermore, Gazprom, the giant Russian energy company, demanded that Ukraine immediately pay its past dues. At the same time, Moscow promised Ukraine inexpensive natural gas and new loans, if it joined the Russia-Belarus-Kazakhstan Customs Union. Given Kiev's dire economic situation, the threats and promises were very hard to ignore. The EU's effort to attract Ukraine into its orbit failed. An association with the EU would have been a first step toward Ukraine's full membership and possibly NATO membership. The Vilnius summit was a victory for Russia and a loss for America and the West.

Ukraine's reversal triggered huge protests in Kiev

There had been demonstrations prior to the summit, but in support of European association. The decision to reject Europe and to remain in Russia's sphere of influence triggered enraged public protests. Hundreds of thousands of people took to the streets in Kiev and other cities. The media emphasized the determination of the Ukrainian people to break out from Russia's shadow and join the European family of nations. At the same time, the leaders of the opposition demanded the impeachment of Yanukovych and the resignation of his government.

The protests turned violent and the police made use of truncheons, tear gas, flash grenades arresting hundreds of people.

Dozens, including some journalists, were taken away by ambulances. As a result, the chief of Kiev's police resigned, but the protests continued. Ukraine's Prime Minister declared the demonstrators had resorted to "illegal methods," that their actions "amounted to a coup" and that the government would take the necessary means to restore order, while Russian President Vladimir Putin claimed the protests had been organized by "outside forces" to topple a "legitimate government."

Interestingly, before going to Vilnius, Yanukovych held a secret meeting with Vladimir Putin, his sponsor and chief backer. No one knows what they discussed, but Kiev's relations with Russia are not rosy and Moscow's offers to attract Ukraine into its new Customs Union are murky. In this political climate, Yanukovych's decision to choose Russia over Europe represents very much his personal interests. If he does not win the 2015 presidential elections he may end up in prison and exchange places with Yulia Tymoshenko, the former prime minister of Ukraine and one of his bitter foes jailed by the regime. Could Moscow help him once again in this new "revolutionary" fervor?

The first days of December 2013 witnessed the largest public rallies in Kiev since the 2004 Orange Revolution. Those events had brought Ukraine temporarily on a westward path. Moscow derailed the pro-western movement then and it is trying to do it again now. Unfortunately, Ukraine is a divided country between those who prefer the West and those who favor Russia, but currently the balance tilts toward Europe. One recent opinion survey reveals that 45 percent of Ukrainians support integration with the EU and some 30 percent prefer closer ties with Russia. While the current American leadership seems to condone Putin's maneuvers, the U.S. public is ill informed. American TV stations, for example, reported little of the great struggle in Kiev. People in the United States who were interested had to turn to the Arabic Al Jazeera station.

The consolation prize

Georgia and Moldova signed association agreements with the EU. Armenia, another country that was invited to the summit, preferred to remain aligned with Russia. Considering a bitter historic enmity with neighboring Turkey, an ongoing territorial issue with Azerbaijan and an economy in ruin, Armenia did not have much of a choice. There were public demonstrations against the government's decision to reject the EU, even in remote Armenia.

As for Moldova and Georgia, they signed EU association agreements and their governments and people rejoiced over their new status. The new agreements should help the two countries increase their exports, eliminate some visa restrictions, and offer them a path toward full membership.

In anticipation of such westward moves, Russia had punished these two republics in the past, seizing some of their territories and subjecting them to intense pressure and blackmail. In this regard, the regions of Abkhazia and South Ossetia of Georgia and of Transnistria in Moldova, which had split from these two countries, remain in Russian hands. For now Moscow is quiet; however, the two countries fear this is just a temporary reprieve to help secure a peaceful atmosphere before the Sochi Winter Olympics in February. After that, Moldova and Georgia expect renewed Russian pressure.

Moldova's special ties with Romania

Moldova used to be part of Romania and its ties with Bucharest are very special. Returning home from the Vilnius, President Traian Basescu of Romania stopped in the Moldovan capital of Chisinau, where he met President Nicolae Timofti. The two leaders share the same language and strong national feelings. The very next day, December 1st, was Romania's National Day and Presidents Basescu and Timofti commemorated it at the Romanian embassy in Chisinau. December 1st was celebrated both in Bucharest and in Chisinau. President Basescu declared for the first time after joining the European Union and NATO, Romania's next project was to reintegrate Moldova with Romania.

Reunification is a delicate issue because Russia opposes it strongly, Western Europe is hesitant and does not want to upset Moscow, and the United States was not committed until recently, when Secretary of State John Kerry paid a short visit to Moldova and declared Washington's support for its European integration. During the meeting, President Timofti asked Kerry for help to insure the security of the region, since they fear Russian efforts to destabilize the country.

In this complex political climate and in view of the continuing Russian threat, even the leaders of Moldova are split. While Timofti spoke warmly of brotherly Romania, in an interview given to a group of Russian journalists, Prime Minister Iurie Leanca preferred to speak of meeting Romania in the European Union. However, public pressure is growing. A large number of people demonstrated in Chisinau, during the Romanian National Day rejoicing Moldova's association with the European Union and demanding reunification with Romania.

And there is something else. Since the 1940 Soviet annexation of Bessarabia and the establishment of the Soviet republic of Moldova, Moscow has claimed that the local people speak a language called Moldovan. Now, on December 5, 2013, the Constitutional Court of Moldova pronounced its decision on the language question. It is Romanian!

World Order, Henry Kissinger. Penguin Press, New York, 2014. March 3, 2015

A recent book by Henry Kissinger *World Order*, suggests that America should grant Russia its own sphere of influence. Yet, history shows that whenever Russia was given a hand, it grabbed everything. Can the U.S. trust Russia? We start this book review with a view of the world and then focus on Russia and East Europe.

Henry Kissinger, the well-known and highly acclaimed American diplomat has published a new book entitled *World Order*, a much needed volume at the beginning of this troubled century. Born Heinz Alfred Kissinger in 1923 in Fürth, Germany located in the Bavarian region of Europe, Kissinger encountered growing anti-Semitism during that turbulent period causing his family to seek refuge in New York when he was 15 years old. Thus, in 1943 as a naturalized U.S. citizen, Henry Kissinger, remarkably in only five years, served in the U.S. armed forces both in France and Germany during the Second World War. Later educated at Harvard University, Kissinger went on from academia to statesmanship and became an influential American policymaker. Consequently, his book was awaited with anticipation by both his admirers and his critics. Not unexpectedly, *World Order* is well-written, informative and provocative. While the author is an accomplished historian and a knowledgeable man who helped shape some of the most important and tragic foreign policy of the latter part of the 20th century, his world vision can be described as soundly "establishment" and his legacy as questionable.

As National Security Adviser and Secretary of State, Kissinger was instrumental in America's controversial opening to China, in the negotiations to end the Vietnam War, and in the peace process between Egypt and Israel. In his vision, all of those dealings brought about a more secure world. But, did they?

As a former refugee from Eastern Europe and as a geographer, I read with interest Kissinger's theories and his views of the events that he personally witnessed and shaped. I also followed his endeavors to promote a safer world order along with his philosophical conclusions. What can we learn from this book and how does it prepare us for a better future? The quick answer is that we learn a lot from reading it, and, yet, we remain unprepared for the future. Actually, at the end of the book the author writes that when he was young he wanted to find "The Meaning of History." Now, he concedes, the meaning of history is yet to be found.

The book offers a good review of history, geopolitics and international relations starting with antiquity and ending with the ongoing events of these very days. In his search, he focuses on the idea of 'world order.' In this regard, Kissinger is solidly embedded in the European post-Westphalia order established in 1648 following the 30 Years War. The Westphalia agreements set up the modern state as a cornerstone for order and the concept of the balance of power for maintaining international peace. The system was a compromise between 'power' and 'legitimacy' and between the small and large European countries of the time. In Kissinger's opinion, the Westphalia system endured, acquired global acceptance, and although challenged by a perpetually changing world, it remains the best model for securing international peace. He mentions that "no truly world order has ever existed" and that the old Westphalia system is now challenged from many sides.

As an adviser to several American presidents, as well as a diplomat and negotiator, Kissinger is admired and criticized at the same time. One can admire him for his knowledge, for his analyses, and for the attempt to put his ideas into practice. Yet, he is criticized for having been cynical in a world of increasing humanitarianism and idealism and for negotiating treaties that in the end were detrimental to America and the West. Indeed, if his ideas were so thoughtful and beautiful, why was applying them so ugly? Kissinger received a Nobel Peace Prize for his contributions to bringing peace to Vietnam and South-East Asia. Yet, instead of bringing freedom, millions of people were arrested, massacred and enslaved following the 'peace' that he helped to negotiate.

Kissinger was also instrumental in opening America to China claiming that a mutual engagement would bring about international cooperation and more security. Recounted elsewhere, it was this very rapprochement with Beijing that caused a permanent rupture in Kissinger's valued relationship with his mentor since 1943, of whom he says, *"Fritz Kraemer was the greatest single influence of my formative years. His inspiration remained with me even during the last thirty years when he would not speak to me."*

Kissinger was convinced that such an approach would lead to a split between Beijing and Moscow. And what really happened? The two powers are colluding against America. Where is the international peace and cooperation that he envisioned? And with regard to the Middle East, where he was deeply involved in peace negotiations, it seems that we are now further away from peace than ever before.

In *World Order*, Kissinger avoids criticizing any American President apparently to keep open his 'advisory capabilities' and to preserve his link with the White House for future benefits. He even praised President Obama for his foreign policy choices and for maintaining good relations with Russia's Vladimir Putin. Actually, Kissinger boasts that he enjoys a friendly relationship with Putin and advocates a dialogue rather than a confrontation with him. In this vein, he took a soft approach with regard to Moscow's claims on Ukraine, recognizing, somehow, Russia's right to a sphere of influence. Is this appeasement toward Russia or promoting his own undisclosed interests?

In spite of this criticism, the book is a good source of knowledge. The reader finds out that some ancient Asian countries were equally or even more advanced in their international dealings than the European states of the time. The political and moral principles advocated by Cardinal Richelieu or Machiavelli in medieval Europe, for example, had been espoused two thousand years earlier in India. Some medieval societies produced their own wise statesmen, but are their recommendations universally applicable? How can one reconcile power and legitimacy or democracy, dictatorship and terrorism? Kissinger offers many case studies and gives priorities to some of them, but he offers few solutions. Perhaps that is the distinguishing difference between the statesman and the strategist.

With regard to the U.S., the author embraces the idea of American 'exceptionalism' based on democracy and government by consent, but he admits that there is an innate ambivalence and contradiction in U.S. foreign policy. He tries to justify America's current world preeminence, but is this preeminence going to last? In fact, any growing superpower appears driven by a sort of a natural law to achieve global domination. Historically all great powers that have tried to expand as far as possible, have failed in the end. Is the world any different today? It is in a way. Today, the world has the capacity to destroy itself. Reminiscent of his 1957 book *Nuclear Weapons and Foreign Policy*, Kissinger is worried and cautious about nuclear weapons and their proliferation. For examle, he vehemently opposes Iran's efforts to achieve nuclear capability.

As for the contemporary world, the author mentions the transformation of the former Soviet Union, but does not explain why the Soviet system collapsed. *World Order* also focuses on the coming of age of Asia and the changes Russia and China are bringing to the new world order. The global geopolitical order went from bi-polar at the end of the Second World War to uni-polar at the end of the Cold War with the U.S. as the sole superpower. The world is now slowly moving toward multi-polarity and uncertainty. How the world is going to change in the future is a theoretical question without a practical answer. Although, one thing is clear: America ought to remain strong and engaged internationally and must try to keep the world in balance. But it is not going to be easy. In this context, Kissinger offers a statement by President Reagan's

Secretary of State George Shultz who said: *"Americans, being a moral people, want their foreign policy to reflect the values we espouse as a nation. But Americans, being a practical people, also want their foreign policy to be effective."* Can these opposing values be reconciled? They were successfully combined under a strong leader. At the height of the Cold War Ronald Reagan had a vision and he was capable of transforming his vision into reality!

The reader can see the knowledgeable historian and the astute statesman in this book, but what is Kissinger's philosophy at the end of a long career? He admits that we live in a contradictory world of cooperation and confrontation and we need wise leaders to navigate the dangers surrounding us. In a digital world of instant information and with a population increasingly demanding participatory democracy, the task is not easy. Other than that, is there a sense and purpose in history? In Henry Kissinger's *World Order*, the author does not tell us. Perhaps we must look elsewhere for the answer.

It is in his eulogy to his mentor and Pentagon strategist, Dr. Fritz Kraemer, at the Fort Meyer Chapel on October 8, 2003 that Kissinger reveals the divergence between the policymaker and the ancient prophet. *"The prophet thinks in terms of crusades; the policymaker hedges against the possibility of human fallibility. The policymaker, if he wants to avoid stagnation, needs the prophet's inspiration, but he cannot live by all the prophet's prescriptions in the short term; he must leave something to history."*

At the end of the day, the erudite cannot substitute for the strategic approach in American foreign policy. And so, as Kissinger approaches his 92nd year, he pursues "policymaking" via his 'advisory capabilities' through his firm Kissinger Associates, Inc. This includes the promotion of globalization, which is the process of international integration through trade, investments, and the outsourcing of manufacturing and information technology. Yet, globalization largely favors the wealthy, the powerful and the influential, otherwise known as the "establishment" and brings about even more socio-economic inequities which in turn may trigger political upheavals. Are we advancing toward freedom and free market cooperation or toward societal confrontation?   We shall see! Nevertheless, with regard to Russia, all we can see now is a resurgence of Moscow's old ambitions.

Ukraine: A New Battleground between Russia and the West. March 3, 2014

Ukraine represents the real core of Eastern Europe and it is currently a bone of contention between Moscow and the West. With an area almost as big as France, a population of 46 million people, with good agricultural land and huge industrial complexes, Ukraine is a country of utmost importance. Yet, recent bloody events in Kyiv's Maidan, or the central square better known to the West as Independence Square, have shown that Ukraine is badly split and is prone to remain a problem. The solution to the current Ukrainian crisis rests with its own people, with Russia, and with the West, America included. And none of these potential solutions is easy to address.

History and geography have not been kind to Ukraine, and recent politics and geopolitics have worsened the fate of the country. To begin with, the land that is today Ukraine has been historically inhabited, conquered, divided and partitioned by a variety of peoples and invading states that have prevented and delayed the formation of a modern Ukrainian nation. In the more distant past, a good part of the land was controlled by Poland, by the Tatars and by the Turks. The rise of Muscovy gave Russia control of the eastern part of the country, while a good part of the western part fell under Austrian control.

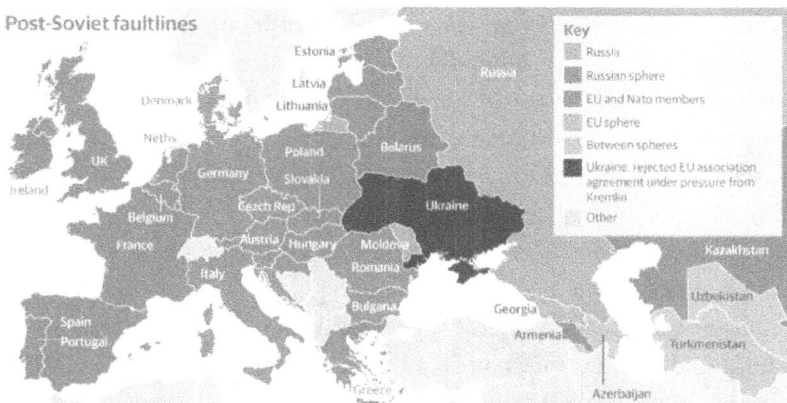

Source: The University of Texas Library

More than three hundred years ago Ukraine decided to unite with Russia and that sealed its destiny. Throughout their domination, the Russians looked down at the Ukrainians and repressed their aspirations. An opportunity presented itself after the Bolshevik Revolution when Ukraine enjoyed a brief period of independence. That was followed by the Soviet annexation and by a new wave of repressions. In the 1930s, for example, the peasantry opposed the process of collectivization, which led to Stalin's massive repression, mass starvation and even acts of cannibalism. So cruel was the period that when the Second World War started many Ukrainians sided with the German invaders. That led to more Soviet persecution after the end of the war. Many of those memories are still fresh in the minds of the people who after the dismemberment of the Soviet Union opted for independence. However, the 1991 independence did not lead to a break with Moscow or to real democracy and a better life. As a result, recent events represent a new attempt to break away from Moscow and to join Europe and its values. Nevertheless, there are many obstacles.

Ukraine is to a good degree an artificial country forged together by the Soviet Union at the end of the Second World War. It consists of lands that used to belong to neighboring countries, as well as lands inhabited by non-Ukrainian minorities. The strategically important Crimean Peninsula, for example, was gifted to the Soviet Socialist Republic of Ukraine in 1954 by the former Soviet leader Nikita Khrushchev. Ethnically, however, Crimea is dominated by Russians and by Tatars. While the Tatar minority was surprised by the turn of recent events and may have divided loyalties, the Russians are strongly pro-Moscow. Another region of dispute is eastern Ukraine. This region was developed economically under the Soviet regime and maintains some of Russia's biggest military and heavy industry complexes. Moscow is not going to lose control of this strategic area any time soon, where many local inhabitants are also Russian. For the time being, however, Crimea is the hottest problem. The local Russians are waiting for any sign of encouragement from Moscow to break away from Kyiv. And Moscow under Vladimir Putin is probably the biggest obstacle in Ukraine's struggle for sovereignty and independence. In fact, Russia considers the recent uprising in Kyiv to be instigated by outsiders and warned the West not to interfere. For Moscow, the country is within their exclusive sphere of interest. That brings us to Russia and the crux of the problem.

Under the Soviet regime, Moscow nurtured global aspirations and managed to gather an empire that reached to the very center of Europe. The dissolution of the Soviet Union took the Kremlin by surprise. Russia is somehow the last colonial empire of Europe and it cannot reconcile with the loss of its former territories. And nowhere is this state of mind more obvious than in Ukraine. To a certain point, Russia is right. The two peoples are closely related ethnically, culturally and linguistically and have developed together for about three hundred years. Psychologically, it is almost impossible for average Russians to accept the idea of a totally separate Ukraine. And it is also extremely difficult to separate physically the two ethnic groups in the eastern and southern areas of Ukraine. Furthermore, Moscow is still enmeshed in a 19th Century geopolitical mentality, and Vladimir Putin's plan to recreate a Eurasian Customs Union embodies this mentality.

President Putin has already lamented openly the breakup of the USSR. He has also reintroduced the former Soviet anthem and is playing up the nationalistic aspirations of the Russian people. Apparently, the Kremlin continues to fear Europe and its democratic values and Ukraine is Moscow's buffer to the west. Without Ukraine, Russia would no longer be the important world power that it is today. Putin understands that clearly. And if Ukraine joins the European Union and NATO, Russia would forever lose its influence over its neighbors. Consequently, unless the Russian people and leaders change their mentality, and mentalities take decades if not longer to change, Russia will not freely allow Ukraine to get away. And Putin is the man that represents current Russian nationalism.

How could events in this situation unfold in the near future for Ukraine? There are several possible scenarios:

1) Return quietly to the status quo ante, find a way of living with Russia, and keep the country together. The possibility is limited because this is why people revolted against the Yanukovych regime in the first place. Furthermore, the country is polarized deeply between pro-

European Ukrainians in the west and a pro-Russian population in the east. The dire current economic situation of the country does not help either;

2) Continue the stalemate and risk civil war and a possible partition of the country;

3) Accept a partition, instigated by Moscow, with the eastern and southern regions splitting from Kyiv and uniting with Russia.

As the end of February arrived, Crimea, home to the Russian Black Sea fleet, was already considering a split from Ukraine. The new government in Kyiv had lost control of Crimea's main civilian airport as Russian troops arrived by the thousands and attack helicopters landed. The early days of March witnessed Russian troops surrounding a Ukrainian military base and *BBC News Europe* reported pro-Russian activists were "blocking sailors from coming to work" at Ukrainian naval headquarters. These events followed Putin's order for Russian military maneuvers on the Ukrainian frontier. Ukraine's acting president Oleksander Turchynov, Chairman of the Ukrainian Parliament, described Russia's deployment of troops in Crimea as an invasion.

Before closing this essay some questions may be asked: What did the leaders of the United States and the former Soviet Union discuss and agree upon at the Malta Summit in 1989, when President George H.W. Bush and Communist Party Chairman Mikhail Gorbachev deliberated? While the Cold War was declared at an end, was Ukraine granted to Moscow's sphere of influence? And what is America planning to do now, if events get out of hand?

Ukraine: American Illusions and Russian Delusions. May 7, 2014

There are several contradictions, incompatibilities, and potential clashes worldwide at the beginning of this 21st Century. There is the contradiction between nationalism and internationalism; the clash between economic expansionism and national sovereignty; and, the deepening gap between the rich and poor countries. One such incompatibility with a potential confrontation is between the American *illusions* and the Russian *delusions* that confront the two powers in Eastern Europe.

In March and April of this year, I spent six weeks in Eastern Europe, mostly teaching in Romania. My visit occurred during the radical events that shook Ukraine followed by the Russian annexation of Crimea. The Russian aggression jolted Romania and adjacent Moldova having chilling effects on other European countries bordering Russia, especially the three Baltic countries. Obviously, Moscow continues to consider Eastern Europe as part of its exclusive sphere of influence. Armed with a "Eurasianist" agenda, if not a new doctrine, Vladimir Putin seems determined to reestablish the former Soviet Union, wherever ethnic Russian speakers reside in significant numbers. In this regard, it appears that Crimea is only the beginning, and the Russian people approve of the annexation unreservedly. Even the former Soviet leader, Mikhail Gorbachev, concurred and said that Putin should not stop at Crimea. However, the conflict in Ukraine is nothing but a proxy fight between Russia and the West, although some fear it could lead to the Third World War, unless Putin is deterred.

Russia has been unable to match the development of the West. Fearing American economic power and influence, Moscow is responding with westward territorial expansion further into Europe long ignoring Ukraine's political independence and territorial integrity. Ironically, the Russian Federation constitutes the largest national landmass on earth. If the breakup of the Soviet Union had left Russia solely upon the European Plain with the Ural Mountains as its eastern border then Putin's insecurity might be more understandable. But that is clearly not the case.

There is, in fact, a clash of interests. The West led by the United States is looking for economic globalization, while downplaying the importance of the traditional nation-state. Russia, however, is still set in the framework of 19th Century geopolitics. That means sheer territorial annexations when possible, spheres of influence at the periphery, and buffer zones to separate Russia from other powers. This time, the battleground is Ukraine. With Crimea already annexed, Moscow is eying the Donetsk and Odessa regions. Odessa, however, could also incorporate Transnistria and may reach the Danube, thus bordering Romania. This is where Romania is worried and apprehensive, as I found out for myself on multiple occasions. For now, it may be just a matter of perception, but Romania knows all too well Eastern hypocrisy and brutality.

To further intimidate Kyiv, Vladimir Zhirinovsky, the deputy speaker of Russia's Lower House and head of the Liberal-Democratic Party of Russia, reminded Ukraine that it has inherited lands belonging to its neighbors, including Romanian lands. And he alluded to the possible further dismemberment of Ukraine. While annexing Crimea, President Putin assured Kyiv that Moscow would react severely if Romania dares to make a territorial claim. It was not the first Russian threat against Romania. Previously, Putin had warned Romania that it would suffer grave consequences, if it accepted the new American missile shield on its territory.

The Russian annexation of Crimea and the fear of further territorial expansion are alarming for all those countries that have known repeatedly Russian aggression. Moldova and the Baltic states fear military interventions similar to those preceding the Second World War. Transnistria, a small region of Moldova located mostly on the left bank of Dnestr River, has already been under Russian control since the dismemberment of the USSR. Like Ukraine, Moldova is not a member of NATO and thus it feels vulnerable. In addition, Latvia and Estonia have large Russian ethnic minorities and fear Russian intervention under the pretext of defending those minorities.

As for Romania, all officials strongly support the American position with regard to Ukraine, stand by NATO, and denounce the Russian aggression. On an intellectual level, the analysts stress the past Romanian experience and insist that Moscow cannot be trusted. But they are apprehensive, especially after President Obama renounced the installations of the American missile shield in Poland and the Czech Republic and after 'resetting' Washington's relations with Moscow. Some analysts even question the reliability of Western Europe and the North Atlantic Alliance. As a rule they trust NATO, but ask themselves how soon would Romania be defended in case of a surprise Russian attack? And professors of history and geopolitics remind people that Romania received territorial guaranties from France and Great Britain before the Second World War only to be brutally trampled by Moscow and Berlin.

Ukraine's territorial guaranties under the 1994 Budapest Memorandum on Security Assurances have been violated by one of the three guarantors consisting of the United States, the United Kingdom and the Russian Federation. In return for its political independence and territorial integrity, Ukraine gave up its nuclear weapons arsenal.

In Romania, the attitude of the average citizen is more nuanced. Instinctively, and for good reason, ordinary people do not trust Russia and its intentions, but they have also lost their trust in the West. They embraced the European Union with open arms only to see their former industrial enterprises ruined, their employment gone, and many of their dreams dashed. There is freedom and more democracy in Romania, but the communists of yesterday are the new rich and crooked political class of today. Corruption is widespread and immorality is king. All this with the acquiescence and even the participation of the West.

These days Romania seems to be an experiment on how to subdue and control a country. Nationalism and economic isolation are no longer real options for the small countries like Romania. Communism is gone, but some ordinary people are already nostalgic for the old system. Only a small layer of the population has benefited from the post-communist changes. Economic globalization is not helping the small and underdeveloped countries like Romania. The West and the United States must do more to win over the hearts and minds of average people. This is true for most Eastern European countries. Russia, however, is a different ballgame. It sticks to its nationalism and it has the resources and apparently the will power to oppose Western domination of the world.

Ukraine, is now the battleground between Russia and the West. If it chooses to join the European Union, Ukraine will have to radically reform its economy. Consequently, numerous factories in the highly industrialized East that are currently uncompetitive will have to close. I have seen scores of such ruined factories in Romania and they look as if they were ravaged by war. Millions of Ukrainians will become unemployed and for a while they will have a hard time adjusting to a new order. That will be dangerous in a country already split between pro-Russian and pro-Western tendencies. Although some may disdain the 'old' regime of Viktor Yanukovych and its strong ties to Russia, in the end they may experience a change of heart, and opt for Moscow.

Chapter 6
The United States, Romania and Russia

In Europe's Shadow: Two Cold Wars and a Thirty Year Journey Through Romania and Beyond, **Robert D. Kaplan, Random House, New York 2016.** August 9, 2016

Romania is a key country in south-east Europe and it is the place where East meet West. In the past, Romania traditionally looked to France and Western Europe for models of evolution and development. Currently, the country looks to the EU and America for models of future evolution. The recently published book *In Europe's Shadow* helps the reader better understand post cold-war Romania and the new Romanian-American relations.

Robert Kaplan is a journalist and a writer who possess a good understanding of the world and has a special interest in Eastern Europe. His new book, *In Europe's Shadow*, focuses on Romania, but reflects his wide knowledge of the entire area of East-Central Europe. The book addresses a host of regional issues and is many-faceted. It takes up historical questions, old and new challenges, socio-political and philosophical issues, as well as contemporary worries, politics and geopolitics. Equally important is that Kaplan thinks journalists should be completely detached and objective and should approach their missions 'impersonally.' Can anyone be one hundred percent objective?

For Kaplan, Romania is key to understanding Southeastern Europe and is of real geopolitical importance in the present confrontation between East and West. He sees Romania (together with Poland) as the pivot of America's policy against the new Russian aggressiveness. The author reveals a nuanced sense of history and a good grasp of current events.

Robert Kaplan is fascinated by the uniqueness, culturally, historically and ethnically, of Romania. Coming from Hungary, he writes, Romania is an Eastern country, but coming from Moldova and Ukraine, it is a Western country.

In fact, Romania is both and thus is even more interesting. He admires Romania's Byzantine inheritance and is puzzled by its unique diversity. He also wonders at the survival of the Roman and Latin roots of the people. Romania, he writes, *"constitutes one of those indigestible ethnic nations…that have miraculously survived the millennia despite being oppressed, overrun, and vanquished."*

Obviously, he has studied the country and visited it several times both under the old regimes and since the fall of communism. He also visited other countries of the area and was able to make pertinent comparisons. For Romania, he notices, geography was a nightmare and history was a tragedy. He puts Poland in the same category and recommends that the two countries be strengthened as outposts of NATO in the new East-West balance of power.

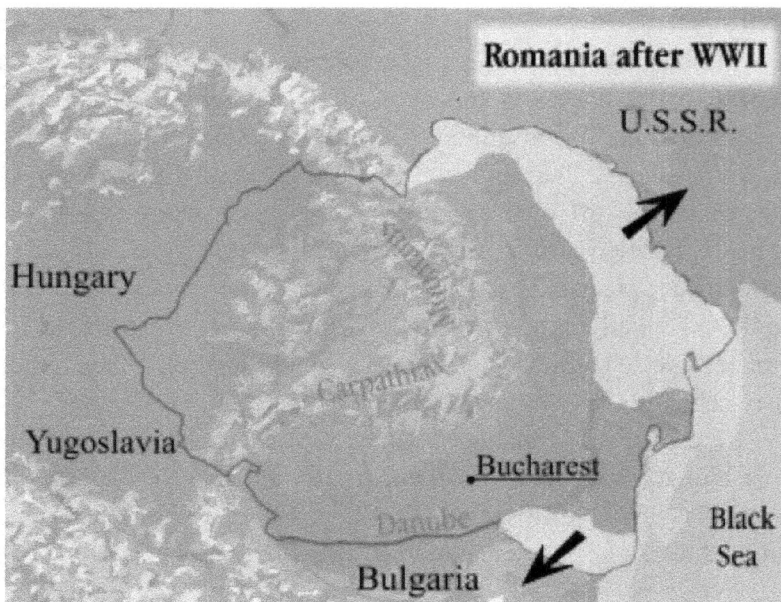

Romania is the sole Eastern European country that in its recent past was subjected to three invading powers: The Ottomans, the Germans, and the Russians. Currently, Romania is again threatened by Russia. In this vein, he cites several Romanian leaders who are worried about Moscow's new aims and provocations. Among others, he consulted George Cristian Maior, former director of Romanian domestic intelligence and currently ambassador to Washington. Maior stressed that presently Moscow is buying influence with Eastern European media and politicians and is trying to subvert again the region. Russian influence is already strong and growing in Serbia, Bulgaria, Hungary, and even beyond. Furthermore, Romania's former province of Bessarabia (Moldova) is still under Moscow's thumb, while its split region of Transdniestria (Transnistria) is directly under Russian control. These days, Moldova and Ukraine represent the primary battle ground between NATO and Russia, Kaplan writes. And he adds that Russia is not giving up the two countries and there is little the West can do.

In the opinion of this reviewer, the murky state of affairs of this area started with the new partition of Europe decided by the U.S. and USSR at Malta in 1989 under the administration of then-President George H.W. Bush. For reasons not shared with the public, Moldova and Ukraine were left in a limbo as a neutral zone between Russia and Europe. Nonetheless, this region could trigger a grave international conflict. Moscow's ongoing war of attrition in Ukraine proves the point, particularly after Putin's annexation of Crimea.

Robert Kaplan cited a rich bibliography and consulted a good number of Romanian leaders, writers and analysts. Many of them are well-known to this reviewer who was a journalist with Voice of America.

However, Kaplan relies too heavily on the opinions of those who, after the fall of communism, veered toward the new internationalist trend. Yet, except for some subjective tilts, the book is a valuable source of information and offers a welcome contribution for the understanding of what is going on in the region. A good number of Romanians, for example, regret the end of the old communist regime that gave them a sense of social security. However, they only have to read the pages written by the author about the gloomy situation in Romania of 1981 to reconsider their misplaced nostalgia for the communist past.

As a native Romanian myself and a former political refugee, I visited Romania in 1990, less than one year after the fall of Ceausescu. At the time, the country was a disaster and many people seemed almost de-humanized. I was thinking then that thousands of years ago when our ancestors left the caves they probably smiled with happiness when they saw the beauty of the sun. In 1990, the Romanians looked as if they had just gotten out of a cave, but were not sure if they were free to enjoy the sun.

The Romanians did survive the 'communist ice age,' as Kaplan writes, but I realized then that surviving is not a virtue. One must be a winner! Twenty five years after regaining their liberty, the Romanians are still suffering and are still far from being real winners. Kaplan admits that not everything is well in the new Eastern Europe, but he does not analyze deeply the danger for the future of the current dissatisfaction.

In Romania, for example, the old industry was completely destroyed, the agriculture was ruined, and over three million young men and women left the country to work in the West. The situation is similar throughout Eastern Europe. To be sure, there is freedom now, but there are also many split families and abandoned children. And there is unemployment, prostitution, pornography, moral decay, and other social ills, many of them imported from the West. The result is that countries like Romania have been deprived again of their national dignity. Is this the future?

The author may exhort the process of globalization, but all is not well in the new Europe. And Vladimir Putin is already exploiting this dissatisfaction to Russia's advantage, while Obama's America is ambivalent to say the least.

As for some aspects of the book that could be considered one-sided, the author dedicates a disproportionate amount of space to the evolution of the Jews in the area. As a Jew himself, and as an American and Israeli citizen, his attitude is understandable. However, his sources and numbers are incomplete and some are biased. He admits, for instance, that during the Second World War the Romanian Jews were saved by not being sent to Nazi concentration camps, while the country was led by General Ion Antonescu.

In this regard he writes, and I quote: "Antonescu kept, by some statistical reckonings, the largest number of Jews away from the Final Solution in Axis-dominated Europe." Nevertheless, Kaplan demonizes Antonescu and calls him consistently a murderer of the Jews. He refers primarily to Bessarabia, Transdniestria and Odessa. Some prominent Jews do not agree with this assertion, and the author only marginally mentions some of them.

When, as a young man, I became a political prisoner in communist Romania, I met many former officers and soldiers who had fought on the Eastern Front alongside the Germans. I learnt that the Romanian troops did kill a number of Jews, but the real pogroms were triggered by the German Army.

Robert Kaplan should have also read the writings of Paul Goma, a Romanian refugee from Bessarabia married to a Jewish woman, who now lives in Paris. He would have learnt the Romanian side of the story and would have acquired a more balanced view. He would have also discovered what the Bessarabian Jews did to the Romanians, when the Soviet Army invaded this province in 1940, following the Ribbentrop-Molotov pact.

Many of those who Kaplan cites as sources of information cooperated with the communist regime in the past and have switched sides mostly to benefit from the new global trends. Actually, to a very large extent, the new political class of current day Romania is compromised and corrupt and is stridently pro-Western, chiefly to cover their murky past and to gain international legitimacy. Most likely, such people stretched their answers to satisfy Mr. Kaplan.

And a closing point; the author condemns, unequivocally, ethnic patriotism and nationalism and even any form of order and discipline that could lead to extremist attitudes and eventually to anti-Semitism. But, he should have also researched the roots of extremism to make sure that this scourge would not haunt us again in the future. Instead, he advocates internationalism and globalization, precisely what the Britons have recently rejected in their Brexit referendum.

Perhaps this UK vote to leave the European Union will provide the necessary escape valve from their problems of immigration and centralized control by helping to release the societal pressures that have gradually grown as a result of the Schengen agreement's open border policy and Brussels' over regulation. While Romania is a signatory to Schengen, it has yet to implement its provisions.

However, Kaplan admits the potential attraction of extremist movements even in this age *"in a world where the masses, unable to sufficiently benefit from globalization, reject globalization outright."* Yes, extremism is a danger in Europe and Moscow is already exploiting it!

Does globalization bring the promised fruits to the average citizen? Or does it bring advantages mostly to a small established elite group? And then, how are we to reconcile Western internationalism with Eastern nationalism, in an era of increasing inequity and polarization?

It should be remembered that the West won the Cold War with the unreserved help of eastern patriots and nationalists. Yet, in the new Eastern Europe, those patriots were denied from sharing the fruits of their own sacrifices. Unless America and the West change their globalist policies, it is possible that in another confrontation between East and West the God-fearing patriots and the nationalists may not let themselves be used, abused, and abandoned again.

The United States and Romania: Security and Mutual Interests. June 14, 2013

Stratfor is a professional electronic publication that deals with geopolitical issues and global intelligence. Its founder and chairman, George Friedman, is well-informed and aware of contemporary Eastern European affairs. On May 29, 2013, he published an article entitled, "The Search for Belonging and Ballistic Missile Defense in Romania," about Bucharest's search for a solid post-communist anchor. From the start, Mr. Friedman states that *"during the Cold War Romania confused all of us"*... the country was *"hostile and uncooperative with the Soviets"*... yet Ceausescu ruled with *"ruthless irrationality."* Now *"Romania longs to be better integrated into the international system,"* especially into the European Union and NATO. *"No matter how flawed*

Europe is today," writes Mr. Friedman, the Romanians want to belong to the West and they pin their hope on America.

In many ways Romania is no different than the other East European countries, the author writes, remembering his own parents in Hungary listening to Voice of America (VOA) in 1944 and hoping to be saved from both the Germans and the Soviets. Throughout the Cold War *"Eastern Europeans listened to VOA and imagined liberation from the Soviets. When that liberation finally came in 1989, it was unclear whether and to what degree the Americans had precipitated the Soviet collapse."* Mr. Friedman underscores that *"the concept of liberation is fixed, and despite all of their concern for the European Union, the United States remains the redeemer..."* Eastern Europe, he adds, *"is perhaps the last place in the world where the United States is still seen as noble and invincible,"* stressing, however, that *"power is complex and distorts even the best of wills...,"* and America is no different.

In Mr. Friedman's opinion, Romania is now somehow different and it encounters more difficulties in its Western orientation than other countries in the region. He suggests that the Romanian leaders should adopt a more realistic attitude and rely more on the country's own possibilities to achieve stability and security rather than on seeking them from outside. In this regard, he claims that NATO is weak and the EU is flawed, thus, overreliance on them is risky. He also has doubts about basing in Romania the American anti-missile shield. Instead, he recommends better economic relations with American business companies. Indeed, Romania is looking for a quick political fix for its current problems, but Mr. Friedman's suggestions are easier said than done. Socio-political development requires decades of disciplined and wise policies most of the time involving private businesses. Political agreements are quick arrangements, but they do not have the depth of solid multilateral relations. With an economy in disarray, in a state of social internal confusion, and unable to find its own way through the EU maze, the Romanian leaders opted for strong political relations with the United States.

As a Romanian-American who grew up listening to VOA, and then as a Voice of America editor, I feel compelled to offer a few additional clarifications. First, to paraphrase and juxtapose the former British Prime Minister Disraeli, no country has permanent friends, but only permanent interests – and America is no different. For fifty years, the Eastern European countries were abandoned to Moscow and to communism. In this regard, nobody ever revealed the real provisions of the Yalta agreements, nor why communism collapsed without firing a shot 50 years later. In fact, no one fully explained to the public either what was decided at the Malta meetings in 1989... Now, the Eastern Europeans are expected to be grateful for being "liberated," but few Western leaders want to remember the communist atrocities and their consequences.

Alongside Poland and Ukraine, Romania was one of the most abused countries of Eastern Europe. Moscow's troops invaded Romania no less than 12 times in recent history and the province of Bessarabia, most of it part of the newly created republic of Moldova, is still under Russian control. No wonder Romania does not trust the Kremlin and wants to belong to Europe. After such foreign abuses, Bucharest has very few options. The only choice is anchoring itself to the West and America represents Romania's best hope.

There are problems, however, and Mr. Friedman is right in saying that Romania is somehow different. There were no communists to speak of in Romania before the Soviet occupation. According to official communist statistics there were less than 1,000 party members in 1944 and overwhelmingly those communists were non-Romanian ethnics. They sympathized with the USSR and turned with vengeance against the Romanian nation. For about ten years after the Soviet occupation, ethnic Romanians shunned the communist party and the secret police hoping for an American liberation. Only after the failed Hungarian revolution of 1956 and after witnessing the indifference of the West, did the ethnic Romanians begin to join the communist authorities. And most of those who did so did it for personal gains. However, the result of those early communist years was disastrous for the country. The formal cultural, economic and political elite were devastated and replaced by a class of opportunists. After the collapse of communism, this class took over the political leadership of the country masquerading as social-democrats.

And America and the West embraced them as true democrats. Then, with the blessing of various Western institutions and under their condoning eyes, this new political class pilfered and thus ruined the economy of the country by enriching themselves.

What moral model did America and the West offer for the remaking of Romania during the post-communist years? Where were the Nuremberg-like tribunals to expose and judge those guilty of murdering countless innocent people? And there is growing skepticism among Romanians about Washington's attitude toward the former Romanian province of Bessarabia, now under Russian influence and control.

The social reality is sad in today's Romania. There is indeed freedom and democracy, but people have found out that democracy without a strong economic foundation is an empty shell. While the average monthly salary for those who still have jobs is about 300 dollars, members of the former secret police and party hierarchy enjoy monthly pensions of thousands of dollars. It is true that Ceausescu's regime was ruthless, but now many people say that at least they had jobs and security during those years.

I returned to Romania in 1990, after 22 years of exile, and thereafter have continued to visit periodically. Most of the time I was visiting as a VOA reporter and I had the opportunity to meet the new leaders as well as former political prisoners and many average citizens. Yes, Romanians had unrealistic expectations of the West, but for the most part they were let down again. While the West encouraged the process of democratization, it condoned the new political class and it turned a blind eye to their behavior and abuses. These new leaders would sell the country to anyone in order to remain in power and protect their ill-gotten gains. As for the people, they are increasingly becoming cynical. A few years ago, when I attended a meeting of a democratic party, a young man asked me if I still believed in the flag that I was wearing on the lapel of my coat; it was the American flag.

Romania is integrated now in the EU and NATO, but for security reasons and for their own interests the new leaders also want to link the country militarily to the United States. The decision of the Obama administration to cancel the plan to install a U.S. anti-missile shield in

Poland and the Czech Republic was a blow to East Europe. It was then that Bucharest rushed in to accept the same anti-missile shield on Romanian territory. That decision enraged Moscow which reacted bitterly, especially in Moldova. Moscow's reaction made some Romanians question what Bucharest gained from Washington for accepting the anti-missile shield on its territory?

Mr. Friedman concludes that *"the United States spent the last half of the Cold War baffled by Romania, and Romania has spent the time since the fall of communism baffled by the United States."* And, he suggests that the United States and Romania focus on "cold calculations of national interests." And here is the difficulty. In this time of need, Romania requires assistance and is pinning its hopes on America. It needs primarily economic help domestically and international support to address the old question of Bessarabia. However, America does not seem to understand, or refuses to understand, these real problems. The American policy toward Romania is seen through Washington's security interests. The Romanian leaders lump together their personal interests with the needs of the country and that makes a dialogue between Washington and Bucharest difficult. In the end, the Romanian leaders risk to alienate themselves from the people and America risks losing one of its last friends in Eastern Europe.

Russia's Opposition to U.S. Missile Defense in Romania. June 2, 2016

On Thursday May 12 the United States and Romania inaugurated the first American Missile Shield in Eastern Europe at a military base located in the village of *Deveselu* in southwest Romania. The project, under construction for a number of years, has elicited Russia's angry protestations to a missile system on its doorstep. America did not budge but went ahead with the base as planned, and also started to build a similar one in Poland. With Poland to the north, Romania at the Black Sea, and Georgia in the Caucasus region, they form NATO's front line of defense in the region.

The event received widespread press coverage in Romania, internationally and in Russia, but Moscow's point of view was different, as expected. *AP*, for example, mentioned that the U.S.-NATO defense system aims at "protecting Europe from ballistic missile threats," whereas Moscow sees it as a new attempt at surrounding Russia militarily. In this context, Moscow stressed in the past that if Romania went ahead with the plan as intended, it would expose itself to deadly consequences. And further, if NATO proceeded with building a similar missile shield in Poland, Russia would deploy its own *Iskander* missiles in Kaliningrad, the heavily militarized Russian territory between Poland and Lithuania. The Russian missiles have a range of about 300 miles and would threaten a large part of Poland. However, Warsaw officials were not impressed. They believe that Russia already has such missiles in Kaliningrad remaining from previous exercises.

The *Washington Times* reported, "While the Kremlin doesn't view the NATO missile defense system as a threat to its nuclear forces in its current limited shape, it fears that the U.S.-led missile shield may eventually erode the deterrent potential of Russian nuclear forces when it grows more powerful in the future."

According to *Romania Libera*, Prime Minister Dacian Ciolos, Defense Minister Mihnea Motoc, and other officials participated in the inaugural ceremonies in *Deveselu*. Other participants were the former prime minister of Norway and current NATO General Secretary Jens Stoltenberg along with U.S. Deputy Secretary of Defense Robert Work. The Romanian prime minister declared that *Deveselu* will be fully integrated in the overall NATO defense system before the July 8-9 NATO summit in Warsaw. The base was a former Romanian military installation. Transforming it into a modern facility cost the United States 800 million dollars. As for the missile base in Poland, Stoltenberg announced that the very next day (May 13) he would travel to *Redzikowo*, close to the Baltic Sea, to open the works on the Polish base.

According to *AP*, Stoltenberg stated at the opening ceremony that Deveselu is not directed against Russia adding that the interceptors are too few and too far from Russia to be able to intercept intercontinental missiles. Nevertheless, the retired Russian admiral Vladimir Komoyedov, chairman of the State *Duma's* Defense Committee, declared for *Interfax* that the new American installations in Romania and Poland are a direct threat to Russia. "They are 1,000 percent aimed against us," he declared. And according to *AFP* of May 13, President Putin warned that Russia would consider any measures in order to "end threats from American anti-missile systems that were recently activated in Romania." Neither Poland, nor Romania budged. And both countries have strong reasons to fear Russia. The recent war in Ukraine was a wake-up call.

With a tragic sense of history at the hands of the Russians, Romania welcomes any opportunity to strengthen its national security. However, there are also dissenting voices and some of these voices sound very logical. Thus, it is hard to say whether such voices speak from the heart or they echo Moscow's agenda.

Active News of May 9 reported that reserve Colonel Marin Neacsu claimed that the Romanian military would be used as *cannon fodder* for U.S. interests adding that Romania has become an annex of America to be used whenever and however needed. The colonel also accused Washington of using Romania's aspiration of reuniting with Moldova just to challenge Russia without helping the Romanian national cause. By doing this, he continued, Romania would expose Moldova to increasing Russian threats without obtaining anything in return. One of his letters addressed 'to the Romanian people' was widely circulated on the Internet.

Another analysis posted recently on the Internet startles readers even more. It is entitled, *Is there a plan to disband Romania? (Se Pregateste Pulverizarea Romaniei?)* The analysis focuses on the last 25 years of transition that have ruined the old economy without replacing it with a new one leading to a ravaged Romanian socio-demographic fabric. Unfortunately, almost all the arguments used in the analysis are real. Yet, the analysis may very well be concocted in Moscow to disorient Romanians. Moscow does it all over Eastern Europe. It is an ongoing method of PSYOPS, or psychological operations.

According to the analysis (*Stiri exerne.ro* and *http://gandeste.org*), Romania gained nothing by joining NATO and the EU, which are both considered tools of the current process of globalization. On the contrary, Romania's sovereignty is threatened. Morally, the West is compared to Sodom and Gomorrah, while the political leaders of Romania are considered corrupt puppets of the West. As a consequence, the analysis claims, Romania's traditional military, industrial, agricultural, banking system and many other institutions have been completely ravaged. In only 25 years, the analysis continues, from a position of having no international debts, Bucharest has amassed some $150 billion in international debts.

The analysis is not signed, but retired Colonel Vasile Zarnescu provides commentary. He considers the analysis as a correct mirror of the "last 25 years of criminal transition." In his conspiratorial view, some international circles have: purposely impoverished the people; compelled the youth to immigrate; and, encouraged a wave of third world migrants to replace the indigenous population. He concludes that the purpose is to promote globalization in order to control the world.

Moscow's disinformation campaign is a form of psychological warfare intended to influence Romanian public opinion and ultimately government policy. Such PSYOPS are targeted squarely at Romania's membership in NATO and the European Union, intertwining the factual with the fabricated, hoping to cause anxiety among the populace.

Moldova: Between Russia and the West. March 8, 2017

The Republic of Moldova is a small and poor country that has existed since the 1991 dismemberment of the Soviet Union. The country is of limited importance to the world, but it is a battleground between the expanding Russian ambitions and the apparently shrinking interests of America in Europe.

In spite of its pro-European manifestations, last November Moldova elected Igor Dodon, a strongly pro-Russian president. Moscow's choice in Moldova reflects Russia's traditional geopolitics and intelligence operations. While Putin rides on a wave of nationalism at home and encourages Western European nationalists, Russia promotes pliable leaders around its periphery. Moldova is the latest case. Shortly after his election, Mr. Dodon went to Moscow and was received by Vladimir Putin.

The visit should not have rung alarm bells, but in the new international situation it did. The two leaders discussed issues of bilateral interest and addressed Moldova's plan of joining the Moscow-led Eurasian Union. President Putin stated that Moldova is an important partner of Russia and stressed the 'historic' relations between old Russia and the medieval Principality of Moldova. The less informed reader should know that Moldova together with Wallachia and Transylvania, inhabited largely by Romanians, united to make modern Romania.

However, Russia occupied the eastern part of Moldova and later made it into a Soviet republic. Ever since, Moscow has used this province for its political purpose. President Putin did not miss this opportunity, either. He offered Dodon a framed map of historic Moldova including the larger part that is in Romania. It was a veiled territorial threat against Bucharest. Then, according to the TASS news agency, Mr. Dodon showed the map to the Russian journalists stressing that Moldova's relations with Russia are crucial.

There were immediate reactions against Dodon's statements and some of them were from elected Moldovan officials. According to *Moldova.org* of January 22, even before his departure for Moscow the Liberal members of the Moldovan Parliament initiated the procedure to suspend him. Then, several organizations and notably *Tinerii Moldovei*

(The Youth of Moldova) began to protest against the president and vowed to keep denouncing him. They affirmed, ironically, that Moldova is not 'Dodonia' and rejected Dodon's opinion that Moldovans are different than Romanians. The official Soviet position was for decades that Moldovans are a separate nationality. *Tinerii Moldovei* rejected any such distinction and adopted the slogan… I *speak Romanian I do not care for Dodon!*

Another issue that was discussed in Moscow was the future of pro-Western Chisinau that prevailed prior to Dodon's election. Over the last several years Moldova received substantial financial aid from the European Union, but during his visit to Moscow Dodon played down the importance of the association with the EU. Instead, he proposed trilateral negotiations between Moldova, EU and Russia. According to *Moldova.org*, Brussels rejected the idea and made it clear that the Association Agreement is only between EU and the Republic of Moldova.

Romania is recently overwhelmed by a series of anti-corruption protests, but its leaders are worried by Putin's attitude and actions in Eastern Europe. The chief of the PSD governing party Liviu Dragnea and Prime Minister Sorin Grindeanu rushed to America and on January 19 they met Donald Trump. During the meeting, they expressed their fear for the future of the Strategic Partnership of Romania and the United States. However, President Trump answered promptly: '*We will make it [the partnership] happen.*' For Romania, this reassurance is important in light of a possible rapprochement between the new Trump administration and the old Putin team.

In the larger European scene, the election of Donald Trump, just after the exit of Great Britain from the EU, has encouraged the nationalist movements and anti-EU trends. However, a rapprochement between the new Trump administration and Putin, as reported by the press, could be tricky for the West and dangerous for the East. Such a move would offer Moscow new opportunities to increase its influence over the European continent. Moldova may be of little importance to America, but Western Europe is a different story. And there are reasons to worry because Europe is approaching a series of significant national elections.

On March 15 there will be elections for the Dutch Parliament and the conservative Party of Freedom could win more seats than expected. In April and May there will be presidential elections in France and the National Front of Marine Le Pen is making big inroads. Later this year there will be elections in Italy and Germany, and in both countries nationalists are increasingly vocal. And in Germany, Chancellor Angela Merkel may lose the election because of her open pro-immigration policy.

Of all these countries, France is of particular interest because many citizens are tired of terrorist acts and may decide to vote for Marine Le Pen. And it is risky because Le Pen and Putin are friends and France may tilt the European political balance of power toward Russia.

While Moscow is supporting European nationalism, the United States continues to embrace the process of globalization, multiculturalism and internationalism. A war for the hearts and minds of Europe is already ongoing. The new Trump administration will have to act very wisely if Washington is to retain its position in Europe. Resetting relations with Putin will not do it.

Fixing a U.S. Diplomatic Gaffe. September 20, 2016

No international subject is more sensitive for Romania than the problem of Bessarabia, the eastern half of the old Principality of Moldova, and the fate of those circa four million Romanians living there. The province was first annexed by Tsarist Russia in 1812, reunited with Romania in 1918, invaded by Soviet troops following the Ribbentrop-Molotov pact in 1940, but retaken by Romania in 1941, only to be re-annexed by the USSR in 1944. Based upon its territory, Moscow organized the Soviet Republic of Moldova, which became independent after the dismemberment of the Soviet Union. The international conditions of the time, the Soviet-American agreements signed at Malta and the lack of vision of the post-1989 Romanian governments left the Republic of Moldova in limbo.

While Romania joined the European Union and NATO, becoming a loyal ally of the United States, Moldova remained under

Russian control. Nevertheless, every specialist knows that Moldovans are Romanians and their aspiration is reunification. From a Romanian point of view, reunification is natural and imminent, although its timing may require some patience. Yet, the recent statement of the U.S. Ambassador in Chisinau, the capital of Moldova, triggered dismay and indignation at almost every level in both Moldova and Romania.

On August 26th on the occasion of Moldova's 'independence,' America's Ambassador to Chisinau, James Pettit, gave a televised interview. He stated that Moldovans are a distinct nation with their own history and traits and have their independent country. He also said that Moldova must remain a sovereign state and therefore, it is not good for the people to think of joining Romania because "union is not a practical solution." By making this statement, Ambassador Pettit reiterated the old Soviet point of view. His pronouncements raised questions about America's policy and reliability upsetting some of the highest institutions of Moldova and Romania.

Speaking at Moldova's Academy of Sciences on August 31st the very President of Moldova, Nicolae Timofte, responded, *"I am of Romanian origin as were my parents, my grandparents and all those who live on this land. We are ethnic Romanians, although we call ourselves Moldovans. This truth should be accepted once and for all,"* he concluded. At the same time, The Writers' Union of Moldova issued a statement underlying its moral obligation to take a stand and denounce the U.S. ambassador *"for distorting the truth and for offending the 'holy of holies' of the Romanian national identity – the unity of language, history and culture."*

Similar reactions were reported virtually at every social level in Moldova and Romania and were published by the press and aired by mass media. A few titles from the press read: *Stop Abusing our National Ideals, Defend us God from our Friends, What 25 years of Independence? Why do Americans claim that Moldovans are not Romanians?*

Some of the articles asked clear and pertinent questions: Is it possible that America does not know the truth about Bessarabia? Is it possible that it does not know about the people of this province, mostly

Romanians, arrested, killed or deported to Siberia? Is it possible that the State Department does not know about the Ribbentrop-Molotov Pact? Ribbentrop was hanged after the Nurnberg trial, but apparently his infamous pact has remained. Does the U.S. ambassador to Chisinau want to perpetuate the consequences of this pact and alienate Romanians in the process? Is this the official position of the State Department?

The diplomatic uproar also upset the Senate of Romania, which sent Washington a letter of protest. The letter stresses that the Senate is the supreme representative body of the Romanian people and it mentions clearly, "The Romanian Senate rejects without equivocation the declarations of the U.S. ambassador to Chisinau regardless if they represent his personal opinion or the official position of the American Government." And the Senate asked for clarifications.

The clarification came immediately from the American Embassy in Bucharest, and it was not very pleasing for most people stating, *"The U.S. has long supported the sovereignty and territorial integrity of the Republic of Moldova. The United States applauds Romania for its continued leadership and collaborative approach to support Moldova's democratic development, reform efforts, and further integration into the EU according to the desires of the people. ... Drawing broader interpretations of our policy goes beyond the scope of our policy."*

Most Romanian and Moldovan newspapers reacted with various interpretations and began to doubt America's commitment to Romania. Some editors even suggested that in the grand scheme of international events, the U.S. might even trade Romania to Russia for stability in Europe. A pertinent analysis in this vein was authored by Dan Dungaciu, head or Romania's Institute for South-East European Studies. He concludes that the State Department is under the influence of specialists that embrace the old Soviet view point which, in his opinion, is damaging America's diplomacy. The analyst stressed that if the ambassador's statement represented the official views of the State Department, *"then we could see the huge difference between the position of a great American president, Ronald Reagan, and the administration of President Obama."*

Meanwhile, in Chisinau somebody wrote on the car of the American ambassador : *'Bessarabia is Romania.'* And in Bucharest, at a public rally in the University Plaza, young people collected thousands of books about Moldova to be sent to Ambassador Pettit to educate himself on the topic.

Yet, the uproar had a positive outcome. Ambassador James Pettit had a meeting with Mihai Ghimpu, leader of the Moldovan Liberal party and most likely candidate for next month's presidential elections in Moldova. According to cotidianul.ro of 5 September, Ghimpu explained to the ambassador in very clear terms that Moldovans are Romanians and that the aspiration of most of them is to reunite with Romania. He also said that in 1991 he personally voted for the independence of Moldova because union was not possible then, but people like him saw in the independence just a step toward union. "If we do not reunite with Romania," Mihai Ghimpu added, "we will be occupied by Russia the same way Crimea was occupied." The ambassador listened and then said that by making the statement of August 26, he did not want to offend the aspirations of the people. *"If the Moldovans want to unite with Romania, he would respect the decision and the ideal of the unionist movement."*

EU Enlargement, Russia and U.S. Policy. August 12, 2013

On November 27 and 28 representatives of the European Union will meet in Vilnius, Lithuania, to discuss the prospects of expanding its borders eastward. The enlargement will also bring with it the expansion of NATO, which makes Russia jittery and compels the United States to take a stand. On the one hand, Moscow is trying to neutralize Western Europe with beneficial economic deals, and on the other, it opposes strongly NATO's expansion into its former area of influence. This trend places Russia and America in opposing camps once again. Currently, however, Russia has become increasingly assertive, while under the Obama administration the United States has become soft and accommodating. What should be expected?

The new Russia under President Vladimir Putin resembles the old Soviet Union. Domestically, the Russian press has been muffled and the democratic process has been very much halted. Economically,

Putin's Russia resembles again the former USSR. According to the July 13 *Economist* "Castles in the Sand" the site of Moscow's Sochi 2014 Winter Olympics looks like a giant Soviet project which is costing the exorbitant amount of $50 billion. A big part of this huge expenditure at the Black Sea resort of Sochi is going into the pockets of various Russian oligarchs connected to Putin. No one dares oppose it, writes the *Economist*; it is Putin's pet project and his regime's way to legitimize itself. And geopolitically, Russia is engaged in a deadly struggle to retain control over its former republics and to prevent the EU expansion into those areas.

The European Union, however, has an open policy of eastward enlargement, and after the integration of Croatia this summer, it made clear that the door remains open. *"For all its trouble,"* wrote the *Economist* on June 29, 2013, the *"EU is still a family that others want to join. And the lure of membership remains a powerful incentive for economic and political reforms among its neighbors, including in countries in the former Soviet Union."* In this regard, the Vilnius EU summit will gather the six countries of the "Eastern Partnership," Belarus, Ukraine, Moldova, Georgia and Azerbaijan, and will begin firm negotiations for their future integration. Yet, Moscow is intent on blocking the process.

For the time being, Belarus is solidly in the hands of President Lukashenka, an unreformed pro-Moscow communist. Ukraine is also under a pro-Russian president Viktor Yanukovych, but with many Ukrainians preferring to join the EU, the country is split. Moldova is under tremendous Russian pressure. As for the republics of the south Caucasus, Armenia has no choice but to stay aligned with Russia, Georgia is territorially mutilated and incapable of maintaining its sovereignty following the 2008 invasion, while Azerbaijan is isolated and feels virtually abandoned by the West. As of now, we do not know what changes the Vilnius summit will bring to the region, but Russia is already using all its powers to retain its dominant positions on the geopolitical chessboard. And Moldova is a good case in point.

As a former Romanian territory and with most of its people being ethnic Romanians, Moldova is split between its European aspirations and the local communist minority that prefers Russia. This split has been Moldova's problem ever since its independence. To compound the local geopolitical scene, Moscow instigated Transnistria, a multi-ethnic region of Moldova, to break away from Chisinau. And to further punish Moldova's pro-Romanian aspirations, it also instigated the minuscule Gagauzi minority, to declare its autonomy. (The Gagauzi live in southern Moldova, are of Turkish descent, but are Christians.) Economically, Moldova is the poorest European country with neither prospects of self-development nor advancement. Politically, since independence, Moldova was led by Western-oriented governments at the beginning, by leftist-oriented agrarians later, by unreformed communists a few years ago, and again by pro-Western leaders presently. The current leaders, President Nicolae Timofte and Prime Minister Iurie Leanca, seek to draw Moldova closer to Romania and into the European Union.

Making himself an emissary of the EU, President Traian Basescu of Romania visited Moldova in July and again encouraged it to join the EU. According to *Romania Libera* of 17 and 18 July, he was received warmly and with full military honors by the president of Moldova and he also met with many opposition leaders. While meeting the local people, a young woman stressed that the road to the EU is long and bumpy and asked: *why not reunify first Moldova with Romania?* Mr. Basescu answered simply: *"Demand it and we will do it."* Otherwise, the Romanian president had a conciliatory tone toward Moscow. Nevertheless, under a cool façade, Russia is working hard behind the scenes in contravention to the independent republics to strengthen and enlarge its own Eurasian Customs Union.

As for Russia, it continues its unpublished agenda. As reported by the *Romanian Global News* of July 17-18, and the *Romanian Breaking News* of July 16, Moscow even claimed that Romania itself could join this community and in the process it would reunite with Moldova. Nevertheless, during his visit President Basescu said that the Moldovans are part of the Romanian nation, they share the same culture and history, and the land should join the EU, not the Eurasian Customs Union. And, he even added sarcastically that "he did not meet any Moldovans with slanted eyes."

Yet, as reported by *Moldova Weekly News Buletin*, of July 24, Russia's Foreign Minister Sergei Lavrov warned Moldova that it would suffer consequences if it decides to join the EU. All this time, Moscow's foreign policy... "stayed its course" by consolidating the "near abroad" and projecting power internationally. For example, according to the Russian magazine *Kommersant* and as reported by *Romania Libera* of July 25, President Putin will visit Iran in mid-August and the visit is expected to consolidate the Russo-Iranian relations. Among other things, Russia may increase its assistance to Iran's nuclear research and may even deliver to Tehran the dreaded S-300 rocket system. Then it will be interesting to see how President Obama will or won't respond.

Chapter 7
New Russian Maneuvers and Policies

Putin's Ukraine Policy is Dividing Europe. July 21, 2014

The ongoing crisis in Ukraine is dividing Europe and creating more friction with the United States, and could lead to a new international alignment. Putin's Russia is engaged in a multi-layered offensive policy with these aims in mind, while Washington is cautious and reactive rather than pro-active. A case in point is Russia's annexation of Crimea, which seems to have been already accepted as a *fait accompli*. Current negotiations are focusing on ending the violence in Eastern Ukraine and on compelling Russia to stop supporting the rebels. But, did Moscow trigger the conflict just as a cover up to annex Crimea, or annexing the peninsula is only the beginning of a new policy? The current *status quo* raises serious questions about the determination of the United States to oppose Putin. However, Russia's aggression also places Putin in a difficult dilemma. An article published by the *Christian Science Monitor* on July 7 summarizes the situation: *With Ukrainian rebels on the ropes, some Russians ask: Where is Putin?* Problem is, how far can the West and Russia stretch their interventions in Ukraine without risking a potentially devastating war?

For now the international confrontation consists mostly of declarations and sanctions, but the conflict may take on a life of its own and get out of hand. *Associated Press* of July 3 remarked that Moscow has toned down its threatening rhetoric recently, but many Russians expect Putin to take resolute action against Ukraine. Indeed, Putin cannot let down his supporters without eroding his political power base. He accused the West of having caused the crisis and said that he had no choice except to protect ethnic Russian in Ukraine because they "feel themselves a part of the Russian world." And Putin promised to use all means at his disposal to defend them. If not honored, this promise may turn against him.

The current crisis started when Ukraine's then-President Viktor Yanukovych refused to sign a treaty of association with the European Union. The decision triggered a violent uprising and the ousting of the pro-Russian president. Moscow's reaction was to encourage rebellions in eastern Ukraine and to threaten the territorial integrity of the country. Now Putin claims Western insistence Kyiv choose between the EU and Russia is responsible for breaking up the country. Yet despite all odds, on June 27, Ukraine, Moldova and Georgia signed association agreements with the EU. As a result, Russia redoubled its efforts, overtly and covertly, to assert itself regionally and internationally, threatening Ukraine with "serious consequences."

Today, Russia's threat of "serious consequences" rings ominously true, following the shoot down on Thursday of the Malaysian passenger jetliner Flight 17 killing 298 innocent people over eastern Ukraine. Perhaps it is truly time to revisit Putin's role in the Smolensk air crash of April 10, 2010, which involved "the deaths of Poland's president, and almost one hundred members of the military and political elite of a key U.S. – Central European ally on NATO's border with Russia" and largely overlooked by the West.

What Russia dreads is that in the future Ukraine may become a NATO member and will threaten its regional hegemony. Apparently, to placate Russia's fear, NATO announced that it was not going to expand any further in the near future. However, Moscow does not accept this pronouncement and continues to take drastic measures to foster its ambitions. Thus, Ukraine will be pressured economically and kept under a permanent threat of further dismemberment if it continues a pro-Western policy; Georgia, which was already punished militarily in 2008, is now kept under observation; and Moldova is under strong Russian economic pressure and is blackmailed with dismemberment.

As the poorest European country, Moldova's economic existence depends on exporting several agricultural products and on receiving gas and oil from Russia. The very day Moldova ratified the EU association agreement Moscow banned the imports of its agricultural products and began to harass Moldovans working in Russia threatening them with deportation. The European Union reacted by easing Moldovan exports to the EU and by eliminating visas for Moldovan citizens. The country is currently caught in a state of economic war between Russia and the West and its impoverished population is already feeling the pain.

Politically, Russian pressure is open and direct, as well as indirect. On July 2, for instance, the Moldovan Parliament ratified the association agreement with the EU with a majority of 59 votes. Knowing that they would lose the vote, 39 communists and ethnic Russians, members of the Chisinau legislative body, boycotted the meeting. These members, however, are working hard to turn the population against the West. Furthermore, since Moldova was once part of Romania, Moscow fears the reunification of the two countries, thus bringing NATO closer to Russia. To prevent such an outcome, Moscow intensified its relations with the break-away Moldovan region of Transnistria. It also began to incite the small Gagauz minority of southern Moldova to split and possibly try to join Russia as Crimea did. At the same time, Moscow is taking shrewd measures to isolate Romania economically and to punish Bucharest for siding with Washington.

Russia is also dividing Eastern Europe by enticing some countries with favorable energy deals. Bulgaria, Serbia and Hungary have already signed up for the Russian energy project "South Stream." Other Balkan countries, including the NATO members Greece and Turkey, have also joined the project. For now, Moscow's efforts are mostly economic, but the implications are political as well. Slovakia, located strategically in central Europe, is highly dependent on Russian gas and is also siding with Russia. In fact, these countries did not condemn Moscow for its aggression and instead have advocated accommodation with Putin's policy. Russia is splitting indeed Eastern Europe and the title of an *Associated Press* release in this regard is very illustrative: *EU's United Front on Russia Falling Amid Gas Needs.*

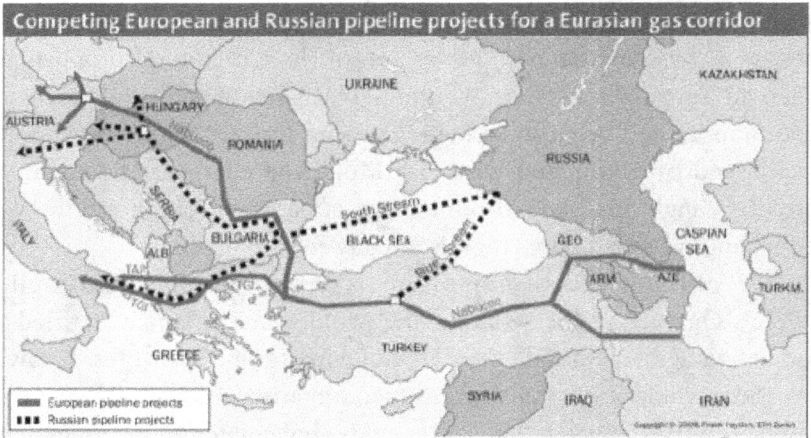

Competing European and Russian pipeline projects for a Eurasian gas corridor

In this new climate Romania and Poland have remained the best American allies in Eastern Europe and the strongest supporters of Ukraine independence and integrity. There are, however, certain misgivings and hesitations even in these countries. For example, Boreslaw Sikorski, Poland's Foreign Minister, stated in a private discussion with a former finance minister that *"the Polish-American alliance is worthless, even harmful, as it gives Poland a false sense of security."* According to *Time* of June 14 this statement was taped, leaked to a magazine and published on June 22. Such a statement reflects Poland's disillusion after President Obama's "reset" of U.S.-Russian relations and the canceling of the project of installing an American anti-missile shield in Poland and the Czech Republic. As for Romania, the government is deeply divided between a strongly pro-American president and an ambiguous prime minister who is trying hard to suspend the president, while the population at large is becoming increasingly cynical about Washington's policy in the region.

Putin is also cozying up economically to Germany and France with the covert aim of isolating America. A case in point is the deal signed by Russia to buy advanced French navy ships of the Mistral type for Russia's Black Sea fleet. The United States accused France of violating an international embargo, threatened the French banks with huge sanctions, and asked Paris to cancel the transaction. The largest French bank, *BNP Paribas*, admitted that it violated the sanctions, but refused to cancel the deal. According to *Bloomberg News,* France's president, Francois Hollande, also refused to cancel the transaction. Reacting to Washington's interference with the deal, Putin declared that America is trying to blackmail its own European allies.

The late Nobel Prize winner, Alexander Solzhenitsyn, a well-known Soviet dissident, once said that the Second World War never ended, but continued in different forms. Apparently, he was right. Since that war ended, the world went through a long period of cold relations, a rather short period of relaxation, and is confronted now with an era of neither war, nor peace, but some kind of a new realignment. In Asia, for instance, President Putin is warming up to China and Iran to attract them into what can only be a new anti-American bloc. And all that while in a typical Russian style Vladimir Putin wished President Obama a happy Fourth of July and called for improved relations. In the meantime, the stalemate in Ukraine continues and these days Kyiv appears to have the upper hand. Will Russia stand idly by? That's always been doubtful and, indeed, it appears it has not.

The Black Sea – New Battleground between Russia and NATO. Nov. 19, 2014

The Black Sea is located at a geo-strategic intersection between Europe and the oil-rich Middle East and between NATO and the Russian Federation. The annexation of Crimea by Russia and the ongoing conflict in eastern Ukraine add new significance to this disputed body of water. The issue of the Black Sea and the current Russo-Ukrainian conflict were discussed amply by the NATO leaders at their recent meetings.

The Black Sea has been important to Europe since ancient times and it has also served as a commercial hub between the old continent and Asia. Yet, throughout history it was a disputed body of water controlled by the Greeks and Romans in antiquity, by the Byzantine and the Ottoman empires during the Middle Ages, by tsarist Russia later, and by the Soviet Union after the Second World War. The sea itself covers 168,500 square miles and it is larger than the better known Baltic or Red Seas. In a way, the Black Sea is an extension of the Mediterranean Sea with which it is connected through the Bosporus Strait and the Dardanelles both controlled by Turkey. Of the two, the Bosporus raises special concerns because it is very narrow and navigation is dangerous, but easy to monitor.

The fall of communism and the disintegration of the Soviet Union led to new dynamics in the area and to hopes of liberalization and cooperation. In 1992 at Turkey's initiative, the riparian countries gathered in Istanbul to set up the Black Sea Economic Cooperation bloc (BSEC). The signatories aimed at transforming the sea into a region of peace and stability. However, a question remained, which I rhetorically raised in a 2003 article published by The *Journal of Social, Political and Economic Studies:* "Would Russia, the main successor state of the former Soviet Union, accept a loss of status and cooperate as an equal partner with the other countries that border the Black Sea?" Indeed, Moscow reluctantly joined the BSEC but for ulterior motives. In fact, Russia's intent was to regain control over the former Soviet republics and to continue to dominate the sea. For Russia, the Black Sea is of utmost importance. It provides ice-free harbors almost year round and it is Russia's sole link with the Mediterranean and the Middle East. While paying lip service to the idea of cooperation, Russia fomented several revolts and wars around the Black Sea until it saw an opportunity to challenge Ukraine and occupy Crimea.

After annexing Crimea, Moscow announced a modernization program of the Sevastopol Naval Base, where the Russian Black Sea Fleet is headquartered, and at the same time, it decided to build a new naval base at Novorossiysk, which is on the Russian mainland close to Crimea. Allegedly to counter America's and NATO's presence in the region, Moscow also decided to increase its Black Sea Navy by 80 new surface ships and six submarines. These decisions made the president of Romania, Traian Basescu, a staunch American ally, declare that Moscow wants to transform the Black Sea into a Russian lake. NATO took notice.

BLACK SEA REGION

Fig. 1

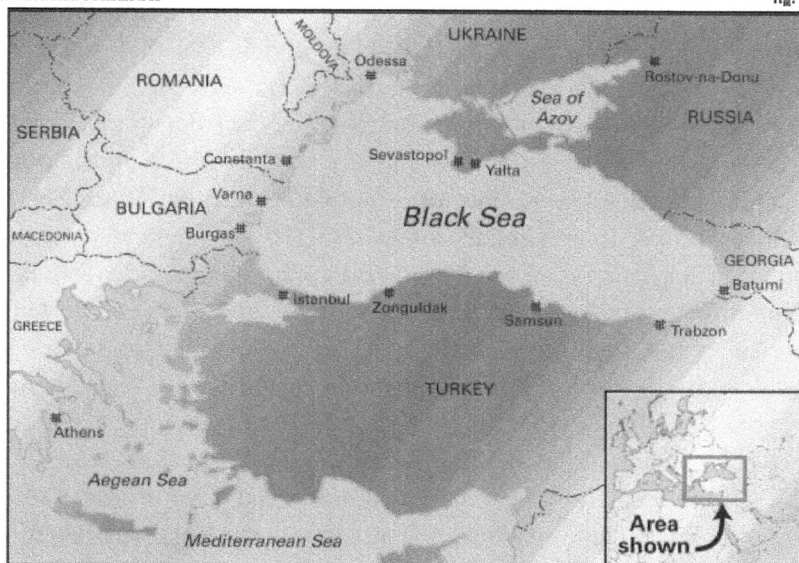

Some Western analysts claim that naval forces are no longer vital in today's age of globalization and inter-continental nuclear missiles. Yet, according to *Romania Libera* of October 10, 2014, at the beginning of the month Russian President Vladimir Putin visited the port of Novorossiysk, where he was met by Vice-Admiral Alexander Vitko, the commander of the Black Sea Fleet. The admiral reported that by 2020 it will have a total of 206 ships, including six new submarines of the Kilo class. He did not mention, however, the modern French Mistral warships for which Paris has contracted with Moscow but whose delivery has been put on hold. According to the admiral, the expansion of the Russian Black Sea Naval Fleet is necessary to counter America's and NATO's threat.

The reality is that Moscow rejects the expansion of the North Atlantic Alliance into the Black Sea through Romania and Bulgaria and vehemently opposes the prospect of further NATO expansion. This is why Ukraine has been punished territorially and is currently being kept under Moscow's permanent threat. Simply put, Putin's Russia cannot accept the idea of losing the Soviet empire and is trying hard to regain its former superpower status.

In the meantime, some American warships have entered the Black Sea and have paid visits to their new NATO allies. Romania in particular welcomes the American visits and insists that a permanent NATO presence be established in the Black Sea. While Ukraine is mortified by the Russian actions on its territory, Romania is afraid that Russia may take Odessa and eventually threaten the Romanian lands. The problem with the presence of military vessels in the Black Sea is the 1936 Montreux International Convention. This agreement places strict limits on the entry of foreign warships. Accordingly, no warships that come through the Bosporus Strait should be bigger than 15,000 tons; no more than nine such ships should enter at the same time; and, these ships should not stay in the Black Sea more than 21 days. The alternative proposed by NATO at its recent Newport (Wales) summit was to rotate such ships in order to maintain a permanent presence.

There is, however, a more daring and revolutionary solution proposed by Turkey, the country that controls the Bosporus. Four years ago, then-Turkish Prime Minister Recep Tayyip Erdogan proposed to build a canal around Istanbul from the Black Sea to the Marmara Sea, thereby bypassing the Bosporus and circumventing the provisions of the Montreux Convention. If realized, the canal would solve not only political disputes, but also important economic and ecological problems.

Furthermore, the Russian Defense Ministry recently announced that the military bases in Crimea will be completely modernized over the next several years. A new airbase located near Simferopol will house modern planes such as Su-25 and 27, MiG-29, Il-38N and will receive attack helicopters and long-range bombers of the TU-22 type. At the same time, the Sevastopol submarine base will be rebuilt and the peninsula will be provided with anti-aircraft missiles and 300 new pieces of artillery. Moscow's plan also calls for bringing to Crimea a number of ground units specializing in chemical, biological and radiological warfare. Such a military build-up practically ends the era of cooperation and poses huge problems not only for Ukraine, but for the entire NATO organization. The Russian geopolitical agenda is on a collision course with the Western economic-political goals.

Meanwhile, the Black Sea retains its strategic and military importance. It is close to Syria, where Russia continues to enjoy the Cold War-era warm water access to the Mediterranean for its naval supply and maintenance facilities at Tartus, an area close to the troubled Middle East and to the Caspian Basin, whose oil must flow through the Black and Mediterranean seas to reach European markets.

Russia, NATO and the New Ukrainian Defense Policy. February 10, 2015

Ukraine is a struggling country caught between Russia and the European Union. Historically, the country has been associated with Moscow and its culture is split between the Russian-dominated East and the European-dominated West. In his book *The Clash of Civilizations and the Remaking of the World Order*, the late Harvard professor Samuel Huntington stated that Ukraine is a cleft country with two distinct cultures. Geographically, Ukraine is a bridge that links and separates Russia from Europe. A bridge, however, he argued, can break at any time, and this is what Moscow did last year when it occupied and annexed Crimea and encouraged eastern Ukraine to revolt against Kyiv.

The recent upheavals and the uncompromising struggle between the pro-eastern and pro-western tendencies show how deeply Moscow is involved in the evolution of this country. If Ukraine wants to join the European Union, Moscow becomes suspicious and is ready to sabotage any move in that direction. However, if Ukraine wants to join NATO, Russia is ready to use any means, military included, and if necessary is ready to dismember the country. The process started by annexing Crimea and by threatening a split of the Donbas region.

In December Moscow adopted a new military doctrine and stressed again that NATO and the United States were Russia's biggest enemies. It also strengthened its military position in the Black Sea, the Caucasus and the Arctic region. Internationally, Moscow also forged closer relations with China and stated that an international war was possible. With regard to Ukraine, Russia demanded 100 percent guaranties that it would never join NATO, but what are Kyiv's choices?

After the bloody events of the last year, the Ukrainian authorities, and more importantly, the people at large, realized that the country was in a dire situation. They understood that on the one hand Moscow did not respect the international agreement regarding Ukraine's borders and on the other the country did not have the military capacity to confront Russia. Yet, the crisis and the armed conflict that already took several thousand lives helped the Ukrainian people clarify their identity and national interests and distinguish friends from foes. The conflict made President Petro Poroshenko, as well as most Ukrainians, look toward Europe for their future. The separatist war and hostilities of 2014 opened a new era in East-West relations. For the time being, the events are unfolding slowly because no one wants a dangerous escalation, but they are moving slowly toward more confrontation.

As reported by AP, on December 24 the Kyiv parliament repealed the 2010 law regarding Ukraine's nonaligned status. That law was mandating a policy of "nonparticipation in any military-political alliances." The repeal was approved 303 to 9 showing an unexpected solidarity among lawmakers. A few days later, President Petro Poroshenko signed the law and stated that finally "a mistake has been corrected." He also said that Kyiv was working to reform the national economy and military forces to meet European and NATO standards.

As for NATO, a spokesman said that "our door is open and Ukraine could become a member if it fulfills the standards and adheres to the necessary principles." General Jens Stoltenberg also stated that Ukraine is a valued partner. And the U.S. State Department announced that *"Countries that are willing to contribute to security in the Euro-Atlantic space are welcome to apply for membership."* NATO has not actually issued a formal invitation to Kyiv for membership in the alliance, but the idea has already alarmed Moscow. Potential membership in the Western alliance would confront Russia in its own backyard and Moscow finds that unacceptable. Consequently, its response was immediate and threatening. Russian Foreign Minister Sergei Lavrov reacted more moderately by stating that the new law would only heat up the current confrontation.

Moscow's newly modified and adopted military doctrine reflects Russia's anxiety. Local observers and Western analysts stress, however, that except for its nuclear capacity Russia's military is weak and its economy is in shambles. In fact, the economy is based almost exclusively on the export of oil and gas. The plummeting global price of oil together with the Western economic sanctions has brought Russia to its knees. The rubble, for example, lost almost half of its value and the stores began to empty themselves of goods as they were during the last Soviet years.

Yet, Russian Foreign Minister Sergei Lavrov who addressed the 51st Security Conference held in Munich, Germany on February 7, warned of confrontation in light of NATO expansion. He said: *"NATO's course on strengthening its military potential and expanding its military presence and infrastructure on the alliance's 'eastern flank' as well as an increase in the number of exercises near the Russian borders creates additional tensions, provoke confrontation and undermine the whole system of Euro-Atlantic security."*

2015 began with some sort of victory for President Vladimir Putin. He inaugurated the new Eurasian Economic Union, meant to be similar to and to compete with the European Union, but even that started on the wrong foot. The countries making up the new union are Russia, Belarus, Kazakhstan, Armenia and Kyrgyzstan. Yet, the *Business Insider* of December 31 posted an illustrative article entitled, "Russia starts the New Economic Union on New Year and it already looks like a Disaster." Belarus, for example, a pivotal member, has criticized Moscow for blocking its commerce with Kazakhstan. As retaliation against Western sanctions, Putin banned many imports from Europe but could not prevent Belarus from importing and resending such goods to Kazakhstan. However, on their way, many such goods are sold in Russia thus, sabotaging Putin's response to the European sanctions.

According to Reuters on December 31 Vladimir Putin has sacrificed the political and economic freedom of the Russian people for the idea of old-style Soviet glory. But he only brought Russia close to economic collapse. Yet, opinion polls show that his ratings are near record highs among average Russians. There is a deep streak of imperialism in Putin's Moscow and of irrational nationalism among Russians that defy reasoning and threaten world peace. Will Russia withdraw from Ukraine and renormalize its relations with the West or will it turn inside and toward China and risk a confrontation with the West? Ukraine is again the bridge between East and West. Will that bridge hold?

Putin Meddling in Eastern Europe and the Middle East. December 5, 2016

This past November, Bulgaria, a European Union and NATO member located strategically on the Black Sea near Greece and Turkey elected a pro-Russian president. Also in November, Moldova, a country that was aspiring to join the two organizations, elected a pro-Russian president that advocates membership in the Eurasian community of nations. Hungary, on the other hand, is increasingly vocal against EU decisions and is flirting with Russia. After the violent dissolution of Yugoslavia, Serbia is also upset with America and is now courting Russia. More importantly, Turkey, a powerful NATO member and a strategic ally of the United States, is warming up to Russia, thus threatening the frail balance of power in the Middle East. To complicate the situation, several Western European countries, such as Germany and France, are cozying up to Moscow, losing sight in the process of Russia's geopolitical goals. In fact, for a number of years, now Russia under Vladimir Putin, has been conducting psychological warfare against American interests. In Europe, only Great Britain identified the danger and denounced Moscow's insidious actions, while the United States was overwhelmingly preoccupied with the presidential elections.

Will President-elect Trump confront the Russian psychological operations in Europe and Moscow's meddling in the Middle East? Will the new administration be capable of strengthening the NATO alliance thus keeping the *Germans in and the Russians out*? Apparently, there is hope.

On December 1st, *Associated Press* reported that the U.S. Congress has become aware of the new danger posed by Russia: The House *"Passed a 93-page intelligence policy bill that calls for a high-level panel to counter Russian political interference around the globe."* The AP wire mentions, however, that *"it is a measure that might run counter to President-elect Donald Trump's pledge to improve U.S. relations with Russia."* The bill, voted 390 to 30, addresses national security threats and has a classified annex. The Senate is expected to take up the issue and most likely pass the bill before the end of the year. The bill provides for *"an interagency panel to stifle Russian attempts to exert covert influence over peoples and governments."* It refers specifically to . . . *"exposing falsehoods, agents of influence, corruption, human rights abuses, terrorism and assassinations carried out by the security services or political elites or the Russian Federation or their proxies . . ."* The question is: Why did Congress not react years ago and instead the Obama administration tried *to reset* relations with the same aggressive Russia?

At this point Russia's intentions appear to be fourfold: 1) organize an anti-American pole at a global level; 2) neutralize Western Europe; 3) regain control over Eastern Europe; and, 4) make impossible an American-sponsored peace settlement in the Middle East. And, so far, Moscow seems to be winning.

In light of recent events in Europe and elsewhere, Washington will have a hard time countering Moscow's operations because the West does not stand on clear moral ground anymore. Take, for example, the process of globalization, which is strongly promoted by America. It has led to the ruining of the Eastern European economies without much to show for a better life except for a small group of former communists who robbed the national economies of their countries and managed to ingratiate themselves to Western corporations. At the same time, in the name of democracy the EU is pushing Eastern European countries to adopt allegedly democratic rights that impinge on their moral values. As a result, certain minority groups are getting more attention and enjoy more rights than the majority of the population. A number of corrupt Romanians, for example, were sentenced to prison. In the new prisons regulated by EU standards, prisoners live by hotel standards, are allowed to order food from outside, are permitted to go to see their doctors, if they claim to be sick, and are freed ahead of time, if they write books. It is ridiculous, but according to the Romanian press some of the prisoners authored several books in one single year. (As a visiting professor in Bucharest this past November, I was asked about life in prison during the communist years. My students were shocked by my own experience in communist prisons. And I referred them to my book, *Journey to Freedom*, published by the Selous Foundation in 1989.)

While in Bucharest in my native country, I watched with keen interest the presidential elections in Moldova. The Russian maneuverings and pressures were felt everywhere. The pro-Russian candidate Igor Dodon was openly helped by Moscow and by the Russian oligarchs. And, because the vote was close, Moscow's agents brought busloads of voters from the Russian-controlled Transnistrian Republic to vote for Dodon. At the same time, numerous Moldovans residing abroad were prevented from voting by the limited number of bulletins each voting center had received from Chisinau. Despite the huge Russian efforts and inflow of financial support, the pro-European candidate Maia Sandu received over 40 percent of the votes. Some analysts considered this to be a great success. Moldova is a very touchy issue for Romania and remains of continuous interest to Bucharest.

A few days before the Moldovan elections, I had a personal meeting with the former President of Romania, Traian Basescu. He served as president from 1994 to 2004 and was a strong pro-American and pro-NATO advocate. He was the only Romanian president who spoke of Moldova as a lost Romanian land and who asked for Moldovan citizenship. The citizenship was granted to him at a public ceremony held at Moldova's Bucharest Embassy, and he was one of the first to vote for Ms. Sandu. However, I noticed certain sadness when we spoke of America's policy in the region. He mentioned that initially, after the fall of communism, America was willing to support the reunification of Moldova with Romania. Why did Washington change its policy and was so soft on Russia during the last several years?

The Kurds and the Question of 'Kurdistan.'
November 4, 2014

The American media frequently mentions the problem of the Kurds and their struggle for survival. Their plea is even more urgent, since this past June when a new jihadist force launched a brutal campaign to conquer Syria and Iraq. These days, the struggle is taking place primarily in Syria and especially on the outskirts of Kobani, a mostly Kurdish town of some 50,000 people located near the Turkish border. The war, however, raises additional problems in a region of already incompatible claims, aspirations and interests.

The Kurds have put up a heroic fight against the superior forces of the Islamic State of Iraq and Syria (ISIS), but the media claims that they need urgent help in order to prevail. According to Associated Press of October 14, the Kurds are hanging on to their lands against all expectations because *"they have a cause and are preparing to die fighting for it."* But, what is their cause?

The Kurds are loyal allies of the United States and the only 'boots on the ground' fighting alongside the Western coalition against the self-declared Islamic State caliphate. From Washington's point of view, at stake in the near future is the very existence of Iraq as a unified country. If ISIS prevails, the order and stability of the whole Middle East would be greatly endangered. However, if the Kurds endure, sooner or later they will demand a country of their own. With the exception of Israel, no one would willingly accept an independent Kurdistan in the center of the Middle East. Either way, the region is in more trouble now than ever before and a return to the *status quo ante* no longer appears to be a viable choice.

Most of the fighting at the end of October was taking place in Syria near the Turkish border. Turkey, a NATO member and traditionally an American ally, concentrated its troops across Kobani, but refused to step in and help the Syrian Kurds. Only lately and reluctantly Ankara allowed some Turkish and Iraqi Kurds to aid their Syrian brothers. On the other hand, the Iraqi Army, which practically deserted instead of fighting ISIS, agreed, albeit reluctantly, to fight along with the Kurds against the newly self-proclaimed caliphate. Why this reluctance to side with the Kurds? Who are the Kurds and what threats do they pose to the current order in the Middle East?

The Kurds are one of the most ancient peoples of the Middle East. They are of Indo-European origin and occupy a huge land area currently divided among Turkey, Iran, Iraq and Syria. Numbering close to 30 million people, they represent one of the largest Middle Eastern nationalities. Yet, they do not have their own country. Their closest relatives in the region would be the Iranians, but while Iranians are Shia, the Kurds are Sunni Muslims.

Throughout their history the Kurds served as mercenaries for the great powers of the region and failed to organize and maintain their own state. Without an educated elite and lacking representation, at the end of the First World War their area was divided among the newly formed countries. Consequently, the Kurds became the largest minority in the Middle East. Nonetheless, the idea of independence survived with them, but it took different paths in the countries that divided them. Thus, instead of asking for independence, they settled for local autonomy.

According to the CIA fact book, there are currently about 14 million Kurds in Turkey, making up 18-to-20 percent of Turkey's population; 7-to-8 million in Iran representing 8-to-10 percent of the population of that country; 4-to-5 million in Iraq making up 15-to-20 percent of the Iraqi population; and 1.6 million in Syria making up close to 10 percent of Syria's population. Apparently, the Kurds have integrated themselves better in Iran and Syria, but have rejected bitterly the assimilation efforts pursued by Iraq and Turkey, where they sought national recognition. However, an independent Kurdistan would carve out big chunks of territory from the aforementioned nations, which is strongly rejected by the respective countries. This is why Turkey is reluctant to help the Kurds in Syria, and this is why Washington has to walk a very fine line when it encourages the Kurds, who have proven to be strong allies.

During the recent decades the Kurds organized themselves separately in each of the four countries and tried to fight for their rights. In Turkey, for example, the Kurdistan Workers Party (PKK) fought fiercely against the government until recently, when the former prime minister and current Turkish president, Recep Tayyip Erdogan, agreed to grant them increased minority rights. The Iraqi Kurds also bitterly opposed Saddam Hussein's brutal dictatorship and as a result they suffered incredibly at his murderous hand. When the United States fought the first Iraqi war, the Kurds became natural allies of America. Then, the United Nations and Washington established a safe zone in northern Iraq, which became an autonomous Kurdish region. The very existence of this region is feared now by the governments in Damascus, Ankara, Tehran and Baghdad as the seed for a potentially independent Kurdistan. This would be an unacceptable threat to their territorial integrity.

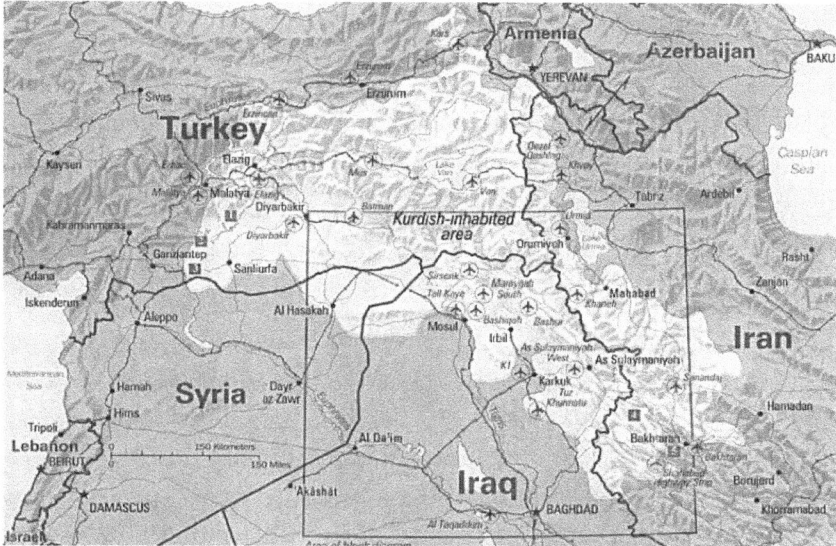

Kurdistan spanning Iraq, Iran, Syria and Turkey

Could America and the West help the Kurds without alienating the other countries and without risking an all-out war in the Middle East? And how long can the world ignore the Kurdish issue? And what will America do, if events get out of hand?

Is Turkey Changing Sides? August 16, 2016

Turkey's recent military coup attempt is worrying the West and there are good reasons for concern. For several decades, Turkey kept a balance between Europe and the Middle East, between Christianity and Islam and between NATO and Russia. Turkey's membership in NATO is very important and a change of sides is hard to imagine. Yet, the daily *Romania Libera* announced that Ankara could leave the alliance.

On July 15 some elements of the Turkish military attempted a coup, apparently, with the intention of keeping the country on a secular track. Turkey's elected president, Recep Tayyip Erdoğan, appealed to the people using social media allegedly to save his democratic regime. The coup failed. In the process 290 people lost their lives and for a short time normal life was disrupted. Judging by the crowds that demonstrated for democracy, the majority of the people sided with the president. His policy, however, is pro-Islamist and his critics accuse him of authoritarian rule.

Certain critics claim that Erdoğan used the coup to impose a dictatorial regime. He accused his former ally, Muslim cleric Fethullah Gülen, of masterminding the failed uprising. And Ankara asked Washington to extradite Gülen, who now lives in the United States. Gülen denies any ties with the coup, while the State Department asked for proof of his involvement.

Erdoğan is caught in his desire for increased power between the Islamist movement and the West. Yet, his regime resorted to wide-spread domestic reprisals. According to AP, AFP and other media sources, over 10,000 Turks were arrested and jailed after the coup and another 50,000 were fired from their jobs. The Turkish *Anadolu* News Agency announced that among those arrested are military men, journalists, judges, professors and members of various institutions suspected to have sympathized with the coup leaders. AP of July 28 mentioned the arrest or removal of 149 generals and admirals and 47 senior journalists. The authorities also closed many newspapers, television and radio stations, and three news agencies. The presidency also decreed a three-month state of emergency. Amnesty International criticized Ankara for violating human rights.

Ironically, Russia defended Erdoğan's policy, while the Balkan countries accused him of wanting to revive the old Ottoman Empire. Based on their historical experiences, most Balkan countries reject Turkey, but Romania, which was victimized historically by Russia, maintains good relations with Ankara. This year Romania's president visited Turkey and President Erdoğan offered to build in Bucharest the biggest mosque in Europe. The Romanians were outraged and the issue is still pending. (The site selected for the mosque is one of the best in Bucharest and is located across the Romanian American University, where I teach as a visiting professor. One can already see crosses erected by people on the site to prevent building the mosque.)

A little history

During the 19th century the Ottoman Empire was considered the sick man of Europe. While Istanbul was Westernized to a certain degree, Anatolia remained an Islamist hinterland. The military defeat during World War I left Turkey in disarray. The country was saved by General Mustafa Kemal and his allies. The new government abolished the Ottoman Sultanate, proclamed the Republic of Turkey and banned the old Caliphate. At the same time, it introduced many Western-type reforms and even banned the traditional Muslim clothing for both men and women. Turkey was on its Western course, but the reforms did not manage to reach deep into Anatolia. Yet, whenever a pro-Islamic government tried to depart from the new secular trend, the military intevened and forced Turkey back on Kemal's pro-Western road.

During the last decades several events challenged Turkey's status quo. Membership in NATO did anchor Ankara to America and Europe, but repeated rejections for membership by the European Union angered the people and the govenment. At the same time, the radicalization of the Middle East and the conflict between Israel and the Arabs fed a domestic Islamist resurgence. Increasingly, more and more Turks began to adhere to a strict form of Islam and to exert influence over the authorities. It was in this climate that Erdoğan's Justice and Development Party came to power and began to change Ankara's policy.

Implications and consequences

Turkey is now at a crossroad. For the last several decades Turkey has been a bridge between East and West, but the route Ankara is choosing will have deep implications for the future. During the Cold War, Turkey was crucial in deterring the former Soviet Union. Currently, Turkey still has the largest NATO military second only to the U.S. It is also in Turkey, at the Incirlik Air Force Base, where the United States maintains a large stockpile of nuclear warheads. According to the July 24th *Los Angeles Times*, this is America's largest foreign stockpile of nuclear weapons. Should Ankara change sides, it would be a huge loss for America and a big gain for Russia and Iran.

Regionally, Turkey and Iran are divided on the issue of hegemony in the Middle East. Yet, the two countries are united by Islam and by their policy of keeping the Kurds under control. They both reject Washington for creating an autonomous Kurdish region in Iraq. On the other hand, dictatorial rule is also very tempting for Erdoğan. He is already one of the richest political leaders in the world and lives in an enviable palace. A change of U.S. policy may make him a sort of sultan for life.

As for Russia, the failed Turkish military coup is even more significant. Putin is deeply opposed to the NATO alliance and to the recent NATO summit held in Poland. He and Russian intelligence are working hard to divide Europe and to remove it from American influence. The recent UK Brexit referendum weakened both the NATO alliance and the European Union. The potential separation of Turkey from NATO would ostensibly weaken the alliance further. Putin greeted both events, while Washington was left to wonder on the side lines.

Alert and ready to act, Vladimir Putin is courting Erdoğan, while outmaneuvered, the Obama administration appears paralyzed and in denial. The question is: Will the next U.S. administration regain its sense of mission?

Waiting for Russia's Next Move in Southeast Europe. May 27, 2015

To a Westerner southeast Europe appears peaceful and changing for the better, but beneath the surface people are struggling and some are worried about Russia. I gathered various impressions during a recent trip to Romania, Moldova, Ukraine and Bulgaria. While Romania and Bulgaria are now members of the European Union and NATO, Moldova is under Moscow's thumb and Ukraine is facing Russian aggression. The ongoing conflict in Ukraine keeps Kiev's leaders on edge, threatens Chisinau, and worries Bucharest.

Ever since the start of the Ukrainian conflict and the Russian annexation of Crimea, the tension between NATO and Moscow is palpable. Russia provokes the NATO allies and even speaks of a possible nuclear specter. Is Moscow just posturing, or is the threat of war real? It is probably both and Russia's military threats are taken seriously by its neighbors. Moscow is conducting masterful psychological warfare which could jeopardize NATO's unity and drive a wedge between Europe and America.

In Bucharest I attended a lecture titled "U.S. Ballistic Missile Defense and Non-Proliferation Policy," given by Frank Rose, U.S. Assistant Secretary for Arms Control. Romania has been threatened by Russia for accepting an American ballistic missile shield on its territory. Moscow alluded that Romania had exposed itself to potential reprisals and it could be annihilated within a matter of hours. On the psychological front, ever since Romania joined NATO, Moscow has spread the rumor that America should not be trusted. The lecture was an assurance that Romania is in no danger and that any threat to a NATO country would invoke the collective defense of Article 5.

Romania makes a good post-communist case study. The Romanians have a justified fear of Russia and a strong pro-Western attitude. Ever since the tsars, Moscow has wanted to reach the Balkans and the Mediterranean Sea. If only Romania would not be in the way. Indeed, the Romanian lands have been invaded repeatedly by Russia. The historical background has changed, but the geo-political situation has remained.

Today's Russia is still looking over its western borders and is luring some European countries. Greece, for example, is strongly dissatisfied with the European Union and went to Moscow for assistance. Serbia has just been visited by Russia's foreign minister and is inclined toward Russia. Macedonia is following suit. Hungary is upset with the EU policies and is now befriending Moscow. Slovakia is tilting toward Russia, while the Czech Republic is caught between East and West. Only Poland, Romania, and the Baltic states are standing fast by NATO and America.

To my chagrin I found my native country, Romania, confused and in doubt. People have begun to distrust America and the assurances Washington is giving Romania. I argued that Romania is not in imminent danger. Russia is not capable of any further expansion and that if NATO would not react, the organization would disintegrate.

I traveled with a Romanian-American friend to his native village in central Moldova, where we were received with great hospitality. In the capital, Chisinau, we also met young Moldovans dreaming of union with Romania and desiring to be part of Europe. There are, however, many poor people in Moldova and the society is split. Without economic opportunities, many local people work in construction in Moscow and favor Russia. The powerful Russian minority of Moldova is also chiefly siding with Moscow. The local Ukrainian minority, generally pro-Russian, is now confused. As for the authorities, they are divided, corrupted and manipulated by Moscow.

We left Chisinau heading south toward the Danube accompanied by a local man who had been an officer in the Soviet Army. He was a tremendous source of knowledge and information about the former Soviet Union. As a native Moldovan with a Romanian passport, he could pass easily as a Russian. He was our driver and guide along the Danube and on to Odessa.

The small region adjacent to the Danube, currently in Ukraine, was part of historic Moldova and, therefore, of modern Romania. After the 1939 Ribbentrop-Molotov pact, Russia annexed the entire province of Bessarabia and for better control over the Danube granted this piece of land to Ukraine.

When Moscow decided to modify the border of the former Romanian province of Bessarabia in favor of Ukraine, it embittered the two nations. Now, in spite of Romania supporting Kiev in its conflict with Russia, privately, Ukraine considers Romania an enemy country. Actually, Moscow has already alluded to this territorial issue and tried to lure Romania on its side. With Odessa on their mind, certain Russian circles even began to mention an independent pro-Russian "Bessarabian" republic along the Danube. A Russian-controlled Odessa together with Transnistria and this region would constitute what some circles call "The New Russia."

Returning to this Danube piece of land, one is shocked by its state of neglect and decay. During the Soviet era, Moscow developed the Danube harbor of Reni, which was an important hub of economic activities. Now the harbor is idle and its big cranes are rusting. The entire area seems to have undergone little development since the Second World War and its roads are almost unusable. The population of the area is ethnically mixed and their main language is Russian. We could not figure out, however, which way this population would turn in case of a Russo-Ukrainian conflict.

Eventually, we reached the Dnestr estuary. A bridge took us over the river and to better roads when we arrived in Odessa. In spite of its neglected buildings, the city appears European and is beautiful and full of history. The Black Sea frontage is also well-kept and the national theater nearby is magnificent. Nevertheless, local people speak predominantly Russian and even have Russian affiliations. Apparently, Ukraine's independence did not help the people of Odessa.

Upon my return to the U.S., I found a number of analyses claiming that Russia is preparing new actions against Ukraine. My sources also thought that the Russo-Ukrainian conflict would escalate in the future, and in their opinion could lead to the disintegration of both countries.

And where is Russia going to stop: Eastern Ukraine, Odessa, or the Danube and the NATO border? It seems that NATO and the United States will not go to war with Russia for the defense of Ukraine. However, Washington should take Senator John McCain's advice and give Ukraine the necessary arms to defend itself.

New Russian Maneuvers. July 7, 2015

The Russo-Ukrainian conflict is far from over and a mutually acceptable solution is hard to achieve. The Russian annexation of Crimea is a fait accompli: Moscow will not willingly return it to Ukraine and Kyiv will not officially accept the annexation.

What Russia really wants is to control Ukraine and to maintain its geopolitical influence in East Europe. And Moscow has many cards up its sleeves. There are the Russian-dominated regions of eastern Ukraine, the Moscow-controlled Transnistria region of Moldova to the west, and the Odessa region to the south. As a sea port, Odessa is vital to Kyiv, but it is also essential for Russia's influence in the Black Sea.

From the Baltic to the Black Sea a new fault line is taking shape between the NATO alliance and Russia. Moscow still speaks of peaceful solutions, but underneath is already plotting new moves. One such move aims at Odessa and the Danube River. Reaching the Danube has been Russia's dream since the tsars. Apparently, Moscow is now reviving the old dream. A brief history is due in this regard.

The territory between the Dnestr and Prut Rivers was part of the medieval Principality of Moldova. Initially, the region adjacent to the Danube and the Black Sea belonged to Walachia, which was led by the Basarab princes. Later, the entire region between the two rivers took the name of Bessarabia.

The Russians reached the Danube in 1812 and annexed the province. However, Moscow's expansion threatened Western European interests, which triggered the Crimean War. Russia lost the war and was forced to return the area to Romania. Then, Moscow re-annexed it after the 1877 war with Turkey, but lost it again to Romania after the First World War.

Yet, in 1940, the Soviet Union reoccupied the province following the Ribbentrop-Molotov pact. Nonetheless, Romania joined Germany during the Second World War and regained its province, only to lose it again at the end of the war. At that time, Moscow reconfigured the annexed territory and gave to Ukraine this piece of land adjacent to the Danube. The land became part of Odessa region, but remained little developed since then offering few economic opportunities to its inhabitants. The population of the area is made up of Romanians, Russians, Ukrainians, Gagauzi and Bulgarians, and is largely pro-Russian. And now, to further blackmail Ukraine and to bait Romania, Moscow is about to invent a "Bessarabian republic."

Petro Poroshenko, the pro-Western president of Ukraine, appointed the former president of Georgia Mikhail Saakashvili as the governor of the Odessa region. In his new capacity, Saakashvili sounded an alarm against Moscow's designs for the region. On June 22, he declared on Ukrainian TV that Russia was inciting the people of the Danube area to proclaim their own popular republic. And he exposed the deep Russian infiltration of the area and the plan to split it from Kyiv. His fear was confirmed by the Ukrainian Security Services (USB), which arrested numerous members of the Bessarabian Popular Council, who were distributing separatist leaflets. According to *Agerpress* of Bucharest and *Timpul* of Chisinau, the USB also confiscated 500 copies of the separatist paper *Novorossia*. Moscow is continuing to infiltrate Ukraine with the intent of disrupting and destabilizing.

The truth is that the NATO countries neighboring Russia are wary of Moscow's threats. This is why the Alliance's leaders have reassured them of unflinching commitment to their defense. Furthermore, NATO decided to station heavy military equipment and troops throughout the entire region. According to Reuters of 24 June, U.S. Defense Secretary Ashton Carter made an announcement to this effect at a press conference held in Estonia. He mentioned military personnel as well as tanks, armored vehicles and self-propelled howitzers, which will be positioned in Estonia, Lithuania, Latvia, Bulgaria, Romania and Poland.

The Western Alliance is also holding military maneuvers envisioning different scenarios. One such war exercise is now taking place in southeast Romania close to the Danube. The exercise involves 1,500 troops from U.S., Romania, five other NATO countries, as well as from Georgia and Moldova. The Independent of June 24 also mentioned the participation of 70 tanks and armored vehicles, 17 airplanes, and four navy ships. Moscow does not like NATO's reactions, but it is downplaying its own provocative maneuvers.

Speaking at a recent Kremlin meeting, Russian President Vladimir Putin vowed to modernize Russia's military forces and threatened with grave consequences any aggression against Russia. NATO did not blink. Announcing that a U.S. Marine Corps unit will soon be stationed in Bulgaria, Brig. Gen. Norman Cooling, deputy commander USMC Forces Europe and Africa, declared to AP that "it is certainly our intent to convince the Russians and Mr. Putin to refrain from aggression and return to the community of peaceful nations." …Putin may be bluffing, but more likely he is testing the margins and NATO must be ready!

Chapter 8
Europe's Never Ending Struggle

Heart of Europe: A History of the Holy Roman Empire, **Peter H. Wilson, Belknap Press of Harvard University, 2016.** March 1, 2017

Europe has been very important to the world since ancient times. And for about 500 years till the Second World War Europe was practically the center of the world. However, the continent has lived though unending struggles and changes and is currently experiencing again very important transformations. What can we learn from the past and what should we expect? The book mentioned above shed some light in this regard, but not much clarification for the future of the continent.

Heart of Europe: A History of Holy Roman Empire is an encyclopedic study covering over one thousand years of Western European Christianity, roughly from 800 to 1806. Peter Wilson did a detailed job chronicling every event and personality that shaped the "Empire." As a geographer, I was fascinated by the changing maps and focused primarily on geography rather than history. Yet, I soon realized that the Empire's fluid geography was as blurred as its history was complex and convoluted. And, I realized once more how different was the evolution of Western Europe from that of my native Eastern Europe. I wished the Empire had been analyzed alongside the full evolution of the Byzantine and Euro-Russian empires. However, the other two were analyzed whenever their history and geography intertwined with the West.

Wilson's text is organized topically into four parts: Ideal, Belonging, Governance, and Society. Each part has several chapters: Christendom, Sovereignty, Lands, Identities, Nations, Kingship,

Territory, Dynasty, Authority, Association, Justice, and Afterlife as conclusion. The thick study has numerous tables, illustrations, princely genealogies, as well as numerous maps and a very useful Chronology section. If one were to draw a quick conclusion, it would be how much Europe has changed over the millennia. And, the aftermath of this thought is that 'change' is the permanent state of affairs in the world, and that 'change' is unmistakably coming again to Europe.

Unlike the Byzantine Empire that fell under the Ottomans and Eastern Europe that fell under the Russians, the Holy Roman Empire remained free and became the heart of today's Western Europe. As such, the same area experienced the Renaissance, Church Reformation, Industrialization and Modernization, and recently, the process of Globalization. More importantly, the area of the former Empire led to the formation of the European Economic Community in the middle of the 20th Century and gradually to the current European Union. In this regard and as the author states at the beginning, *"the Holy Roman Empire's history lies at the heart of the European experience."*

While perusing or scanning the book looking primarily for relevance to our century, I asked myself: What lessons can Europe learn from the experience of its Western 'imperial' past? It is worth recalling that in 1787, when theoretically the Empire still existed, James Madison, the future American President, wanted to get inspiration from the Empire's experience for the organization of the United States. Nonetheless, he concluded that the Empire *"was a nervous body; incapable of regulating its own members, and agitated with unceasing fermentation of its own bowels…"* thus causing licentious behavior of the strong, oppression of the weak, confusion and misery. (p. 2) Aparently, human nature has not changed much! Yet, can the EU draw from past experience and avoid those old traps one thousand years later?

Wilson makes no direct comparisons with the European Union, but some thoughts come to mind. As emphasized, the Empire did not have clear borders and although it was based territorially on today's France, Germany and northern Italy, it did not have a stable heartland. And, it did not have a permanent capital city, unifying political institutions, and most importantly, it did not have a core 'nation.' The

Empire was in many ways a lax confederation of cities and lands that changed loyalties and alliances and survived the vagaries of time rather pragmatically. The struggles between contending princes, between emperors, kings and aristocrats, or between papal claims and secular authorities, were never ending. But, what else could have been done in a 'dark age' when kings considered themselves 'God-chosen' and the populace lacked the most elementary of rights? It was much later that nation-states took central stage in Europe and led to the modern world as we know it. Though, some similarities, differences and contradictions, can still be established between the Empire that according to Voltaire 'was neither holy nor an empire,' and the present-day European Union.

Take identity as an example. The backbone of the Empire was the Germanic people of the old, but they were far from being a homogenous stock. Language was not a unifying element either, since they spoke different tongues and identified primarily with their local states. Customs and mores were also different even among Germans. A chronicler identified among them *"cunning Swabians, greedy Bavarians who lived in poverty, quarrelsome Lorrainers prone to rebellion, and loyal Saxons..."* (p. 237). Then, identification and loyalties shifted over time and were often multiple for the same group. Even the core German area was *"a land of many languages, while political and linguistic boundaries never aligned."* (p. 259) While gradually German replaced Latin, *"the Golden Bull of 1356 specified German, Latin, Upper Italian and Czech as imperial, administrative languages."* (p. 260) Then, what can the EU learn from this almost completely forgotten Empire?

Unlike the Holy Roman Empire, the European Union has a well-defined territory and a capital city. However, like the former Empire, the EU is made up of many nations with different loyalties and identities. Worst still, instead of emphasizing its common European stock and Christian Heritage, the EU refuses to acknowledge either one of the two traits, thus building its structures on shaky ground. Nevertheless, trying to compensate for the lack of unifying laws that sapped the vanished Empire, the EU bureaucrats are enacting so many laws that they are in fact stifling normal everyday life. No wonder England has opted out of the Union!

Two other parallels can also be drawn from the evolution of the Empire. First: England was peripheral to the Empire for most of the middle ages and was also a late comer to the evolution of the European Union. But once it got involved, England became an important European player. Second: For most of their history, the Germans tried to control the Empire the same way Germany is trying to control the European Union today. In this regard, the presence of England is crucial in the EU to maintain a balance of power on the continent and especially between Germany and France. Interestingly, the author traces the rivalry between France and Germany to the ninth Century AD Franks, when Louis II was known as *rex Germanie* and his brother Charles the Bald as *rex Galliae*. (p. 256) Rivalry between France and Germany, the core of the EU, has lasted throughout the millennia. Currently, some European analysts are afraid that Germany is trying to enroll France as a partner to saddle the continent. Therefore, Great Britain is even more needed now to keep Europe in balance and to bring it close to the United States. Other than that, two more important conclusions can be drawn from the experience of the Holy Roman Empire. One is that the idea of unifying the continent is probably as old as history itself. And, another one is that as they did in the past, the Europeans would continue to bicker for a long time to come before finding a new *Modus Vivendi*. After all, this is not such a bad thing. Maybe diversity, democracy and individual cultures will be preserved in Europe!

In the last chapter of the book, the author asks himself if the former Empire can serve as a model for the organization of the European Union. From this point of view, opinions differ. Arguments are pro and con, as they were in the young United States between those who advocated strong federal powers over state powers. America, however, was a particular case. By 1776 there were many nationalities in America, but they did not have their own territorial bases and were already in a *melting pot* on their way to becoming a new nation. Unlike early America, the European nations are strongly attached to their land and languages, and are not looking toward melting themselves into a new nation. Practically, this would be impossible since the formation of national consciousness takes hundreds of years. Instead, the British historian Brendan Simms suggests that the EU should become *The United States of Europe* with clearly defined federal and state prerogatives that would suit better the future evolution of the old continent.

In conclusion, the book is too detailed for the average reader, but useful for the scholars of the field. The bibliography is also comprehensive, and as a whole, the study makes a good reference for any library. The author should be congratulated for his laborious work and dedication to the subject.

Europe's New Challenge: Wake Up or Break Apart! March 19, 2016

For more than forty years the Eastern Europeans lived under Soviet repression. During those years they dreamt of becoming free to rejoin the rest of Europe. At long last, communism collapsed, the Soviet Union imploded, and the Eastern countries regained their independence. Yet, the same countries now question Western European and especially EU policies. Why is Eastern Europe turning against the European Union?

The change in attitude toward the West has been caused by the unrealistic expectations of the Eastern countries and by the cynical attitude of the West. Politically, the West accepted the new Eastern governments although they were still under the control of the former communists. This recognition led to duplicity and hypocrisy in both regions – Eastern and Western Europe.

Economically, the West demanded the privatization of state enterprises, but the process triggered chaos and huge unemployment. Morally, the West imposed human rights as a substitute for religion and new and questionable norms of conduct. The ensuing process of globalization also undermined the newly gained independence of the Eastern European countries and threatened the very existence of their nationhood.

The reaction to the EU policies has been slow, but steady and mostly negative. While the West abandoned religion and traditions, Russia returned to old values and began to exploit the dissatisfaction of the East. Most Eastern Europeans reject Russia's new advances, but they are increasingly displeased with the West. And the recent refugee crisis and the decision to impose refugee quotas for each EU country have made some leaders take a strong stand against Brussels. In fact, the European Union is now challenged both in the East and in the West and from both sides of the political spectrum – the right and the left.

Great Britain, for example, may opt out of the union. The refugee crisis has only added fuel to the long simmering fire. The upcoming June referendum will be at least a wake-up call, if not the beginning of a painful break-up. Greece on the other hand is in a double bind – a financial crisis coupled with a flood of refugees.

Although Greece is led by a leftist government, it is deeply displeased with the EU policies. At the right of the political spectrum, the recent terrorist attacks in France and Belgium have given a boost to the right-wing movements in Western Europe. These movements also question Brussels' policies. Something is rotten with the EU and many people are up in arms. The former Soviet dissident Vladimir Bukovsky actually wrote that the EU's bureaucracy works as the former Politburo of the USSR. And, he sounded an alarm regarding the future of individual EU countries.

Opposition to the EU in Eastern Europe is currently strong in Hungary and Poland, but it is also boiling in Romania and elsewhere. Poland was the first to oppose the idea of accepting refugee quotas. However, it was Hungary that denounced the EU. Prime Minister Viktor Orban compared the EU with the former Austro-Hungarian Empire and the Soviet Union saying that those two empires were sick and destined to dismember. On March 15, Orban delivered an anniversary speech in Budapest reaffirming Hungary's national identity and blaming the EU for the current crisis. In a way, he spoke for the entire region and his long list of woes reflects many common worries in Eastern Europe. Orban emphatically declared: *"Today in Europe it is forbidden to speak the truth; to say that those arriving people are not refugees; to say that tens of millions are ready to set out in our direction; to say that this immigration brings crime and terror; to point out that masses arriving from other civilizations endanger our way of life, our culture, and our Christian traditions; to say that Brussels is now stealthily devouring our national sovereignty... Today enemies of freedom are cut from a different cloth than those who ran the Soviet system; they use a different set of tools to force us into submission...*" Orban expressed all his country's worries, but ended on a hopeful note saying, "*the task which awaits the Hungarian people, the nations of Central Europe and the other European nations which have not yet lost all common sense is to defeat, rewrite and transform the fate intended for us.*"

Each Eastern European country has its own problems, and the closer they are to Russia, the more threatened they feel. Given its geopolitical location near Russia, Romania does not dare to officially criticize the EU. However, its intellectual leaders are increasingly critical of Brussels. Gabriel Liiceanu, for example, a leading philosopher, is accusing the EU of a "*lack of leadership and determination*". According to the Romanian media, he wrote "*it is regrettable that beyond a few ridiculous and ritualistic statements, Europe was unable to come up with any plan to address the current refugee crisis.*' And further he stressed that '*many of the current refugees are incapable of respecting Europe's values while Europe's leaders are incapable of saving Europe.*"

Another leading Romanian personality, Ana Blandiana, a renowned poet and human rights activist, compares the current European crisis with the end of the Roman Empire... "*What is going on presently in Europe is beyond any logic,*" she stated recently at Cluj-Napoca University. And she continued... "*We are in the middle of a clash of civilizations and Europe has lost its faith and has denied its Christian roots....*" Then she stressed the traditional importance of the nation and of family values and criticized the 'politically correct trend' imposed by the EU. She said that Brussels is trying to impose '*new kind of families which are unable to produce children.*" Obviously she referred to LGBTs, but in the new political climate she did not dare mention them by name. And, as reported by the Romanian media, at the end of her speech she compared the EU with "*a pod of whales swimming toward an unknown shore only to commit suicide...*"

There are many people in Eastern Europe unhappy with the EU's policies. They complain of a host of issues from stressful consequences of globalization to negative effects of micro-management. They fear a new form of European socialism that could be in the end as poisonous as the old Soviet brand. And many people are revolted against their own governments for accepting centralized policies contrary to the interests and aspirations of their own nations.

It is shocking and it is sad. The former West European communists of the fifties and sixties are posing as socialists these days and are largely in charge of the EU. The former communist parties of Eastern Europe changed their names and now pose as socialists. Together they act as comrades in arms and appear prone to build another 'utopian Marxist society.' What the Soviet Union did not achieve through sheer brutality is being achieved now with kid gloves by the new authorities in Brussels. As of now no East European country has decided to leave the EU, but the seeds of discontent have been sown. Will the EU change its policies and stick together, or will Brussels stick to its gun and risk breaking up the union?

Ethnic Fragmentation in the Global Era: The Case of Catalonia. October 17, 2017

New tendencies in the world push the existing countries toward two contradictory directions. On the one hand, different countries join together in regional blocks mostly for economic reasons. On the other, some ethnic minorities, well rooted on their historic land, vie for political independence. Europe is a good case in point. Several new countries aim to adhere to the EU, while several autonomous regions are trying to become independent, but to remain part of the European Union.

On October 1st news broke that, Catalonia, an autonomous province in the northeast region of Spain and once an independent region of the Iberian Peninsula, voted in a referendum to pursue independence once again. Madrid declared the referendum illegal and warned Barcelona of consequences if it pursued secession. Catalonia may or may not succeed, but the centrifugal force toward independence lives on in Europe and elsewhere. Are we witnessing a fragmentation of the world? Some analysis is necessary.

Ethnicity is a very important factor and it is both objective and subjective. It involves a group of people who inhabit a certain territory and who share such common traits as language, culture, history, and aspirations. Our modern world is made up primarily of large ethnic groups organized in nation-states. They are the world's building blocks.

However, ethnic groups have evolved differently from place to place and not every group enjoys statehood. Granting independence to everyone would be impossible and would make the world chaotic and ungovernable. Consequently, in today's world, small ethnic groups are granted autonomy and minority protection. Yet, what should be done when large populations, such as 7.5 million Catalans, push for independence?

Recent history and current events show that there are limited options when coping with breakaway ethnic groups. One option is to grant them independence and accept the new reality. It is the case of several countries in post-communist Europe.

Another option, especially for parent countries, is to respond with military force and to try to control the pro-independence movements. It did happen in the former Yugoslavia originally consisting of a federation of six republics. Yet, one other is to resort to ethnic cleansing in order to get rid of the problem. It is the case with the Rohingya minority in today's Myanmar. Nevertheless, what could the world do in the case of the 30 million Kurds who straddle Iraq, Turkey, Syria and Iran and who aspire to independence? And what should we expect in the case of Catalonia? What is Europe's response and what is America's position?

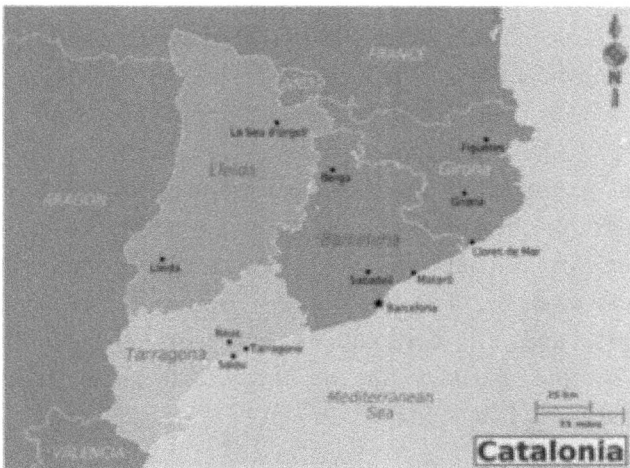

It should be recalled that it was President Woodrow Wilson who formulated the principle of self-determination of nations at the Paris peace conference in 1918. Since then, Washington's position has become somehow ambiguous. In more recent times, President Bill Clinton stated that America supports the independence movements, but only in those countries that do not respect human rights and minority rights. At the dissolution of Yugoslavia, then-Secretary of State Madeleine Albright said that Washington is against organizing the new states based on ethnic criteria. And later, President George W. Bush declared that America does not support any actions leading to the ethnic consolidation of the new states. Nonetheless, later, Washington aided the consolidation of the new Balkan nation-states to Moscow's objection.

The big question is: When is a country truly independent?

The answer is simple, but the reality is complex. A new country is considered officially independent when the United Nations recognizes its independence. For example, Kosovo was recognized as such and is now a member of the UN, but only a few countries have recognized it and Serbia considers it as part of its own territory. South Sudan was also recognized by the United Nations after a bloody and protracted war. Yet, after securing its official independence, South Sudan has been embroiled in a bloody civil war of its own. On the other hand, Somaliland, a former British colony, is a *de facto* independent country without any international recognition. The truth is that small ethnic groups can become independent and recognized as such only as long as it suits the interests of the big countries. And many times, the price for independence is paid in blood.

The current process of globalization also contributes to the world's instability. For example, the economic interests of trans-national corporations foster local aspirations, but this trend conflicts with the existing nation-states. Therefore, local aspirations, existing national governments, and big corporations must struggle continuously to maintain a fine balance among them. Otherwise, regional and international peace is in jeopardy.

In the case of Catalonia, Pandora's Box has been opened and the perspective is complicated and risky. On October 10 Catalan's president stated that the province will pursue independence, but on a more conciliatory note, he offered to negotiate with Madrid. It should be stressed that within Spain, Catalans enjoy full democratic rights and have their own regional parliament restored through the 1979 statute of autonomy. They are economically prosperous, more so than Spain as a whole. And, therein lies the rub; Spain's economic crisis requires wealthy Catalonia to pay billions of euros in taxes to Madrid inuring to the greater benefit of the European Union.

A further push for independence, however, would trigger Madrid's severe reaction and could throw the province into dangerous internal strife and further divisions. Economically, the future country would likely suffer consequences and risk international isolation. Several corporations have already announced their intent to leave Catalonia. Secession would also trigger the greater negative reaction of the European Union, which is already confronted with a host of other problems. And there is one more point: Russia is instigating the process in order to weaken Europe.

Squeezing the Buffer Zone between NATO and Russia. March 16, 2016

Cooperation between Russia and the West has been limited since the war in eastern Ukraine and since Moscow annexed Crimea. Currently, there is an uneasy peace between the two sides. Yet, while Europe is divided and accommodating toward Russia and America is focusing on the election year, Moscow is expanding its influence from Eastern Europe to the Middle East.

In Eastern Europe, Russia's goal is to keep the Baltic republics under threat, to maintain Ukraine in a state of impotence, and to gain full control over Moldova. This republic represents a grey zone between Russia and NATO. Until 1989 it belonged to the USSR, but its recent aspirations have been to join Europe.

Moldova is the poorest country of Europe, is divided ethnically and politically, and is extremely corrupt. Last year, for example, 1 billion dollars disappeared from the country's three main banks *(Unibank,*

Banca de Economii, and *Banca Sociala)*. This is a very large amount for
a country whose annual PIB is 7-to-8 billion dollars. The Romanian
ProTV station called the fraud "the theft of the century." According to
AFP, the mission chief of the EU in Moldova, Pirkka Tapiola, asked
himself in disbelief: *"How is it possible to steal such a huge amount of
money from such a small country?"* And he demanded a full
investigation, justice, and the recovery of as much as possible of the lost
money.

Faced with a public scandal and anti-governmental
demonstrations, Moldova's government commissioned an investigation
that was conducted by the American firm Kroll. The result of the
investigation was leaked to the press and showed that a number of
Moldovan leaders held stock in the banks involved. The investigation
confirmed the fraud, but could not say where the money went. The press
believes that it went most likely to Russia and to various offshore banks.

Revelation of the fraud triggered huge anti-corruption rallies.
The demonstrators demanded the arrest and prosecution of the
perpetrators. Last October, former Prime Minister Vlad Filat was
arrested for allegedly receiving $250 million in bribes for his part in the
fraud. The event is complicating Moldova's already confused political
scene.

According to *RFE/RL*, many international observers are
convinced that Russia is exploiting the protests to weaken Moldova's
pro-European tilt. In fact, many Moldovans see no way out of this
conundrum and demand reunion with Romania. However, the fraud
boosted the pro- Russian political parties and made some of their leaders
accuse the West of fomenting the crisis. To some observers, the scenario
recalls the Kiev protests of two years ago.

Expressing a Russian point of view, *Moscow Times* of 28
October 2015 stressed that this fraud by a pro-Western coalition led to
the disappointment of many Moldovans. However, it added that the local
electorate is already split and will continue to remain split. In fact,
Moscow controls Moldova through the local Russian minority, the
former Communist Party, a number of front organizations, and a network
of highly-paid agents. On one hand, Moscow is working hard to

destabilize Moldova, and on the other, it is preparing some opposition groups to take over and to bring the republic back in Russia's fold.

Moscow is also manipulating Moldova through the self-proclaimed Republic of Transdniestria (Dnestr Republic or Transnistria). While this small republic is a bone of contention between Russia and Moldova behind the back of Ukraine, Moldova itself is a battleground between Russia and NATO. Given its location, Transdniestria could be used against Ukraine, Moldova, Romania, and NATO.

Russia has already challenged NATO and the United States in the Baltic and Black Sea basin. With regard to Eastern Europe, it is said that NATO's eastern flank could not resist a Russian attack. Nevertheless, as reported by the *AP*, at a February 10 NATO meeting in Brussels, the alliance secretary general, Jens Soltenberg, acknowledged Russia's aggression and made some clarifications. He said that he wanted *"to reassure skittish allies and to deter Moscow without completely alienating the Russians in the process."* It is a step by step process, but is it achievable?

Previously, on February 2, Washington announced that it would quadruple spending on U.S. troops in Europe. Among others, America will store tanks and other military equipment in Western Europe to be airlifted and used anywhere on the continent in case of a crisis. At the Brussels meeting NATO also decided to boost *"the defenses of front-line alliance members most at risk from Russia."* In this regard, NATO mentioned the formation of a multi-national military force. *The Christian Science Monitor* of 11 February wrote that the plan provides for *"1,000 troops each in Lithuania, Latvia, Estonia, Poland, Bulgaria, and Romania, backed up by a rapid reaction force of up to 40,000 air, naval, and special operations personnel."* Some of the military and the heavy equipment will be placed in Romania. But Russia is not standing idly by.

According to confidential sources leaked to the media, Russia is currently consolidating its military forces in Transdniestria. The Bucharest TV station *Realitatea* announced that Russia modernized, militarized, and expanded the Tiraspol Airport. Tiraspol is the capital of this republic. The landing strip of the airport was lengthened to 2,500 meters to accommodate big military planes while many new military barracks were built in the area.

Allegedly, at a special session of the Russian Supreme Security Council held on January 22, President Putin was informed about that buildup and was told that everything was ready for the *'Tuman'* operation. No one knows what this operation means. At the same time, Tiraspol's Ministry of Defense announced in February that its own military forces organized important maneuvers involving tanks and other heavy equipment. Concomitantly, the leader of the Moldovan Russians, Alexandr Kalinin, appealed to President Putin to save the Russians living in Moldova. Mass media noticed that a similar appeal was addressed to Putin before the annexation of Crimea, raising the question of whether the Obama administration will react with the same lack of determination as it did with Crimea?

Eastern Europe: An Area Divided and Exposed to Russian Threats. Sept. 19, 2017

After the decision of Great Britain to leave the European Union, Europe is struggling to maintain its purpose and unity. The North Atlantic Alliance (NATO) is also confronted with new challenges, and America is faced with an increasingly aggressive Russia.

In that new climate, Eastern Europe is, once again, a bone of contention caught between East and West. The balance of power between the two camps is maintained by NATO with the United States as its chief guarantor. According to several analysts, Poland to the north and Romania to the south represent America's strategic shield against Russia. However, Moscow is trying hard to destabilize the region, and Washington has few options opposing Moscow and maintaining local stability.

Unfortunately, Eastern Europe is a mosaic of countries and nationalities with contradictory and often hostile interests. Poland, for example, is ethnically a homogenous country and is less prone to Russian subversion. But Warsaw is worried about the prospect of international destabilization and Russia's intentions. Consequently, Poland is consolidating its military power. Romania, on the other hand, is a nation divided with a large number of ethnic Romanians living across its eastern border and with a large Hungarian minority living inside its borders. That makes Romania easy prey to Russian subversion and instigation. Yet, because of its strategic location at the Black Sea and because of its natural resources, Romania is important to America and to the West.

With a long history of victimization, Romania mistrusts Russia and is strongly pro-Western. The country wrestles with ethnic and territorial issues which Moscow exploits. Romania's eastern-most province, currently the Republic of Moldova and formerly Bessarabia, is still under Russian control. Moscow is using this republic to blackmail Bucharest and to destabilize the region. In 1944 the American diplomat Malborne Graham wrote that this region represents *"the most critical territorial problem bequeathed to the present generation as a direct legacy of the age-old Eastern Question." A* bone of contention indeed!

When the USSR dismembered in 1991, Moscow offered to let the newly independent republic of Moldova reunite with Romania, if Bucharest would not join NATO. Nevertheless, Bucharest opted for the West and allied itself with the United States. Russia reacted bitterly with threats, with more political interference in Moldova, and with instigating Hungary to reopen its territorial claims on Transylvania.

Take Moldova for example. During the last several years, Moldova was pursuing a pro-Romanian and pro-NATO policy, but Moscow would not tolerate it. During this year's elections, Moscow mobilized its local Russian minority and the pro-communist groups, rigged the polls, and elected a pro-Russian president.

The new president rushed to meet Vladimir Putin in Moscow and after his return reversed Moldova's pro-Western tilt. The new authorities also muzzled the press, stopped its cooperation with NATO, and began to harass the pro-Western Moldovan leaders. They also arrested Dorin Chirtoaca, the mayor of Chisinau, who is a strong pro-European advocate. That made the democratic opposition appeal to the European Union for remedial measures, but so far to no avail. Here is an excerpt from the letter sent to Brussels by the leaders of Moldova's pro-Western parties, namely, the European People's Party and the Alliance of Liberals and Democrats for Europe:*"We are bringing to your attention a major problem concerning recent political events that have occurred in the*

Republic of Moldova. The legally elected mayor of Chisinau, Dorin Chirtoaca, was arrested under false accusations and is currently detained... We are witnessing with increasing concern the deterioration of the rule of law and democratic standards in the Republic of Moldova... Instead of seeking to advance the country toward democracy the socialists have chosen to strengthen autocracy... "

Regarding the Republic of Moldova, and also Ukraine, in his book *In the Shade of Europe* published last year, Robert Kaplan claims that the two countries remain under the thumb of Russia. A possible reunion of Moldova with Romania is not possible under the present conditions. As for Transylvania, located in western Romania, when interviewed by the newspaper *Romania Libera* on February 26, 2017, Kaplan answered that Moscow is instigating Budapest to revive the idea of *Greater Hungary* to the detriment of Romania and possibly of Serbia and Slovakia. Kaplan stressed that Russia is further determined to divide and control Eastern Europe.

In his view, Serbia, Bulgaria, and the other Slavic countries of the region have linguistic, cultural and historic links to Russia, while Romania is isolated and targeted. On the other hand, Hungary is under Russian influence and manipulation. Kaplan does not believe that *Greater Hungary* is a viable option, but he thinks that deep in their hearts the Hungarians still dream of recuperating their lost territories. Transylvania is their first target. Not surprisingly, President Putin's recent visit to Budapest has increased Bucharest's worries.

Russia's influence over Hungary recently manifested itself when Budapest opposed Romania's admission to several Western European multilateral organizations. For example, this September Hungary opposed the integration of Romania in the European Organization for Cooperation and Economic Development (OECD). Obviously, Moscow knows how to divide Europe, while Washington is confronted with a challenge keeping the old continent together and safeguarding America's interests.

A Little Publicized Meeting Took Place in Romania. May 10, 2016

A conference, Our Europe-A Europe of Nations, took place unexpectedly on April 16 at Sinaia in Romania, the renowned mountain resort of Peles Castle and the former residence of Romanian kings. The meeting was organized by the new Romanian nationalist party *Forta Nationala,* and was attended by delegates representing several countries, including Marine Le Pen, president of the National Front in France. The event received limited press coverage from the traditional media, but it was well-covered by social media, including the *RBN.ro* and by *pressone.ro* on April 20.

The meeting was strange because true nationalism in Romania is in retreat, while a form of 'parade' nationalism is encouraged by certain forces, and especially by Russia. Among the Romanian participants were Laurentiu Rebegea, currently a member of the European Parliament, and an active member of Le Pen's faction, Europe of Nations; Victor Craciun, a dubious individual with strong ties to Moscow; and, Mircea Chelaru, an honest Romanian patriot, but apparently with little political acumen. There were also many enthusiastic young people, as well as older men described by the press as nostalgic for the old times.

The atmosphere of the Sinaia meeting was festive, and the event was apparently well-orchestrated. However, the main topic of the conference was both anti-West and anti-European Union. In her speech, for example, Marine Le Pen assured Romania that the country would be better off if it left the EU, which she described as 'a drifting ship without a compass,' and 'a total failure.' Le Pen questioned the EU's future, calling it 'a threat to its inhabitants.' Instead, she proposed a Union '*from the Atlantic to the Ural Mountains*'... a Europe that would also include Russia.

The conference was well-attended. Among the important foreign participants were: Ludovic De Danne, spokesman for the French National Front and secretary general of the Europe of Nations group in the European Parliament; Marcel De Graaf, Dutch member of the European Parliament and co-president of the same group; Tomio Okamura, president of the Movement for Liberty and Democracy from the Czech Republic; Riccardo Molinari, vice-president of the Northern League of Italy; Johannes Hübner, representing the Liberal Party of Austria; and, Zbigniew Jarząbek, representing the New Right Party of Poland.

While the speeches condemned the European Union and the policy of the West, the attendees kept applauding apparently without much thinking or reasoning. Nevertheless, there is a dangerous duality afoot in Eastern Europe. On the one hand many people are justifiably wary of the EU's current policy. On the other hand, Russia is working hard to influence European hearts and minds against the EU, America and globalization. Within this political climate, the Sinaia conference was most likely staged with Moscow's support. While the Romanians do not trust Russia, Moscow has its own agents everywhere and sadly, it also has some real arguments on its side.

The journalists who covered the conference understood the ploy behind the event and asked some probing questions. They asked Marine Le Pen if her organization is financed by Russia and what are her relations with Moscow. Ms. Le Pen answered laughingly that when she needed help to finance her campaign neither French nor Western banks would grant her any loan. Then, she said that she found a Czech-Russian bank that offered her a loan. And she asked the journalist: '*Do you know any Romanian bank that would give me a loan? I will sign the contract immediately...* '

The reality is that for a good number of years Russia has been working to secure support throughout the EU including Southeastern Europe. In neighboring Moldova, for instance, Russia has the upper hand and is buying power and influence. Yet, the Moldovan/Romanian majority of the republic is struggling to oppose Moscow and to link with Romania and the West. To the south of Romania, in Bulgaria and Serbia, Russia is using its common ethnic and cultural roots to draw the population to its side. And Hungary, located west of Romania, is already vocal against the EU. As for Romania, throughout its history the country has been a thorn in Russia's expansion toward the Balkans. This is one of the reasons why Russia has changed its strategy and now is trying to enlist the Romanian nationalists for their opposition to America and the West.

However, a tragic history has taught the Romanians to be wary of Russia's intentions. This is why after 1989 they placed their hope with America, NATO and the West. Would the West let them down again as it did in the 1940s? Apparently not. A recent U.S. decision seems to justify this trust.

According to Romanian media, elements of two American cavalry regiments will arrive at Iassy, the historic capital of Moldova located in Romania, where they will join a Romanian motorized battalion. Together, they will then cross the Prut River toward the city of Balti in the Republic of Moldova, where they will be joined by a Moldovan military unit. On May 9, when Moscow celebrates with great fanfare its victory at the end of World War II, the combined military force of the three countries will parade together in downtown Chisinau to present America's modern military technology. The U.S. military will remain in Moldova until May 29 as part of the larger maneuvers known as Atlantic Resolve. This participation will be a boost to the pro-Western aspirations of the Moldovans and a warning for Russia's aggression in Eastern Europe.

A word of caution is still necessary. America and the West will have to change their political, economic and moral policies in the region. Otherwise, Russia will make even more inroads.

Is Romania Approaching a Second Revolution?
February 13, 2017

Since the beginning of February, Romania has been rocked by an unprecedented series of protests causing internal turmoil and attracting minimal international attention. Largely unreported in the United States, over 200 thousand people demonstrated daily against governmental corruption in Bucharest and another 200 thousand protested in 20 different cities across the country. Romanian expatriates also organized public protests in several Western countries, and in Sofia the Bulgarians organized a rally of support condemning at the same time corruption in their own country.

What triggered such huge rallies? Is Romania facing a second revolution? To answer these questions, one has to understand what communism meant for Romania and Eastern Europe. This is even more important today since the Western media is acting as if it wants to forget communism; as if nothing out of the ordinary happened under those hated regimes.

Communism was forced upon Eastern Europe by Soviet tanks. No country would freely and willingly elect or accept a communist regime. By imposing communism in East Europe, Moscow aimed at expanding the Soviet geopolitical sphere and at annihilating growing nationalism. As for Western Europe, Moscow helped the local communists against a revived Europe, especially against America. Interestingly, the former Western European communists have rebranded themselves as socialists or social democrats and are now in control of the EU bureaucracy.

Romania is a typical Eastern European example of post-war Soviet occupation. By 1944 when the Soviet troops occupied the country, Romania had close to 20 million inhabitants and a miniscule communist party numbering less than one thousand. Of those members and by official communist statistics, some 80 percent were non-Romanian ethnics who hated the Romanian nation. With Soviet help, those individuals imposed one of the most brutal Stalinist regimes. Then, after about 20 years of Soviet-type communism, Nicolae Ceausescu took over the party and imposed his own ruthless regime. By 1989, during the European uprisings, Romanians were fed up with their dictator and joined eagerly the public protests against his regime. They had hoped that once toppling Ceausescu, they would get rid of communism all together. They were wrong!

By changing their name to social-democrats, the communists remained in power. Ceausescu was replaced with Ion Iliescu, a communist who had studied in Moscow where he had been a colleague of Mikhail Gorbachev. With Iliescu in power, the former secret police, *Securitate*, changed its name and with a few internal rearrangements remained behind the new authorities.

What followed was a travesty of justice and democracy. Economically, the former communists ripped off the country. That meant faked privatizations to suit their interests, embezzlements, traffic of influence, nepotism and acts of corruption at the highest level.

By taking over the economic reins, they also managed to manipulate the political elections. At the same time and to protect themselves, the new authorities cultivated a pro-American image and courted Western businesses to engage in profitable operations in Romania. Consequently, for a long while the population was quiet, but underneath the surface the dissatisfaction was boiling.

In 2015, Romania elected a new president who had not been a communist. The population was again enthusiastic hoping that this time the country was finally on a course correction. However, soon after his election, President Klaus Iohannis fell under the influence of those who manipulate the power behind the scene. Then, following the December 2016 parliamentary elections, the Social-Democrat Party (PSD, former communists) won a plurality and designated Liviu Dragnea as prime minister. But Dragnea had a suspended prison sentence for corruption and was not eligible for the position. As chief of the PSD, he appointed Sorin Grindeanu as prime minister to act as his proxy.

Late, during the night of 31 January the newly sworn-in government secretly approved a controversial ordinance (*Ordonanta de urgenta* 13/2017) that would pardon certain crimes and would modify the Penal Code. The ordinance amnestied many previous cases of corruption and watered down the current law, decriminalizing any case involving less than about 48 thousand dollars. (The average monthly salaries in Romania are 300 to 400 hundred dollars. For most Romanians, $48 thousand is a huge amount). This decree triggered the current furor and numerous rallies of protest. Wisely, President Iohannis sided with the protesters announcing that he would challenge the decree in the Constitutional Court.

The government tried to contain the demonstrations, but when it did not work, rumors were spread that Romania is under threats of dismemberment and the protesters are weakening the country. Indeed, the new pro-Russian Moldovan president alluded recently, in a threatening way, to the Romanian-held part of the historic Principality of Moldova. At the same time, Russia's President Vladimir Putin paid a visit to Budapest and inferred support of the Hungarian claims over Romanian Transylvania. Yet, the protesters did not budge. On February 6, seven days into rallies, the *Guardian* interviewed many protesters and published a well-documented article. According to the British newspaper, the protesters, the majority of them young people, would not trust the government and cited as causes 27 years of corruption, as well as huge unemployment, deteriorating public education and a very poor public health system.

After several days of demonstrations and confronted with a situation in a way similar to the 1989 revolt that toppled Ceausescu, the prime minister announced that he would rescind the decree. In his words, the government would send a proposal to the Parliament for debate and review of the case. The protesters would not believe him and demanded the resignation of the entire government. And the slogans and signs they have been carrying speak for themselves: *'PSD is communism,' 'the only solution is another revolution,'* and an English sign reads *'Make Jilava great again!'* Jilava is a big prison near Bucharest. (I know it because I was held there as a political prisoner).

It is hard to compare the current revolt with the 1989 revolution. In 1989 the West pursued and helped to bring about radical changes in Eastern Europe, probably in anticipation of the globalization process that followed. Now, the West wants only cosmetic changes to fit the policy and interests of the European Union. Many Romanians disagree with some of the EU laws and rulings, but they do not want to leave the organization. As for the policy of the United States, people are worried because of the allegedly good relations between President Donald Trump and President Vladimir Putin. In this regard, the Romanians are waiting apprehensively to see how the future American-Russian relations are going to evolve and affect Europe.

Chapter 9
Recent American Policy and Attitudes

Obama's Multicultural America and the Transformation of a Nation. Sep. 29, 2015

Since the end of the Cold War relations between Washington and Moscow have fluctuated from open and amicable to cool and suspicious. Presently, they seem to be contradictory and difficult to grasp, though, one thing is sure: Russia is doing everything to keep the "Near Abroad" under its control while harassing American interests globally wherever it can.

Washington is promoting a number of policies that are rejected, however, by a good part of the world. This poses a risk in the global psychological warfare for the hearts and minds of the people and risks isolating America.

From a cultural point of view societies are seen as pyramids. At the very base of the pyramid are the social relations among people and the relation between societies and the environment. This level of daily *Behavior* represents *what* we do for a living and *how* we do it. It is mostly a visible and measurable world easy to understand. It is at this level where societies *negotiate, agree, disagree and compromise* on various local or international issues. At the top of the cultural pyramid is our *World View,* meaning, what we think the purpose of life is. This is an invisible realm where concepts and consciousness reside and which answers to the question, *what is true or what we believe truth is.* And at this level negotiations are very difficult and compromise is virtually impossible.

The gap between *what we* do for a living and our *world view* is bridged by *Beliefs* and *Values.* Beliefs are important because people do believe in God and have faith. While beliefs are stable, our values tame our behavior and put us in harmony with our world view. In an increasingly globalized world, challenging beliefs and values can undermine everything and can push the world toward chaos. Unfortunately, America is increasingly challenging traditional views.

In God We Trust may now read *In God We Trusted*. It is obvious that the society of today is no longer a God-fearing and Christian values oriented society. Many people have lost their faith, some churches are now empty, and values have been turned upside down. Some fifty years ago America was a stable democracy, feared God and opposed God-less Communism. Now, the classic *beliefs* have not been abandoned, but traditional *values* have been emptied of most content. Officially, America no longer professes Christianity. President Obama has discontinued the Christian Prayer Week that used to gather Christians from all over the world. And, Obama is just one symptom that confronts the society. A recent poll shows that only about 10 percent of the people trust Congress. What kind of representative government is this if Americans do not trust the very people they elect? The truth is that something is wrong, and people are restless and looking for answers. Here are some controversial issues Washington is condoning that confuse the world and feed our enemies.

America is divided on the issues of immigration, multiculturalism and minority rights. Responsible people would like to control immigration and maintain a balanced society. Liberals favor freer immigration and embrace multiculturalism and minority points of view. Yet, multiculturalism is diluting national feelings without fostering democracy or cementing a new sense of nationhood. Another touchy issue is promoting minority rights. Imposing LGBT precepts transformed as rights, for example, is now the new normal for most of the media and for authorities. Thirty to forty years ago one would find a Bible by the bedside of every hotel-motel room. Now, some schools distribute condoms and 'morning after' pills to students. What moral message is America transmitting to the world? Most countries reject this trend. According to reliable statistics between 95 and 99 percent of the people in Africa reject these social policies. Yet, African governments are chastised regularly by U.S. officials for violating human rights.

The concept of human rights is a welcome code of conduct. Respecting human rights is strongly demanded by the State Department. Human rights, however, is a *horizontal* code that governs relations among people. It cannot replace religion, which is a *vertical* code connecting us to a spiritual realm. There is nothing wrong with human rights, except that it misses out God. It was during a God-fearing era when John Paul II was pope and Ronald Reagan was president, when American society combined spirituality with morality and brought communism to its knees. Today, we should heed President Reagan's warning: *"When we will forget that we are a nation subordinated to God, we will simply become a subordinated nation."*

These days the world is again divided and Russia is engaged in subtle but discernible psychological warfare against America. And Russia is now using both spiritual and moral values arguments. Moscow is attempting to gain the support of the political right by appealing to spiritual values and of the political left by defending the downtrodden.

While Russia is openly anti-gay, for example, and rejects the new mores imposed by America and the West, Eastern Europe is vulnerable to Russia's schemes. The truth is that freedom in Eastern Europe came with a host of socio-economic woes. And there are social ills, prostitution and promiscuity unknown before. People are already questioning the intent and purpose of Western values. While many people are looking for a moral shore to drop anchor, America is promoting same-sex marriage as human rights. This flawed approach has already alienated many friends and has fed into existing anti-American attitudes. If Russia should ever win the current psychological warfare, it is only because of the weaknesses of America and the wickedness of the West. Where is that exceptional moral America that stood up to God-less Communism and won the Cold War?

Facing a Crucial Election Year: Will Traditional Values Survive? February 29, 2016

The American dream ended on November 6th, 2012 in Ohio, declared Reverend Franklin Graham. *"The second term of Barack*

Obama has been the final nail in the coffin for the legacy of the Christian males who discovered, explored, pioneered, settled and developed the greatest republic in the history of mankind... Feminists, gays, government workers, union members, environmental extremists, the media, Hollywood, uninformed young people, the 'forever needy,' the chronically unemployed, illegal aliens and other fellow travelers have ended Norman Rockwell's America..."

In Franklin Graham's opinion, traditional America will never out-vote these people. Conservative Americans, he continued, are now politically irrelevant and will probably never be able to legally challenge the new trend. In his view, the American Constitution has been replaced with Saul Alinsky's *Rules for Radicals* and with the views of such people like the international socialist George Soros. They and their acolytes have brought us 'Act 2' of the New World Order, he said, and, paraphrasing a passage from the Declaration of Independence, he added: *"Those who come after us will once again have to risk their lives, their fortunes and their sacred honor to bring back the Republic that this generation has timidly frittered away due to white guilt and political correctness."*

Reverend Graham is not alone. In fact, many God-fearing patriots have foreseen and feared this God-less evolution of American society. In his 2009 book *Liberty and Tyranny- A Conservative Manifesto*, author Mark Levin also observed that morally, politically and economically the United States has departed from its original purpose and is going on a dangerous path. And he quoted George Washington, who wrote that religion and morality are indispensable to political prosperity. One may legitimately ask: where is morality in today's world?

The new political tendency in America is toward some form of state interventionism and socialism. If 20 to 30 years ago this trend was hidden, today the leftist leaders make no bones about it. The reality is that such individuals try to use the state for their own goals. All this is allegedly done in the name of the people and for the benefits of the masses. In this regard, C.S. Lewis wrote: *"Of all tyrannies, a tyranny sincerely exercised for the good of its victims may be the most oppressive."*

Levin also quotes Alexis de Tocqueville, who observed that *"Democracy and Socialism have nothing in common but one word – equality."* But there is a difference. *"While democracy seeks equality in liberty, socialism seeks equality in restraint and servitude."* Is America going this way? It seems so, and Reverend Graham is right to be worried. Traditional and Christian America has already changed. The present is murky and the future is risky. President Barack Hussein Obama has renounced the Congressional Christian Prayer Week.

The situation of Western Europe and the European Union is even worse from a moral point of view. For instance, the traditional Brussels Christmas Fair has already changed its name. The Western European media is avoiding any references to Christianity, while the leftist leaders avoid being photographed with a church or a cross in the background. As for the Christmas greeting cards, the new trend is to use *season* or *winter greetings* to avoid offending Muslims. And, there are increasing voices to ban altogether Santa Clause and any reference to Christmas. All these trends occur, while millions of Muslim immigrants flood into Europe and display openly their abhorrence for Western and Christian values.

Together, with a strong anti-Christian campaign, there is also an endless effort in Europe to promote the collective rights of LGBTs and to enforce strong laws against those who criticize this group. For example, a law debated recently in the Romanian Parliament provides fines of up to US $25,000 (100,000 *Lei*) for anyone who criticizes LGBTs even on the Internet or on any social media, such as *Facebook*. An average monthly salary in Romania is about 300 US dollars.

As reported by Romanian media, Gabriele Kuby, a German sociologist, a mother of three and a writer, came to Romania to promote her new book, *The Global Sexual Revolution: Destroying Liberty in the Name of Liberty.* In her opinion, Western Europe is virtually a lost cause but there is still hope in Eastern Europe. Among others, she warned her audiences that early sexual education ruins the childhood of the kids; the much advocated new gender orientations destroy family values; and the new sex trends in the West turn Christian values upside down. In her opinion, these are done purposely to destroy Europe's traditional values. Can America and Europe oppose this trend? Or will they succumb to the left's dogma of political correctness in a new dark age of social debauchery and political instability?

The late American sociologist and Harvard professor Samuel Huntington warned us over 20 years ago that the future could trigger a clash of civilizations. Have we arrived at that future? He also wrote that the decay of the West may occur gradually, but he cautioned that it may slide on an S curve, slow in the beginning and rapid thereafter, and thus come up very quickly as it did in the former Soviet Union. As for signs of decay, Huntington cited increasing crime and violence, drug abuse and social disintegration. One may add these days another dangerous sign – social polarization.

America of *anno domini* 2016, a year of crucial elections, is at a historic crossroad. The society at large and its political leaders are divided and polarized as never before. Will the upcoming presidential election be an attempt at returning to traditional values, or a fall into the socialist abyss guarded by the left's dogma of political correctness ending forever Reverend Franklin Graham's American dream? The day of reckoning is upon us.

President Trump's Foreign Policy: The Case of Eastern Europe. July 25, 2017

Washington's foreign policy under President Trump must address a series of global challenges. One of them is confronting Russia's attitude in Europe.

Moscow is using the carrot to lure Western Europe away from America and the stick to threaten Eastern Europe – defined as the former Soviet satellite countries plus the three Baltic republics that regained their independence after the dissolution of the Union of Socialist Soviet Republics (USSR). These countries stretch from the Baltic Sea to Central Europe and further south to the Black Sea. Their integration into NATO has upset Russia, and the newly created American military bases in Poland and Romania have enraged it. What has led to this new East-West confrontation and what is to be expected?

Except for Ukraine, an Eastern European country that Moscow will never give up willingly, Poland, Romania, Lithuania, Latvia and Estonia are the countries that historically suffered most at the hands of the Soviet Union. To safeguard their independence, these countries joined the North Atlantic Alliance. As a candidate, Donald Trump downplayed the importance of NATO giving the impression he would cozy up to Moscow. He was less vocal toward the Russian annexation of Crimea and showed little interest for Eastern Europe. This attitude created confusion and concern among many Eastern Europeans. However, once in the White House, he had to face the cold reality of the world as it is. And Europe figured high on his international agenda.

Several political analysts have stressed the importance of Eastern Europe in what is a new period of chilly U.S.-Russian relations; analysts such as George Friedman of Stratfor, Robert Kaplan, Marek Jan Chodakiewicz and Richard Haass. They have stressed the importance of the 'Intermarium,' the land between the Baltic and Black seas, in deterring Russia's new aggressive posture. The area was also stretched to the Adriatic Sea. In the view of these geopolitical analysts, Poland and Romania represent the new pivots of NATO's defense. They stress that the two countries are strongly pro-American and staunch NATO supporters. Indeed, the United States has focused militarily on Poland and Romania. And, as president, Donald Trump has shown good sense and realism toward these countries.

On June 9, President Trump invited Romania's President Klaus Iohannis to the White House and reassured Bucharest of U.S. support and cooperation. On the same occasion, President Trump reaffirmed his support for Eastern Europe and for strengthening NATO. Iohannis was the first Eastern European president hosted officially by President Trump. Then, in July Trump went to Poland, the first East European country visited by the new commander-in-chief. Addressing an enthusiastic audience in Warsaw, President Trump's speech was inspiring. The speech was posted on the White House web site and reported by many newspapers. Mr. Trump declared: *"I am here today not just to visit an old ally, but to hold it up as an example for others who seek freedom and who wish to summon the courage and the will to defend our civilization.... Today, the West is also confronted by the powers that seek to test our will... We urge Russia to cease its destabilizing activities in Ukraine and elsewhere... Americans know that a strong alliance of free, sovereign and independent nations is the best defense for our freedoms..."*

Following Trump's visit, Poland and Romania increased their military spending and decided to acquire American Patriot missile defense systems. President Trump's speech was reassuring. Yet, we should remember what Chodakiewicz wrote in his 2012 book, which I reviewed: *"Moscow's aim is to re-impose its control over Eastern Europe... an area where the United States lacks a coherent geopolitical vision."* And he added a warning: *"America may no longer take for granted the support of its foreign policy by the nations of the post-Soviet sphere..."* That was in 2012. We are now in 2017 and there still are questions that need answers. It is now all in the hands of President Trump.

Trump Hosts Romania's President, Klaus Iohannis.
June 20, 2017

In 2014 Romania elected a new president and many people were hoping for a break with the long period of murky transition from its past as a captive nation in Eastern Europe under Soviet domination to an independent nation. But the enthusiasm was short-lived. President Klaus Iohannis wanted to consolidate Romania's relations with the European Union and to fight domestic corruption. However, even if Iohannis had the best intentions, he found himself enmeshed in an already corrupt system surrounded by individuals whose interests were to stay in power and get rich at any price. The former secret police and party apparatchiks have remained the *gatekeepers* for any change.

As for the people, most Romanians have become wary about globalization and the evolution of the EU and about the Russian infiltration of the continent. Consequently, while many Romanians continued to admire America, some started to doubt Washington's policy. Romania's importance to the United States, both strategically as a NATO ally and bilaterally as a partner, and economically for its resources and potential, prompted the invitation of Iohannis to the White House.

Of all the problems confronting Europe under the new U.S. administration, most concerning are Russia's cozying up to Western Europe, America's commitment to NATO, and President Trump's perceived relationship with Putin's Russia. These problems worry the Eastern Europeans. Thus, there are increasingly more people questioning the attitude of their government in economics and foreign policy. Many Romanians, for example, question the blind submission of their country to Western and American interests.

Meanwhile, the Russians are using the dissatisfaction of the people to influence Eastern European politics. So far, Moscow has succeeded, especially in Hungary, and is now encroaching upon and threatening Romania. Confronted by an ever-hostile Russia and without real friends, Romania has turned again to the United States. With this background, on June 9 Donald Trump hosted Romania's President Klaus Iohannis at the White House.

The visit was very well-covered by the Romanian news agencies and to a lesser degree by the American media, but largely ignored by Western Europe. The event represented a boost to Romania's prestige and to the legitimacy of its leadership. During the visit, President Trump reiterated America's commitment to the Atlantic Alliance, to Romania, and to Eastern Europe. The two presidents also discussed the need to fight international terrorism, to continue to combat corruption, and to strengthen NATO.

Following President Trump's insistence that Alliance members should increase their financial contributions, Iohannis promised to increase Romania's military spending to over two percent of its GDP. He also emphasized that Romania is the most pro-American country in the European Union and asked Trump to help the Republic of Moldova with its pro-Western efforts. President Trump praised Romania and stressed the importance of further developing bilateral relations.

For Bucharest, the event was a publicity coup. For Washington, it was an opportunity to clarify certain controversial declarations previously made about NATO. For example, asked at the joint press conference by a journalist whether he thought the United States should act under Article 5, if any Alliance countries were attacked, President Trump answered without hesitation: *"I am committing the United States to Article 5 and certainly we are there to protect."* Previously, at a NATO meeting in Brussels, he was vague on this issue and actually lambasted the Alliance members for not spending enough money on defense.

Iohannis' visit was reassuring for those Eastern European NATO countries that feel threatened by Russia. For the Western European leaders, the message sent by President Trump was that they must meet the two percent of GDP standard annual payment for defense requirements. An implied message was that the European leaders should stop cozying up to Russia and remember that America kept peace and fostered prosperity on the continent for more than seven decades, while Russia threatened Europe and is now trying to divide it. At least one book, as well as a number of articles published recently point to Moscow's hostility.

Thoughts at the End of an Important Year.
December 15, 2017

In January, many Americans were enthusiastic about the election of a new president – Donald Trump. Like any new administration, the track record is mixed but in Trump's case not for lack of trying to enact his ambitious agenda to "Make America Great Again."

The American economy is robust. Government regulations have been slashed. The Dow Jones Industrial average has gained well over 30 percent, while the S&P 500 is up more than 20 percent. Economic growth is up and unemployment is markedly down. While the Republican-controlled Congress failed to repeal Obamacare (socialized medicine), it appears poised to pass significant tax cuts for the middle class, the first since President Reagan's 1986 tax cuts.

President Trump has filled the Supreme Court vacancy left by the death of conservative jurist Antonin Scalia with the equally conservative Neil Gorsuch and appears likely to fill several others with like-minded appointments before the completion of his first four years in office.

The White House has had mixed results with border control, illegal immigration, and refugee resettlement. The European Union on the other hand has begun court actions against Poland, Hungary, and the Czech Republic over migrant quotas, which they reject.

Yet, the White House has experienced persistent opposition from the Establishment and resistance from elements of both political parties. The country is deeply divided; the Republicans and the Democrats talk over the peoples' heads.

Politically, the presidency is embroiled in what can be described as "probe politics" suggesting a murky affair over its alleged deals with Moscow, when none are evident a year after taking office. At the same time, it has been brought to light that the previous administration was responsible for spying on the Trump campaign and for selling 20 percent of America's valuable uranium supply to Moscow.

Internationally, the world is increasingly troubled. North Korea, in league with Cuba and Iran, is headed by a rogue leader and an unpredictable regime threatening the world with nuclear weapons. China is reluctant to intervene, and Russia is most likely enjoying America's predicament. There are problems everywhere. Over six hundred thousand Muslim refugees are in Bangladesh; half-a-million African refugees in Libya want to cross the sea into Europe; and hundreds of thousands of Arab refugees in Turkey also want to come to Western Europe. The Donbas conflict in eastern Ukraine where pro-Russian partisans seek union with Russia is ongoing and remains unresolved since 2014. The Obama-Clinton failed 'reset' policy led directly to Russian expansion and the annexation of Crimea. Can the world cope with such calamities?

Meanwhile, big American and international corporations seeking cheap labor continue to push for globalization's open borders. Did they ever explain to the world what globalization's consequences might be? What we observe so far are: polarization, inequity, godlessness, irrational behavior, extremism, and international terrorism. The 'rational' response of many citizens in the U.S. and in Europe is a growing anti-establishment attitude.

Something is wrong, and many people sense it, but they are not sure of what to do. However, change is coming. In the 2016 Brexit Referendum, Britons decided to seek a divorce from the European Union, and the decoupling process that is ongoing will continue through 2018 and beyond. France elected a young inexperienced president who promised to change the political system. Many Germans are questioning the chancellor's open borders and immigration policy. In response, nationalism has made important inroads in several European countries.

In a recent article published by *The Washington Times*, the American Middle East analyst Daniel Pipes examines the new wave of European nationalism and comes to some insightful conclusions and warnings.

Nationalist parties, he writes, *"now have a toehold everywhere from Italy to Finland raising fears the continent is backpedaling toward the kinds of policies that led to catastrophe in the first half of the 20th century."* In this regard, he adds, many Jews fear *"a real threat from populist movements across Europe."* Pipes realizes, however, that the new trend in Europe is primarily caused by the recent uncontrolled immigration. Jews are fleeing Europe and Islamist France in ever increasing numbers. Yet, Europe is in a double bind: On the one hand, it needs immigrants to man its economy, and on the other, it is unwilling to address the real causes of its problems. The result is dissatisfaction with centralized EU official policies expressed more and more openly in Eastern Europe.

Ana Blandiana, a well-known Romanian social activist, stated recently that the EU is committing suicide. In her opinion, Europe has lost its traditional [Christian] faith and it does not believe in anything anymore. Further, she wrote, the current political correctness is placing the very liberty of expression under a big question mark. (*Active News*, 28 November 2017). No wonder Romanians are reasserting their own identity and nationalism is growing. A new study done by the Romanian Information Service warns that the birth of a nationalistic party is imminent. The situation is similar in most Eastern European countries that experienced Communism. Nationalism is taking a firm stand against a god-less European Union and against globalization.

The questions are: Who is behind globalization and why is America continuing to embrace it? Worse still, some people liken the current trend with the defunct policy of global Communism advanced in the past by the USSR. Hopefully, such people are wrong. The year 2018 should start to shed some light on the future direction of our nation and the world.

America's Policy: U.S. Romanian Common Interests. February 26, 2018

The United States has vital economic and security interests in Eastern Europe from the Baltic Sea to the Black Sea and further to the Caucasus region. This is the fault line where NATO and the West meet Russia and the East. With Russia displaying an increasingly aggressive, yet, sometimes subtle, attitude towards Europe, Washington must take a stand. It is obvious that Moscow is not giving up control of Ukraine, and it is also obvious that the three Baltic Republics cannot withstand Moscow's pressure by themselves, especially with Kaliningrad to their immediate south. Therefore, NATO's and America's defense line in the East rests mostly upon Poland and Romania. And the importance of Romania in south-east Europe has grown recently after Turkey began to focus on its own geo-political goals that are different from those pursued by the United States. Consequently, Washington's relations with Bucharest have intensified.

American-Romanian relations are geo-political, economic, and military in nature. Geo-politically, Romania is wary of Moscow's intentions. It is this danger that opened Romania to military cooperation with the United States. At the same time, the Trump administration stressed the U.S. commitment to expand its missile defenses and to cover Eastern Europe. And this is where American-Romanian military cooperation began. As a result, the American military has already been welcomed at the *Mihail Kogalniceanu* Air Base by the Black Sea and at the *Deveselu* base in southern Romania. Subsequently, Romanian and American armed forces have organized joint exercises near the Black Sea. According to *Ziare.com* of February 14, 2017, some 500 American soldiers accompanied by a tank unit arrived in Romania on that date. In addition, American navy warships began to visit the Romanian Black Sea Port of Constanta.

The most important American military installation in Romania is located near the town of Deveselu, where the site hosts the Lockheed Martin-built Aegis Ashore Ballistic Missile Defense System. It became operational in May 2016 and it is the first of two such East European interceptor sites. The second one will be completed this year in Poland. Both systems display technology used on U.S. Navy destroyers and cruisers to protect against ballistic missile threats. In this regard, on December 7, 2017, the Hudson Institute held a special meeting hosting George Maior, the Romanian Ambassador to Washington, who emphasized the common interests of the U.S. and Romania. On the American side, Rebeccah Heinrichs, senior fellow of the Hudson Institute, discussed the goals and progress of U.S.-Romanian missile defense cooperation.

During the post-communist years, Romanian media have shown real interest in cooperation with the United States. Most articles offer objective data and are generally favorable to increased bilateral relations and military cooperation. For example, *Hotnews.ro* of June 25, 2015, mentioned that in 2014 there were 620 American military personnel stationed in Romania and that their number was expected to grow. Russia, however, considers this military presence as a direct threat to its territory. Accordingly, on May 15, 2016, *Evenimentul Zilei (evz.ro)* published a picture of an angered Vladimir Putin accompanied by a Russian general threatening Romania. The article's title speaks for itself (translated): *"Romania could become the victim of a nuclear war. The message comes from Russia. Moscow is boiling after the American military activated the Deveselu Base."* According to another newspaper, *Cotidianul.ro* of December 15, 2017, Moscow warned Romania that Russia's newly built ballistic rockets could devastate the Deveselu base. On the other hand, *Flux 24* of October 6, 2017 cautioned its readers that the U.S. Senate may undercut the budget allocated for the Deveselu. This news is questionable, but the Russian disinformation services are hard at work against American interests. To counteract it, on October 8, 2017, the Romanian Foreign Ministry debunked the news as fake.

Romania has become a hub for NATO and American defense activities. Bucharest has also decided to acquire American Patriot missiles and armored military vehicles vowing to increase its military budget. NATO asked Romania to accept the construction in Bucharest of a headquarters for counter-intelligence activities. *HotNews.ro* of April 10, 2017 announced that the Romanian Parliament had begun to discuss the proposal.

American-Romanian military cooperation is deepening, but some political analysts are skeptical. They claim that by building the anti-missile system on its soil the country is exposing itself to more Russian threats and potential retaliations. In this regard, *RealitateaNet* of February 13th published an article authored by a well-known analyst, titled: *"Romania will be sure victim of Russia; America will help only if asked."* The article asks: what is Romania gaining in return? And the analyst blames the Romanian politicians for being too humble and too subservient toward Washington.

American-Romanian cooperation is viewed as favorable by most people, but with some reservation. This reservation is directed chiefly at the political leaders of the country, who have neglected the interests of the population. From now on, improving further the Romanian-American relations will depend, to a large degree, on improving the economic conditions of the average Romanian. And this is something the Bucharest government should do.

Chapter 10
America and the Process of Globalization

About Globalization. July 26, 2012

As a modern concept "globalization" is rather new. The word itself entered our common vocabulary in the 1980's and it gradually acquired a new meaning. The concept is also associated with "the new world order" and free trade, along with the free access to markets. This expression, "novus ordo seclorum" in Latin, is printed on all U.S. dollar bills, but it was introduced in the modern vocabulary by President George H.W. Bush. The concept of globalization has already elicited the attention of many scholars who wrote a number of books and many articles on the subject. Most people have heard of the word, but few are fully aware of what it means. What does globalization represent for America?

This introductory essay will present a short overview of the concept of globalization and will try to elucidate its meaning and potential consequences. The author is drawing his ideas from a number of current writings and from his own personal knowledge. One of the current scholars of the trend, Manfred B. Steger, succinctly characterizes globalization as:

"A social condition characterized by tight economic, political, cultural, and environmental interconnections and flows that make most of the current existing borders and boundaries irrelevant." And also, *"Globalization refers to the expansion and intensification of social relations and consciousness across world-time and world-space."* (Manfred B. Steger, Globalization, NY, London: Sterling, 2007, pp. 10 and 19).

Steger, as well as Peter Dicken (Globalization, NY, London: The Guilford Press, 2007), also see globalization as an elusive concept that refers to a process of changes, a new era, and a new age. However, what we already know is that globalization is caused primarily by modern technology and by new economic forces. The process is supported by national governments and by international organizations. Their agenda is advanced sometimes openly, as with NAFTA, which has been promoted openly by the American government and at other times in a stealthy way. Irrespective of how it is advanced, globalization affects people and governments everywhere. The promoters of globalization are the big Trans-National Corporations (TNCs), which claim that everybody will benefit from it. The most notable international organizations that promote the process of globalization are the International Monetary Fund (IMF), the World Bank (WB), and the World Trade Organization (WTO), as well as various regional integration blocs, all multilateral in nature and all of which call into question the sovereignty of the nation state.

On the practical side, globalization is a natural phenomenon brought about by a myriad of new technologies. At the same time, globalization has led to a number of tangible benefits for most people. There are more goods available now nearly everywhere and the prices are lower. The cost, however, is very high for Americans who have lost their jobs and for the government which is losing some of its prerogatives. And the social cost could be very risky.

From the start, globalization implies a conflicting relationship between large TNCs and Nation-States; between traditional values and (yet little known) New Age values; and, between Western internationalism and local nationalism. Is the world really ready for such a radical change? Is globalization a force for good? Who is winning and who is losing?

Historical experience has shown that many new ideologies are just utopian or are wrapped up with good intentions. But remember what the 17th Century French philosopher Blaise Pascal said: *"the road to hell is paved with good intentions."* We do live in an era of very intense global relations, but did we acquire a global consciousness? The United

Nations estimated that only about one percent of the world population has the knowledge or education to be considered "global citizens." And the most integrated bloc in the world, the European Union, is hardly capable of agreeing on anything, let alone acquiring a common consciousness.

There are currently many TNCs richer and more powerful than most of the countries of the world. The world, however, continues to be organized based primarily on nation-states, not on big corporations. Nation-states and international corporations are in a delicate relationship. They need each other, but the relationship is often acrimonious. The role of the nation-state is chiefly political. Governments exist to assure internal order and international peace. Internally, national governments aim at an even development and at promoting the interests of all their citizens. The TNCs are economic entities. For them, people are consumers and the chief purpose of a corporation is to make money. And the lions' shares of the profits are for reinvestment and corporate growth, the compensation of their CEOs and to a lesser degree for the benefit of the shareholders.

Most importantly, among Western democracies, governments are elected by the people and are accountable to the people. And in a democratic society like the United States, the internal balance of power is maintained by the three branches of the government and is monitored by a free press, often referred to as the Fourth Estate. How are CEOs elected? What are the principles of its corporate governance? Who is watching over TNCs? As a matter of fact, while Wall Street was saved recently by the Federal government with taxpayers' money, financial institutions still opposed any governmental regulation.

On the practical side, what we have seen so far is a trend of de-industrializing America by exporting or outsourcing its manufacturing job overseas and another one of increasing social polarization between high-paying and low-paying jobs. One hundred years ago the ratio between high and low paying jobs was about five to one. Now the ratio is about 100 to one. Such a polarization is dangerous to the stability of the American society. Plutarch, an ancient Roman philosopher, concluded two thousand years ago: *"An imbalance between rich and poor is the oldest and most fatal ailment of all republics."*

The old adage that power corrupts and absolute power corrupts absolutely continues to hold true. Yet, for some people there is no limit for acquiring wealth and power. And when they have it, they can use it for personal or humanitarian purposes or for evil goals. Abraham Lincoln once said: *"Nearly all men can stand adversity, but if you want to test a man's character, give him power."* The reality is that by the time a super CEO of a huge TNC gets all the power, it is too late to test his character.

Is globalization good or bad? It all depends on the whims of those who are at the top of the political and economic world and this is the risk. Are they fair? Are they wise? What have we learned from history? Hegel, a well-known German philosopher, was skeptical. He said: *"The only thing that we learn from history is that we do not learn from history."* What has America learned from globalization? What impact does globalization have on the American middle class? This is the question!

Globalization and the American Patriots. September 10, 2012

An American ambassador was asked once about Washington's position on an important international matter, and he answered that only the President can speak on behalf of all Americans. Who speaks for America on the issue of globalization? The answer is complex.

First of all, we must clarify and define "globalization." This is problematic, for many definitions have been offered. According to the authors of *Pillars of Globalization*, Nayef R.F. Al-Rodhan and Gérard Stoudmann, it may be understood as *"a process that encompasses the causes, course, and consequences of the transnational and transcultural integration of all human and non-human activities."* It is also commonly defined as the universalization of liberal democracy, cosmopolitan identity, and free trade. In fact, the famous political scientist, Francis Fukuyama, referred to the spread of these notions as the *"end of history,"* i.e. the final goal towards which mankind has been consciously or subconsciously striving throughout its entire history.

In practice, globalization is, quite simply, a buzz word used to describe corporate multi-national thinking as opposed to national policy. It is meant to replace (transcend) 'international' in the description of the world economy. Therefore, in the international context, free markets don't work because what they are only 'free' from is government planning and management on behalf of special interests.

Yet, as much as the supporters of globalization wish to portray it as merely a natural and spontaneous process, it is also an ideology, which has functioned under alternatives names, such as internationalism, world federalism, mondialism, or trans-continentalism. The ideologues of globalization often declare that they wish to utilize such tools as international organizations, open borders, mass immigration, and free trade agreements to further international economic and political integration and to create a "new world order" under some form of "global governance."

In the case of the United States, America would become subordinate to global governance, just as States are subordinate to the Federal Government. The globalists readily admit that this entails a significant limitation (and eventual elimination) of national sovereignty and the *de facto* end of the nation-state. They also do not hide their hostility towards the diversity of nationality, religion, and custom that defines the world and which represents a great obstacle to a one-world, globalized system. As Brock Chisolm, the postwar director of the UN's World Health Organization, stated bluntly: *"To achieve world government, it is necessary to remove from the minds of men their individualism, loyalty to family traditions, national patriotism and religious dogmas."*

Is this in any way compatible with American sovereignty and independence under which this nation was founded or the notion of American exceptionalism? Surely, it is an ideology foreign to America and hostile to the Constitution.

The United States was founded - after securing its independence from the British Empire - as a unique republic focused on the welfare of its free citizens. The ideals of freedom, democracy and prosperity expanded and gradually embraced most of the people. In the process, some Americans became very rich and some didn't but the equality of opportunity – without old world class distinction – was always present and available. The majority joined the middle income strata of a free and individualistic society. For some two centuries, this category prospered and became the backbone of the country. However, during the last several decades, the hope to enter the middle income bracket and to maintain that status has diminished. The rich are becoming richer, the poor are losing hope and becoming dependent on the government, while the middle income earners are thinning out. It all seems to be the result of "globalization." The question naturally arises: who benefits from it?

Entrenched globalists admit that, currently, there are some problems with the process, but they claim that, in the future, economic globalization will benefit everybody. That's acceptable only if the individual wishes to be placed on a particular productivity rung of the economic ladder determined not by an individual's free will and opportunity but by the dictates of government policy. As a former refugee from a communist country, I remember that Communist Party activists always promised us future prosperity, which, alas, never arrived. Instead, communism collapsed and was replaced by post-communism and globalization.

And here is what globalization has brought to America: well-paying manufacturing jobs have been lost to overseas outsourcing; young people, including college graduates, have been unable to find adequate jobs; and many available positions pay minimum wages. Globalization has generated a deep chasm, making the American Dream more difficult to attain!

In antiquity, the Greek philosopher Plato argued that the common good required a ratio of five to one between the richest and poorest members of a society. During the previous century, J.P. Morgan thought that bosses should only earn at most twenty times more than their workers. Between 1980 and 2000, however, the average salaries of major CEOs rose to a rate 400 times higher than those of average workers. Is this good for America? Obviously, large trans-national corporations (TNCs) believe it is and lobby the government for more legislation to further globalization. In addition to the disregard for economic patriotism shown by some large corporations, the government and its multiple agencies help push businesses abroad through legislation which increases taxes, labor costs, and regulations.

In the United States, public-private corporations are being created as bridges between private business and government. President Ronald Reagan clearly understood the nature of this problem when he said, *"What is euphemistically called government-corporate partnership is just government coercion, political favoritism, collectivist industrial policy and old-fashioned Federal boondoggles nicely wrapped up in a bright-colored ribbon. And it doesn't work. This kind of approach was tried in Europe."*

To a large degree, these public-private partnerships and the TNCs do not pursue goals beneficial to the public in general, but beneficial merely to themselves. President Theodore Roosevelt understood long ago the delicate relationship between government and big business. Thus, he busted several huge monopolies, such as Rockefeller's Standard Oil, which, at the time, controlled 90 percent of all U.S. oil refineries. Roosevelt argued: *"Great corporations exist only because they are created and safeguarded by our institutions; and it is therefore our right and duty to see that they work in harmony with these institutions."*

Referring also to monopolies and inequality, President Woodrow Wilson wrote in his book, *The New Nation*: *"If monopolies persist, monopolies will always sit at the helm of government. I do not expect to see monopoly restrain itself. If there are men in this country big enough to own the government of the United States, they are going to own it."* Who is currently busting the big trans-national corporations steering the ship of state further along the path of globalization? Who is checking the trend toward monopolization which characterizes modern globalization?

Although little discussed openly, globalization is dangerously dividing American society. The main split is between liberals and conservatives, between atheists and God-fearing people, and between internationalists seeking to destroy the nation-state, and patriots who want to save the Constitution and the America they inherited from their forefathers.

While the liberals seek a new international order, patriots focus on sovereignty, independence and American exceptionalism, reminding us of the very principles on which the country was built. In support of their positions, they invoke the Constitution, the prescribed role of the government, and the Declaration of Independence which reads: *"We hold these truths to be self-evident, that all men are created equal, that they are endowed by the Creator with certain unalienable rights; that among these are Life, Liberty and the pursuit of Happiness."* They also emphasize that the Founding Fathers opted for a government *"of the people, by the people, and for the people."*

Pat Buchanan, a well-known conservative writer and pundit, adviser to presidents, including Ronald Reagan, and former presidential candidate himself, insists that we *"put America first."* Buchanan, along with other critics of globalization, criticizes unreserved "free trade" as a utopian ideal – the word utopia being derived from the Greek *ou topos*, i.e. "no such place."

"Global free trade is a Faustian bargain. A nation sells its soul for a cornucopia of foreign goods. First, the nation gives up its independence; then its sovereignty; and finally, its birthright—nationhood itself..." And *"when the economic levers go, the political independence is sure to follow,"* wrote Buchanan in his book, *The Great Betrayal*.

Economically, to counter the globalist view, the patriots stress that *"an economy is not a country"* and *"trade is not an end, but it is the means to an end."* Therefore, the priority should be the welfare of the American nation not the special interests thriving on government engineered globalization. Other Americans also stress that people are not simply or primarily producers and consumers. As Buchanan pointed out: *"They are members of a nation, with history, traditions, language, faith, culture and institutions to maintain and pass on."*

The internationalists and their atheist allies accuse God-fearing Americans of being retrograde and irrational troglodytes, or, as President Obama notoriously put it, *"angry people clinging to their guns and religion."* Mark Levin in his book *Liberty and Tyranny* rebuts these claims by pointing out that *"science cannot explain the spiritual nature of man... we can explain the existence of consciousness, but we do not know why there is consciousness."* Indeed, American patriots "irrationally" submit to a divine order and place America under God, as did the Founding Fathers.

From a practical point of view, today's patriots want to preserve the American manufacturing industries as a guarantee of national prosperity, sovereignty, and independence. They point out that America is still strong, but the current trends are nevertheless alarming. And they warn that great nations have failed in the past. Could this happen to America? In their book, *The Origins of Power, Prosperity, and Poverty: Why Nations Fail*, Acemoglu and Robinson provide several reasons that ought to give Americans pause: *"Weak governments; hidden private interests; unenlightened leaders; lack of economic opportunities; instability; [and an] uneducated or complacent population."* The authors explain that a nation can shift from a virtuous circle to a vicious circle, where the efforts by elites to aggrandize power and wealth destroy a nation. The ideology of globalization, in fact, creates extractive institutions instead of inclusive political and economic institutions.

What is much clearer is that the notion of American exceptionalism cannot be reconciled with globalization defined as ideology striving towards global federalism. Submerging the United States in a world whose many cultures often prefer the illusory security of servitude over the inevitable risks of freedom poses a threat to America's traditional libertarian culture. In fact, the spreading of an artificial, cosmopolitan universal pop-culture which accompanies globalization amounts to reducing all of the world's cultures to the lowest common denominator, thereby imperiling the great treasure that is the world's diversity.

The Process of Globalization. October 6, 2015

Economic globalization is going to be one of the most critical issues of the 21st Century. The process is advanced by powerful transnational corporations and is often detrimental to average people because it lacks societal roots. Many studies and statistics have shown, for example, that while certain U.S. corporations get bigger and wealthier the American middle class is suffering from low wages and job losses. If globalization runs its full course, the world will be dominated by a few corporations, governments will lose their prerogatives, and people will be heavily indebted to financial institutions. America will be no exception!

The process of globalization has deepened the gap between rich and poor countries and has indebted many nations. The amount some countries owe internationally is staggering. Romania was the only communist country that repaid its full debt just before the collapse of the regime, but the effort ruined it. At the time of repayment, Romania's foreign debt was 10 billion. Today, as a full EU member, it is 170 billion dollars. Yet, Greece is the latest case imperiled by international indebtedness.

A country of only 10 million people, Greece's international debt is 360 billion dollars, a huge amount that Athens could not repay. To avoid a default, Athens received another EU loan worth 90 billion. The truth is that Greece, as well as many other countries, will never be able to repay their debts. This time Athens even tried to turn to Moscow for help, and Russia was too happy to interfere and create new problems for the West.

Who caused the immense current gap between rich and poor countries and between rich and poor people everywhere? The problem is that the powerful business elites in America are now the main promoters of globalization. In a way, the process is like a 3rd International. The first two internationals were communist. The Soviet Union was the center of the communist camp and Moscow's goal was global. The Russian people did not like communism, but they were proud of being in the center of world attention. Communism did not work because it was brutally imposed against the very nature of humanity. Since those days, the tactics have changed, but the purpose of global domination has remained. These global elites want to remain in control. From their point of view, if political communism did not work, economic globalization should.

Globalization is enticing the world with cheap labor, low cost material goods and promises of a better future. Communism relied on the Soviet Union and promised a bright future, but that future never materialized. Is globalization relying now on America? In his well documented 2008 book *Superclass–The Global Power Elite and the World they are Making,* David Rothkopf states that the United States seems prepared militarily to take on the entire world. Is this military readiness for the promotion of the new globalization ideology? Who will the winners be? Maybe some corporations will, but not the American people.

American patriots have already challenged the process of globalization at the grassroots with its attendant loss of jobs and industries moved overseas, along with its established leadership represented by the U.S. Chamber of Commerce, home of the Fortune 500 transnational corporations. These elite business interests want free labor migration, open borders and the end of the nation-state. Free trade no longer means the freedom to trade with other countries but the desire of transnational corporations to be free from rules, unless they have been prefigured in their favor and memorialized in the so-called multi-national free trade agreements. However, if in past decades Washington concentrated on the liberty and prosperity of the American people, now its political elites exhibit an unmatched global avariciousness, while neglecting its own people. Although an avid free trader President Reagan would have never given in to this process. Why is the U.S. supporting the process?

In fact, globalization is only the economic arm of *The New World Order.* It appears that the biggest socio-political division of our time is no longer between rightist and leftist political trends, as it was during the Cold War era. It is between nationalism and greater globalization. Washington is caught between a shift from managed international economics and trade and the new patriotic nationalism at home.

Internationalism is the goal of the socialists. Will America side with Main Street or Wall Street? Will America return to Judeo-Christian values, or will it succumb to libertinism and materialism? Responsible researchers have concluded that if the current trends continue and if the needs of average people and established nations are not addressed properly the world could end up in a crisis of... global proportions.

The Current Refugee Crisis in Europe. September 14, 2015

Unchecked international migration is threatening the national fabric of Europe currently in the middle of a deep refugee crisis. Hundreds of thousands of people are arriving annually, but recently the wave of refugees has gotten out of hand. It is the biggest refugee crisis since the end of the Second World War. The EU authorities are overwhelmed and are trying to make each member country accept specific quotas. This has upset many people and several national governments.

During most of 2015, Italy and Greece were overwhelmed by refugees crossing the Mediterranean Sea. Currently, however, Macedonia and Serbia are assailed by an unstoppable river of refugees from war torn Africa and the Middle East. According to the latest reports, the migrants are crossing the two countries on foot or by various means trying to reach Hungary to enter the EU. Some 160,000 migrants have already reached Hungary this year, and many more are trying to do so daily. Faced with such an influx of migrants, Hungary has complained that its national culture is in danger and its stability is being threatened. Consequently, Budapest has decided to erect a 13-foot wall of razor wire on its border with Serbia. The EU authorities have demanded that Budapest reconsider its plan. Most of the fence is already erected, but refugees continue to enter Hungary by digging under it or by climbing over it.

While thousands of refugees are stalled at the border, others have reached Budapest and have camped near the main railroad station waiting for trains to take them to Germany. Among them, there are many children and elderly people, and the camping conditions are unsafe and unsanitary. The Hungarian public is outrage while the authorities are embarrassed. The situation is not much better further West either. Some 3,000 to 4,000 migrants from the Middle East, Asia and Africa are camped in France near Calais, trying to reach Britain through the Chunnel or on ferries.

The EU acknowledged that Europe has acted too slowly to handle the migrants and stressed that it must work faster to set up special processing centers to identify those in need of protection and those fleeing poverty. The distinction is that political refugees flee to save their lives while economic refugees are looking for better opportunities. However, separating the two categories is not easy. The process is tedious, confusing and time-consuming. When I was a refugee in Austria in 1968 only about 3-to-4 percent received political asylum. The others were processed and accepted by various countries as regular immigrants.

While from a humanitarian point of view Western countries are open to asylum seekers, demographically they are overwhelmed by economic refugees. However, the EU's policy is incoherent and each country applies its own criteria. In the meantime, the wave of refugees continues and various countries are at odds about them. German Chancellor Angela Merkel asked EU nations to stop trading accusations and do more to share the responsibility for refugees seeking asylum. She added that Germany took more asylum-seekers than any other country and pressed anew for quotas to spread the migrants more evenly among the EU bloc. Germany also insists that refugees be processed in Hungary, the first EU country they reach. Refugees, however, want to avoid settling in Hungary in order to reach the richer countries of the West. No country knows how to address the issue.

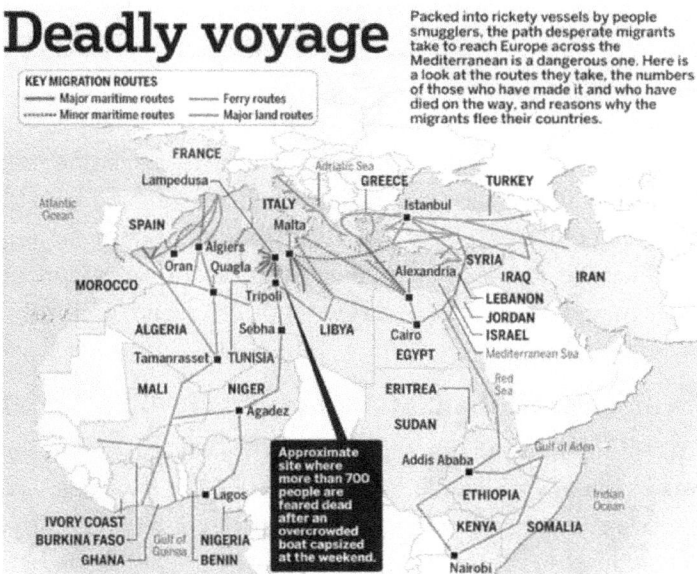

Deadly voyage

Packed into rickety vessels by people smugglers, the path desperate migrants take to reach Europe across the Mediterranean is a dangerous one. Here is a look at the routes they take, the numbers of those who have made it and who have died on the way, and reasons why the migrants flee their countries.

KEY MIGRATION ROUTES
— Major maritime routes   — Ferry routes
···· Minor maritime routes   — Major land routes

The Czech government asked the European authorities to close the Schengen space and demanded that NATO troops defend the EU borders. Slovakia announced that it will never agree with a system that would require EU members to accept set quotas of refugees. Actually, Slovakia, Czech Republic, Hungary and Poland oppose the plan of spreading the refugees all over East and Central Europe. As of this year, Germany alone is expected to receive over 800,000 new people. Nevertheless, recently, a group of Germans booed Chancellor Merkel for being lenient toward the new migrants. On the other hand, after 71 illegal migrants were found suffocated in a truck outside Vienna, a group of Austrians demonstrated for a more humane treatment of the refugees. At the same time, many Germans rallied in Munich in support of the refugees. Obviously, Europe is overwhelmed, confused and divided.

The recent crisis in the Middle East is threatening Europe and some people are blaming America for having destabilized the area without regard to consequences. Libyan refugees try to cross the Mediterranean Sea into Italy and hundreds of them are drowning. Along with them, there are African refugees from various countries. The Syrians come mostly through Turkey and Greece assuming a lower risk. Once in Europe, refugees are confronted with uncertainty and daily difficulties. While controlled migration is necessary for economic development to be mutually beneficial, unchecked migration challenges the stability of the host countries.

Many people in Europe are asking what will happen if tens of millions of refugees flood the continent? There are already a number of Muslim enclaves in Western Europe and most Muslims do not assimilate to the European culture. In fact, they challenge the European authorities by demanding the application of their own Sharia laws and customs. How much longer will Europe survive culturally and politically under such pressure?

America, Globalization and Brexit. June 27, 2016

After hundreds of years of conflicts, during the 20th Century the world was eventually divided into nation-states. The new states represent a more advanced form of socio-political organization and answer primarily to the aspirations of the people. Yet, to avoid further conflicts, the leaders of the world began to think of some new mechanisms aiming at securing international peace.

The first attempt at global organization was the League of Nations proposed by President Woodrow Wilson at the end of WWI. The project failed because Germany challenged the Paris peace agreements and the Soviet Union tried to impose communism upon the entire world. The second attempt was led by the Allied nations at the end of WWII, which set up the United Nations. This also failed because Moscow continued to promote global communism and the UN was unable to cope with the complexity of the world. Mankind needed a new international body endowed with the power to impose its decisions; it needed a new world order.

By 2000 the world entered an era of cooperating blocs and regional integrations that gave meaning to the word globalization. *Globalization*, however, represents just the economic side of the political concept of the *New World Order*. This expression was first used by President Bush Sr. in 1990, when he announced the birth of a *new era.* What does it mean?

The previous attempts to bring about peace and order on a global scale were political. The current idea is primarily economic. However, there is no economic cooperation without political agreement and there is no global peace without addressing geopolitical claims and disputes. Can the new approach solve the problems? It should be mentioned that globalization is an elusive concept and it is both natural and artificial. It is natural because it is driven by modern technology and it is artificial because it is pushed by big corporations for their own interests. The process also results in strenuous relationships between transnational corporations and national governments; it leads to confrontation between national aspirations and international interests; and, it feeds a conflict between traditional values and little known *new age* values.

Currently, America is pushing for globalization. Is Washington's sustained effort for the benefit of the people? Statistically, the average American has not gained from the process. Politically, the society is polarized more than ever before. And geopolitically, the world is again divided and risky. Russia is challenging America in East Europe and the

Middle East, and China is tightening its grip in the West Pacific. Who is winning and who is losing?

The economic polarization of America is already dangerous. Where does the American Republic stand? The American patriots are already opposed to globalization on economic and moral grounds. Can they stop the current trend? The November 2016 presidential elections are crucial. They can make or break traditional America. But there are some hopeful signs. The British have just voted to leave the European Union in order to regain their national independence. For England, the vote marks the beginning of a return to common sense. It is a victory of the God-fearing people over the internationalists who advocate a border-less, God-less and very much a meaning-less *new world order*. We do need an orderly world, but it should be a world of free nations. It is high time for America to regain its sense of nation and sense of mission.

U.S. and the World in the Era of Globalization.
January 2, 2017

During the 19th and most of the 20th Centuries, political leadership took a central stage in national affairs, geo-politics dominated international relations, and economic activities followed the political lead. Consequently, the nation-states and their spheres of influence were the power-centers of the world. The late 20th Century brought about a radical change: Economic activities took over the initiative and big Trans-National Corporations (TNCs) began to dislodge the authority of the government. This new trend led to new international economic blocs, it eroded the power of national governments, and it forced average people to adjust to new realities.

This article explains briefly what is happening on a global scale. A few clarifications are needed. Economy means the production, exchange, and consumption of goods and services. But, there is no economic development without political backing. Politics mean the rules by which a society is governed. Yet, there is a strong link between political and economic institutions. Together, they can make a nation flourish; separate, they can strangle a country. Thus, politics and economics must evolve together to achieve stability and prosperity. This is what happened traditionally in the United States. However, America has come to a crossroad. Should Washington opt for the interests of the big corporations or for the benefits of the average American?

The process of globalization refers to new and strong economic, political, and cultural links that bypass international boundaries. It means new production arrangements and new trade relations, services and marketing activities. All these require renewed international relations and new personal attitudes. Yet, globalization is an elusive concept and is apparently irreversible. The process is caused primarily by modern technology, but it is driven by politics and by economic forces. At the same time, globalization results in a contradiction between big Trans-National Corporations and national governments. And last but not least, it is viewed as a potential conflict between nationalism and internationalism.

In the new economically-dominated world, some pertinent questions should be kept in mind when studying the process of globalization and the role of government. What are the goals of national governments and what are the interests of the big corporations? Who is running the show and who is winning or losing? And what alternatives are there for the world given the globally unifying role of the new technologies? These are difficult questions and the answers are neither simple, nor are they very clear.

Take, for example, the role of national governments and the goals of TNCs. Traditionally, nations are created historically in a natural way from the ground up. They are located geographically on a given territory and have governments that at least in principle are elected by the people. In addition, governments have an inner balance of power between the executive, legislative and judiciary. By contrast, TNCs are created from above without any popular consent, as a rule do not have a local or a national loyalty, and do not have an inner balance of power. While national governments must serve their citizens, corporations serve their interests. Do corporations also serve the interests of the countries where they operate? Yes, but only as long as they first serve themselves. Do national governments always serve the interests of their nations? Not necessarily. Corrupt or inept governments put the interests of their members and their backers before the interests of the nation, thus causing ruinous consequences for the people. Where does America stand these very days between two different administrations with two opposing philosophies?

Is the process of Globalization good or bad? So far we only know some consequences. They are economic domination by some big TNCs, growing gaps between countries, and polarization of incomes between rich and poor everywhere. As attitudes, globalization advocates claim that in the future everybody will benefit, but opponents are skeptical. Until 2016 presidential election, America embraced globalism without reservation while other Western countries were more nuanced and remained strongly ethno-centric. International organizations generally support the process and implicitly help the powerful countries. Many national leaders are caught between a rock and a hard place. As a result, leaders of some developing countries insist on 'Fair' rather than 'Free' trade. Otherwise, poor countries have little or nothing to say. And average people bear the consequences.

The process of globalization has deeply polarized the world. A number of corporations and a handful of individuals have become incredibly rich. The rest of the world is not necessarily poorer than before in absolute terms, but it is being left behind in relative terms. Admitted, globalization entails some benefits for many people: more international trade, more goods available everywhere, reduced production cost, spreading of new technologies, intensified international relations, and hopefully, spreading of democracy. On the other hand, globalization entails negative consequences. It generally creates low-paying jobs, polarizes the society causing social problems, and erodes national sovereignty.

From a geopolitical and geo-economic point of view, today's world is increasingly 'global,' but with three dominant centers: Anglo-Saxon North America, Western Europe, and South-East Asia. The rest of the world is pretty much left (and even kept) behind. That means that some very important countries, notably Russia and China, do not enjoy fully the fruits of economic globalization. They also feel frustrated and respond with aggressive geopolitical actions to geo-economic challenges. It is exactly where the world stands today. If the 20th Century witnessed a switch from geopolitical conflict to economic cooperation, the 21st Century could take us back from economic frustration to geopolitical conflicts. (This article is a succinct summary of Professor Dima's book, *A Brief Study of Globalization*, Exlibris: U.S., 2013).

Chapter 11
Global Problems in a New Global World

***A World in Disarray: American Foreign Policy and the Crisis of the Old Order.* Richard Haas, Penguin Press, New York, 2017**. June 15, 2017

The 21st Century represents a radically different world than anything known by mankind before. It is a drifting world searching for a new political, social and economic order at a global level and for psychological balance at an individual level. Can we find that balance and a new global *Modus Vivendi?* This chapter consists of three critical book reviews and refers to the new global polarity; the relations with a new Russia, which is declining economically, but remains aggressive; and with a China on the rise that seems unstoppable.

A World in Disarray is the title of the book about…a world in trouble. Richard Haass, the author, has an impressive career. He is a former U.S. diplomat, a State Department official, and is now president of the prestigious Council on Foreign Relations. Based upon his credentials and experience, he analyzed the current world and its lack of order. His study is full of cases and examples, but short of solutions? In fact, he advances many possible solutions, but they are mostly suggestions and opinions. And a thought came to mind while reading the book: If his suggestions as a high-ranking State Department official were ignored, as he mentions, who is ultimately in charge of America's foreign policy?

Analytically, the book is organized into three main parts and twelve chapters. The first part deals with the theoretical frame of the Cold War. The second focuses on the post-Cold War years and explains what went wrong ever since. The third part addresses the question of what is to be done? He asks many questions and offers plenty of answers. And some chapter titles are illustrative for the topics discussed: *A Global Gap, Regional Realities, World Order Two, Regional Responses,* and *A Country in Disarray* that is the United States. The book tackles many delicate issues: *the challenge of globalization, the crisis of international migration, terrorism, nuclear proliferation, the complexity of the Middle East, the new Russian aggressive behavior, the divisions that exist within the American society* and others. In fact, the book addresses too many issues and this is a drawback.

Dr. Haass wrote the book out of concern for the evolution of the current world; a world that refuses to obey any order. He presents mostly an American point of view, but the world is still ethno-centric and America is at the center of the world. And what can America do at the beginning of this new century in a world that is more complex and more complicated than ever? He stresses that now, the world is neither unipolar nor multipolar; it is a place in which there are several ascending and descending powers, medium states with local ambitions, inactive little countries, and many dangerous non-state actors. In this new world, the United States cannot afford the luxury to stay aloof. Consequently, the author writes, America's involvement in world affairs is strictly necessary, but insufficient.

The study underscores that our world continues to combine Wilsonian idealism with hard-core realism. That means balancing ambiguous morality, questionable legitimacy, and cynical politics. Such issues as sovereignty and legitimacy are not universally accepted and are difficult to address. Therefore, force is still needed to impose some order and to avoid international chaos. In fact, he admits that some twenty-five years since the end of the Cold War, *'no benign new world order materialized.'* And he adds that currently *'international relations resemble more a new world disorder.'* (p. 5)

The author also admits that the global arrangements set up at the end of World War II no longer correspond to today's humanity. The United Nations, for example, as well as the World Bank, IMF, GATT and WTO and other international institutions, have not kept up with global changes and must be reformed. Yet, there is no consensus on how to change them. On the other hand, nations-states are still the building blocks of international arrangements, but they continue to be self-serving. Will nation-states survive the current process of globalization?

In this regard, he alleges that any new order must respect the sovereignty of the existing states. That means, at least in theory, to allow *'national governments to do much as they please within their border.'* (p. 23). But he adds that the new order must monitor not only the external behavior of the states, but their internal actions as well. Then, what remains of state sovereignty?

Presently, the relations between politics and economics and between national governments and private corporations are very intricate. In today's world some corporations and non-state players are stronger than governments, thus making sovereignty even less relevant. This trend is behind increased nationalism in many parts of the world. Consequently, how can we cope with such contradictory trends? Dr. Haass is not too optimistic. In his opinion, *'the twenty-first century will prove extremely difficult to manage.'* (p.13) ... *'It will not be business as usual in a world in disarray; as a result, it cannot be foreign policy as usual.'* (p. 14) Then, what is it going to be?

He also introduces some new terms or at least tries to give new meaning to several older terms and concepts such as: *Legitimacy and Legitimate anticipation, Sovereignty, Sovereign obligation and Sovereign self-interest, Diplomatic offensive, Nuances of Prevention and Preemption, Naming and Shaming, Managing the Cyberspace,* and even others.

Take, for example, 'legitimacy' and the 1990s wars in former Yugoslavia. He writes: *'One can argue that what the government of Serbia was doing was illegitimate in terms of international law or values and that what the United States and Europe sought to do was inherently legitimate.'* Yet, Russia did not agree. He attempts to clarify the concept: *'What this shows is that it is impossible to define legitimacy in terms of process alone if there is no consensus on norms and rules.'* Then, he introduces a new challenge to legitimacy and concludes: *'the U.N. Security Council itself does not deserve the mantle of dispenser of legitimacy given that its own legitimacy is in question. The problem with the Security Council as currently configured is that it is not representative of today's world...*' (p.197) If the highest global forum is not legitimate, what is legitimacy?

As an author and analyst myself, I would like to add that the current global configuration was largely decided at the American-Soviet summits held in Malta in 1989. The problem is that we do not know what the two sides discussed at Malta. And to add insult to injury, we still do not know the decisions taken by the victors at Yalta in 1945. Then, how can we judge consequences of events that have been kept secret? By contrast, the Helsinki negotiations and agreements of 1975 were open and public. The signatories agreed openly upon a set of values and decisions that are still in force today. One such point is the inviolability of borders. If the Helsinki accords were legitimate, should we conclude that the Malta and Yalta accords were illegitimate? Haass does not discuss this issue!

Another well debated topic is the problem of nuclear proliferation. Who has the right to nuclear weapons, if there is no consensus on legitimacy? Who has the right to decide on how to react to North Korea or to the Iranian nuclear programs? In this venue, the author is tough on these countries. There is no question this is a big dilemma, but Washington should avoid at any price to be perceived as using a double-standard when judging others?

Other analyses undertaken in the book are the problem of spheres of influence, especially those claimed by Russia and China, and of various regional conflicts. From among regional conflicts, the Middle East remains the hottest and apparently there is no solution in sight. Yet, who is responsible for the dire destruction and sufferance in the Middle East, a conflict that threatens to divide and destabilize Europe? As for the spheres of influence, if every major power claims a share of the world, we go back to square one and start bickering again as we did a century ago. Have we learned anything from history? Haass wrote that learning from history is easier said than done.

At the beginning of the 21st Century we do have global knowledge, but we have neither a global government, nor sufficient leaders with clout and global consciousness. Consequently, the world has a lot of gray areas where major regional powers make the rules or interpret them at will. There is a big gap these days between what is desirable and what is possible. In Haass' opinion *'this gap is one of the principal reasons for the disarray that exists in the world.'* (p.150) An old adage says that sometime we do too little too late. In this case the author tries to do too much too early. The world is not ready. We have not acquired, yet, global consciousness and perhaps we never will.

Winning the Third World: Sino-American Rivalry During the Cold War. **Gregg A. Brazinsky, The University of North Carolina Press, 2017.**
September 20, 2017

The rise of China over the last several decades poses economic, political and geopolitical challenges to America and the world. The new book, S*ino-American Rivalry during the Cold War* deals with the evolution of China throughout most of the 20th Century, on the one hand, and America's attitude toward Beijing, on the other. During this critical period, China transformed itself from a feudal society into an industrial giant. And all this time, Beijing championed the right to independence of Asian and African countries. The United States watched this transformation with apprehension and grudgingly adjusted its policy from denying Beijing international legitimacy to eventual full recognition. In his writing, Gregg Brazinsky did a scholarly work, but his book is too detailed for average readers and it requires their total attention. Thus, the reader must keep in mind the big picture: What did China want during the studied period and what did the United States pursue?

The book is organized chronologically, but it also pursues the topics thematically. The introduction offers a brief historical background and clarifies some important ideas. After being humiliating by Japan and the Western Powers throughout much of the 19th Century and the first part of the 20th Century, China wanted to reassert itself and to reacquire a legitimate international status. Siding with nationalist China and rejecting communism, America tried for decades to deny communist China any legitimacy. This stand led to mutual recrimination and confrontation.

The chapters are organized by time periods dedicated to major changes in Beijing's policies and in Washington's reactions: Emergence of a Rivalry (1919-1950); Cultural Competition; Diplomatic Campaign; Economic Competition; and finally, Competition and Cooperation (1968-1979). The Conclusions are also important because they relate to the present situation.

The central theme of the book is that Sino-American rivalry was in essence a competition over status. It should be added, however, that no great power accepts a challenge to its status, and no ascending power can rise without struggling to get to the top. As for the meaning of 'status' analysts disagree on what it exactly means. One definition is *'a recognized position within a social hierarchy, implying relations of dominance and deference...'* (p. 4) Following a century of humiliation, China wanted to regain its status in the world. And communist China (PRC) never lost sight of this goal. Other than that, and to gain international support, Beijing made itself a champion for the struggle against Western colonialism and American imperialism. This attitude brought Beijing in direct opposition to Washington.

The policies pursued by Communist and Nationalist China were irreconcilable. However, even the communists promoted *'the idea that China once stood at the center of world civilization,'* a place that Beijing reclaimed. From this point of view, the author attributes the rise of new China mostly to Mao Zedong and his policies. The United States opposed firmly the new regime, but in the end it had to adjust its policies and accommodate communist China. As one can learn from this study, continuous arguing, in-fighting, maneuvering behind the scene, luring allies and punishing foes, were mind boggling. Accordingly, the evolution of the Sino-American relations, from diplomatic exchanges, cultural contacts, trade and business interests, to real war in Korea or by proxy in Vietnam, was immensely intricate. Most of the struggle, postures, actions and reactions, occurred behind the scene, but they affected virtually the entire world. The United States, for example, wanted an orderly transformation of Asia and aimed at promoting Washington's political and economic agenda. China wanted to re-establish itself as the central power of Asia and fomented revolutionary changes. The overt and covert struggle lasted untill unexpectedly Washington and Beijing reset their relations, and the two giants gradually moved from confrontation toward mutual acceptance and cooperation.

The road for a status change was very bumpy. While America showed determination, China displayed typical oriental patience. In this regard, Zhou Enlai, Mao's trusted Prime Minister, showed flexibility and diplomatic tact, yet was firm toward Washington. When the Geneva 1954 conference tried to find some peaceful resolutions in South-East Asia, Washington was reserved. To be on the safe side, President Eisenhower declared that the U.S. *'had not been party to or bound by the decisions taken by the conference,'* but would *'not use force to disturb the settlement.'* (p. 92) America was right to be suspicious. Beijing promised not to interfere in Indo-China, but it never intended to do so. Then, at the Bandung Conference in 1955, Zhou Enlai stated that in the future *'not even a few countries would be left on America's side...'* (p. 78) Then, gradually and unexpectedly, Washington changed its policy and *'by 1958, even American officials were acknowledging that the PRC would inevitably play an important role in shaping Asia's future.'* (p. 107)

The 1960s and 1970s were crucial for the dramatic change of the Sino-American relations. The relevance of the Korean War began to fade and new conflicts led to new geopolitical configurations. After the Sino-Soviet military skirmishes of the period, Washington and Beijing began to discover common ground and mutual interests. China denounced officially the Soviet Union and called it a *'social-imperialist country.'* Suddenly, the two countries found a common geopolitical imperative – to contain the Soviet Union. For years previously, however, the two sides had intense back-and forth exchanges that were kept secret. Sensing an opportunity for a radical change, President Nixon dispatched Secretary of State Henry Kissinger to Beijing. This first step opened the way for Nixon's visit to Beijing in 1972 and later for full Sino-American diplomatic relations.

Many thorny issues were discussed between the two sides confidentially or in different open forums. Among them there was the fate of Indo-China, where America was embroiled in a protracted conflict, the future of Taiwan, and the question of China's seat at the United Nations. The author rightly concludes that *'Nixon's China visit reconfigured both Sino-American relations and international politics.'* (p. 329). Nevertheless, Beijing always put China's interests first and through shrewd negotiations and duplicity attained most of its goals. Beijing promised to moderate Vietnam's bellicose stand and to respect the neutrality of Indo-China. Yet, Vietnam was abandoned by Kissinger to the communists, and Beijing continued to help the anti-American insurgencies in Laos and Cambodia.

Reality is that the realignment that occurred in Asia during the second part of the 20th Century was complex and in many ways unavoidable. In the opinion of the author neither the United States nor China won the cold war, and Sino-American relations have remained intricate and unpredictable. Despite finding some mutual interests, the author continued, *'China and the United States remained very dissimilar countries with different histories and perceptions of their roles in the world.'* (p. 344).

There is something to learn from the evolution of Sino-American relations throughout much of the 20th Century. First and foremost: never say never to change. The world is in a perpetual state of change and so was Asia. America, a superpower, had to make room for China, a power in the making.

Reconfiguring the geopolitical and economic spheres in Asia was a complex process. During the process, Sino-American relations moved from friendly to hostility and war and eventually to mutual acceptance, economic competition and cooperation. By the turn of this century, a new *status quo* was achieved and for the time being order has been established. Nevertheless, there are still some hot spots, especially in East Asia and the South China Sea. These very days, America and the world need China to contain North Korea, but Beijing will cooperate only as long as it suits its interests. On the other hand, the very neighbors of China are apprehensive and need the United States to countervail the growing military power of Beijing. To avoid further escalations more behind the scene contacts, negotiations and compromises are needed.

What we learn from this book is the huge amount of work and effort that took place during the 20th Century to avoid even worse catastrophes. Maybe similar efforts would save us during this century.

AI Super-Powers: China, Silicon Valley, and the New World Order. Kai-Fu-Lee, Houghton Mifflin Harcourt: Boston, New York, 2018, February 2019

The competition for dominance has moved way beyond the globe; on the one hand in cyberspace and on the other into man's mind. *Artificial intelligence* represents a new frontier and the author of the book, an ethnic Chinese American, warns the United States that China is winning the race.

Artificial Intelligence (AI) Super-Powers shocks the reader and wakes him up to a new world; a world of dramatic changes, global realignments and socio-psychological challenges. We are not facing the 'end of the world', but it is the end of today's world. And what's scarier is that this future is already here although the author gives us about 20 more years to see it implemented.

The author was born in Taiwan and raised and educated in the United States. He is a leader in Artificial Intelligence and is preoccupied with the applications and consequences of the new technology. In his opinion, the world has moved from the age of theoretical discovery to the age of practical applications and from the age of expertise to the age of data. AI is the energy of the new age and it marks the beginning of a new revolution. Resort to artificial intelligence or be left behind!

Artificial intelligence is driven by *deep learning*. Human abilities are very limited in discerning complex signs, signals and various correlations. Machines can do a much better job. *Deep learning* refers to a myriad of nuances in our reaction to different situations that are processed and interpreted by machines. Then, by using complex algorithms, machines spot the most common patterns, make decisions and predictions better than humans do, and apply them to real life situations. The patterns of data are now decisive in determining the accuracy of an algorithm. They are used for various economic activities and for financial profits. It is exactly what is happening now in China at a massive scale, in America more slowly, and to a lesser degree in the rest of the world. This is the future!

Facts

During the 18th and 19th Centuries the world went through the Industrial Revolution. During the 20th Century it underwent a High-Tech revolution. This Century is witnessing a new revolution driven by artificial intelligence! Machines endowed with AI and human-like perceptions are already doing a better job than humans in a range of fields with practical applications: Face and Speech Recognition, Medical Diagnosis and Treatment, Linguistic Translations, Insurance Policies, Granting Loans and others. It should be emphasized that according to informed people, if a new discovery is known to the public, it is already obsolete. And while researchers explore the future, businesses are reaping the benefits.

There are currently seven giants that dominate the world in the research and application of artificial intelligence. They are four American companies: Google, Facebook, Amazon, and Microsoft, and three Chinese ones: Baidu, Alibaba and Tencent. Other big Chinese names are also coming of age. All these companies have developed their own applications and are vying for global domination. The United States is still ahead in the fields of research and innovation, but China is ahead in practical applications. Between the two there is a big difference. American companies are private while the Chinese companies are controlled by the government which is in the hands of the Communist Party.

For China investing in AI is not only of economic importance, but also of political and geo-political importance. By doing so, the government will have more control over its own people and internationally will claim a larger share of the globe. And China is getting ahead because the population is taking its cue from the government. In Addition, Beijing offers subsidies, investment funds, other facilities, and sets up special development zones for AI development. And when China mobilizes its people and resources, results follow suit. In 2007 China had no high-speed trains; ten years later China had more miles of high-speed trains than the entire rest of the world. It has been projected that by 2030 China will become the center of AI of the entire world. And from a techno-military point of view, China could transform economic development into geo-political advantages to the detriment of America.

Existing Applications.

There are currently about 800 million people in China who have access to the internet. That means more people than in the United States and Europe together. Accordingly, Chinese companies 'harvest' each click of the internet user and find patterns of meaning in them. Then, intelligent machines interpret this huge database for correlations that escape the human eye and brain. Finally, specialized companies make practical use of this data. The result is that China is getting ahead in the AI field. (p. 110) For example, the invention of the Smart Phones has given many Chinese direct access to the internet without having to buy a desk computer. There are now more than 500 million smart phones in China and those phones are used for a vast range of operations. Their use has transformed 'online actions into offline services'. Tencent, for example, developed a special super app called WeChat that has taken over the E-commerce in China.

With smart phones many Chinese pay their bills, shop for grocery, order food from restaurants, book their appointments, buy tickets, call taxicabs, send money everywhere, order presents and balance their checkbooks. WeChat has turned entire cities into cashless markets and have changed the urban life. Food ordering, for example, is now widespread and food is delivered hot and quick by hired people riding scooters provided by the IT companies. There are currently ten times more food deliveries in China than in the U.S. and paying by mobile phone is 50 times more often in China than in America. (p. 79)

Another Chinese success story is offered by Mobike. One can get a bike anywhere in a big city, unlock it with the bar code on a smart phone, pay by phone and leave the bike anywhere for the next user. 'Traditional' payment with credit cards requires a fee, is rather expensive and is already considered old-fashioned in China. Paying with a smart phone is easy, quick and there is no fee and no minimum payment either.

Face Recognition and Speech Translation are other two important fields of applied artificial intelligence. A KFC restaurant in China with an up-to-date face recognition app allows customers to pay by simply recognizing their faces and linking them to their smart phones. Payment and bank balancing are then done automatically on the spot. No additional cost!

Another amazing AI application is simultaneous speech translation. Recently, the Chinese program 'iFlyTek' translated almost to perfection president Trump's speech. And it translated not only words and meanings, but also intonation, pitch, patterns and expressions as if he had been born in a Chinese village near Beijing. (p.105). Kai-Fu-Lee claims that 'iFlyTek' has already surpassed its giant American competitors in this field.

Upcoming Applications

The near future looks like a Sci-Fi movie... Based on your family habits, your refrigerator will notice what you need to buy. You go to a supermarket riding an autonomous car that parks itself in the best spot near the store. Then, you get a shopping cart that recognizes you and greets you by your name. That cart has already 'communicated' with your refrigerator and knows what you need to buy. The cart moves by itself in front of you and it takes you to the aisles that you need to visit. Then, it charges the merchandise to your smart phone and it takes the grocery to your car... This technology is here and it could become common practice very soon.

The new wave of artificial intelligence is blurring the line between the digital world of the computer and physical world around us. From being just *automated*, machines are becoming *autonomous*. And endowing them with human-like senses and perceptions could blur the line between humans and machines... For example, a medical doctor consulting a patient could access the global database for a certain illness. Then, a computer would establish with a high degree of accuracy both the diagnostic and the best treatment. Yet, who will be in charge, the doctor or the machine?

Current predictions foresee that in about ten years time machines could equal the intelligence of humans, and by 2045 super-intelligent machines may 'dwarf the intelligence of humans'. The adoption of AI machines is inevitable and the process will have beneficial results as well as dire consequences. Benefits are mostly material and economic, but the chief consequence is that the very meaning of what is a human will be questioned. In fact, the names of two sub-chapters of the book speak volumes: *A Grim Picture* and *The Incoming Crisis of Meaning*.

Consequences

The main consequences of fully adopting intelligent machines are Economic, Socio-Political, Philosophical and Psychological. In the near future such machines will produce material goods quickly and cheaply, will make them available at low cost, and will pretty much 'free' man from labor. Socially, however, the new era will lead to major job losses, social stratification and massive inequality. The future magnates will amass astronomical wealth, but societies will only need a class of specialists and a number of unskilled workers. The rest of the population will be *displaced, not needed* and even *unwanted*. That will result in social disruption and political destabilization.

With regard to America, the author believes that as many as 20 to 40 percent of all U.S. jobs could be lost to artificial intelligence. Global implications will be even worse. Factories and production will likely relocate back in the developed countries to be closer to markets. That will deprive poor country of their most important assets: overpopulation and cheap labor. Consequently, the gap between global *haves* and *have-nots* will widen. Huge unemployment will pose socio-philosophical challenges for governments and psychological problems for individuals. Alarmingly, the author points out that once started, sooner than many of us expect, the social collapse will happen in a very short period of time. (p. 21)

Machines will change the current international political order, but it will also challenge every country internally... *'Dangerous fault lines will emerge within each country and they will possess the power to tear them apart from inside.'* (p. 139) Accordingly, by 2040 we might face a total social disruption.

At a personal level, unemployed people with no hope of finding work would lose their meaning as human beings. People find purpose and fulfillment in their work and achievements. What is the purpose of life if we do not work anymore? Where will be our self-esteem? The author writes about freeing people from the chore of work, but for Christians this is against their core beliefs. We identify with work; redeem ourselves through it; get sense and dignity through our work; grow intellectually and find spiritual meaning through work... Loss of meaning and purpose will almost certainly lead to increased alcoholism, drug use, crime, suicide and a sense of personal futility. This could result in unending social riots, political upheaval and quasi-apocalyptic events.

To soften the future shock, some social scientists propose the introduction of a basic universal income, guaranteed by the government, for every citizen. Some European countries have already started pilot programs in this regard. Other scientists condition the guaranteed income on the pledge that receiving adults will have no children. That idea challenges again the very purpose of life. The author recommends a new Social Contract based on spiritual values, but given the very nature of man this idea is rather utopian.

Closing Considerations

If in the future the line between humans and intelligent machines will get blurred, question is: What does it mean to be human? To be human means to have a soul and feelings; it means to love and to be loved; it means to be needed; it means to strive for personal achievements and for self-improvement; it means to make decisions and assume risks; it means to feel for others and care for them..! Machines will never be able to have human feelings regardless of how super-intelligent they might become. If only people were wise enough to make the right choices!

Bibliographical Explanation

Having been a scholar and a journalist at the same time in my career, I have seldom combined research with reporting. The two endeavors do not really mix, but in all honesty, I gave the sources of my knowledge and information within every of the above articles and essays.

Closing Thought

The world is in a state of change as never before. From America to Russia and from Europe to China, the world is confronted with an alarming array of problems and challenges. We are in the middle of a radical transition and are knocking at the door of the unknown. Yet, while moving into the space age, we are still faced with the age-old human nature: political bickering at home, economic interests overseas, and geopolitical claims in many sensitive areas of the globe. As of this year, 2019, Russia has just won a new battle in Syria that may reconfigure the political scenario of the entire Middle East. That is scary: America and Israel against Iran, Russia, and pretty much the rest of the world! What we need the most these days is honest and competent leaders capable of wrestling with politics as well as with ethics and moral issues. Otherwise, we will not make it into the next stage of human civilization. And the time of reckoning is fast approaching!

www.ingramcontent.com/pod-product-compliance
Lightning Source LLC
Chambersburg PA
CBHW071847270326
41929CB00013B/2127